MOSAIC FICTIONS

Writing Identity in the Spanish Civil War

MOSAIC FICTIONS

WRITING IDENTITY *IN THE* SPANISH CIVIL WAR

EMILY ROBINS SHARPE

UNIVERSITY OF TORONTO PRESS
Toronto Buffalo London

Toronto Buffalo London
utorontopress.com

ISBN 978-1-4875-0142-6 (cloth)
ISBN 978-1-4875-1315-3 (EPUB)
ISBN 978-1-4875-1314-6 (PDF)

Library and Archives Canada Cataloguing in Publication

Title: Mosaic fictions : writing identity in the Spanish Civil War / Emily Robins Sharpe.
Names: Robins Sharpe, Emily, 1983– author.
Description: Includes bibliographical references and index.
Identifiers: Canadiana (print) 20200152564 | Canadiana (ebook) 20200152572 | ISBN 9781487501426 (cloth) | ISBN 9781487513146 (PDF) | ISBN 9781487513153 (EPUB)
Subjects: LCSH: Canadian literature – Jewish authors – History and criticism. | LCSH: Canadian literature – 20th century – History and criticism. | LCSH: Canadian literature – 21st century – History and criticism. | LCSH: Spain – History – Civil War, 1936–1939 – Literature and the war.
Classification: LCC PS8089.5.J4 R63 2020 | DDC C810.9/8924071–dc23

This book has been published with the help of a grant from the Federation for the Humanities and Social Sciences, through the Awards to Scholarly Publications Program, using funds provided by the Social Sciences and Humanities Research Council of Canada.

University of Toronto Press acknowledges the financial assistance to its publishing program of the Canada Council for the Arts and the Ontario Arts Council, an agency of the Government of Ontario.

Canada Council for the Arts
Conseil des Arts du Canada

Funded by the Government of Canada
Financé par le gouvernement du Canada
Canada

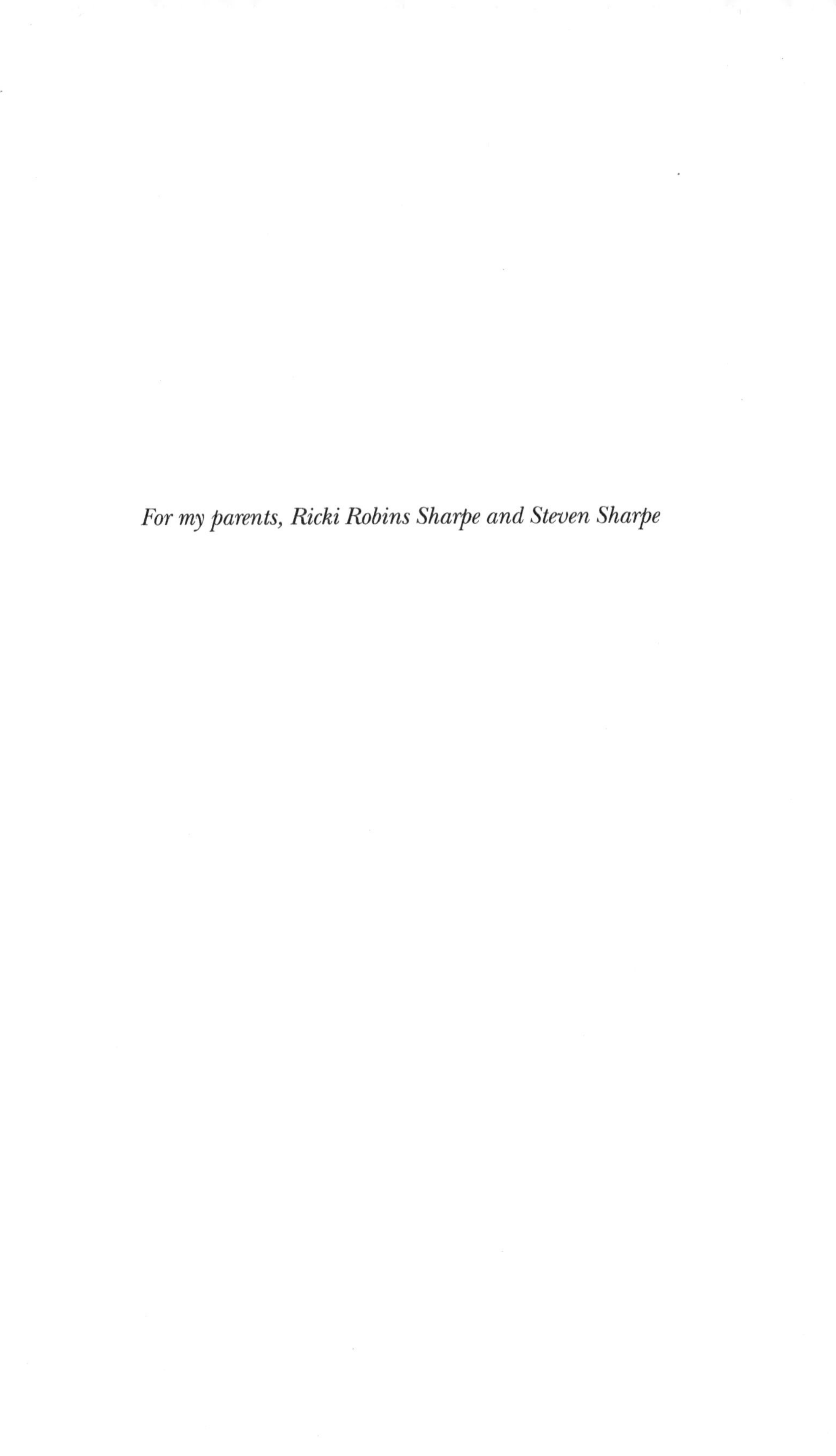

For my parents, Ricki Robins Sharpe and Steven Sharpe

Contents

Illustrations

Acknowledgments

As an immigrant writing about how authors write themselves home within colonized spaces, I am profoundly grateful to have lived and written my book on the ancestral and treaty lands of many diverse Indigenous nations, including the Susquehannock, the Mississaugas of the Credit, the Anishnabeg, the Chippewa, the Haudenosaunee, the Wendat, the Pennacook, and the Abenaki peoples.

This project began in Penn State's Department of English and I would especially like to thank Janet Lyon, who continues to provide unfailing insights and mentorship. I am also grateful to Jonathan Eburne, Mark Morrisson, Benjamin Schreier, and Linda Furgerson Selzer, for their valuable feedback and guidance. My work also benefitted from the support of many other Penn State professors, especially Sean Goudie, Aldon Lynn Nielsen, Sandra Spanier, Susan Squier, and Daniel Walden ז"ל.

The foundations of this study were also laid by my earlier teachers. In high school, Dina Fayerman nurtured my love of literary study; I am thankful for her continued friendship and perceptive readings of my writing. At King's College and Dalhousie, Leonard Diepeveen, Dean Irvine, and Anthony Stewart first introduced me to modernism.

An Editing Modernism in Canada postdoctoral fellowship at the University of Guelph provided vital resources. I am grateful to the School of English and Theatre Studies, especially Susan Brown and Alan Filewod – my incomparable postdoc supervisors – and Jade Ferguson, for their feedback and guidance.

My colleagues, past and present, at Keene State – and especially the departments of English, Women's and Gender Studies, and Holocaust and Genocide Studies, and the Humanities Faculty Research Group – continue to provide me with a thriving intellectual community and immense camaraderie. I thank Carol Adler, Brinda Charry, Anne

Freisinger Cucchi, Nona Fienberg, Sally Joyce, Michele Kuiawa, Anne-Marie Mallon, Kirsti Sandy, Sarah Spykman, and Jan Youga for their impeccable leadership and advice. Jiwon Ahn, Cindy Cheshire, Amber Davisson, Lisa DiGiovanni, Patricia Pedroza González, Ashley Greene, Taneem Husain, Jamie Landau, Mark Long, Emily McGill, Meriem Pagès, Laura Premack, Anna Schur, and Marin Sullivan all provided incisive reflections on my research. Thanks, also, to Jo Dery, Sharon Fantl, Irene McGarrity, Chris Parsons, and Peggy Walsh for discussing work while getting me out of the office.

I am grateful for sustained and sustaining collaboration with many more colleagues who have read drafts, shared insights, and offered inspiration and critique during different phases of this work. A special acknowledgment is due to my Canada and the Spanish Civil War Project comrades, particularly Bart Vautour and Kaarina Mikalson, for the most productive, enriching, fun collaboration I can imagine. A massive thanks to Andrea Cooper for nearly two decades of academic escapades. Thank you, as well, to Leslie Allin, Rachel Bara Sturges, Amy Clukey, Adam Cotton, Nancy Cushing Kennedy, Dustin Kennedy, Kevin Levangie, Hannah McGregor, Richard Menkis, Emily Christina Murphy, Ersula Ore, Katie Owens-Murphy, Ruth Panofsky, Katie Tune Pierrot, Grégory Pierrot, Krista Quesenberry, Patricia Rae, Stephanie Scott, Jennifer Spitzer, Mark Sturges, Michael Thurston, Brant Torres, J.A. Weingarten, Erin Wunker, and all the modernist ladies.

My students at Penn State, the University of Guelph, and Keene State are endlessly impressive. It is an honour to read and think with you.

I have been lucky enough to correspond with many of the authors whose works I discuss here – one of the greatest joys of this project. I appreciate immensely their beautiful writing and personal generosity in discussing the Spanish Civil War's contemporary resonance. My gratitude to Byrna Barclay, Neil Bissoondath, Dennis Bock, George Elliott Clarke, Stephen Collis, Brian Dedora, Mark Frutkin, Susan Holbrook, Maureen Hynes, Jim Nason, Steven Ross Smith, Nicola Vulpe, J.A. Wainwright, and Terrence Rundle West.

The research work for this project has taken me to four different countries. In addition to that of Bill Brockman at Penn State and the committed staff of Keene State's Mason Library, I have benefited from the assistance of librarians and archivists at the University of Toronto's Thomas Fisher Rare Book Library, the Toronto Reference Library, Queen's University's Archives in Kingston, the Tamiment Library and Robert F. Wagner Labor Archives and Columbia University's Rare Books and Manuscript Library in New York City, the Marx Memorial Library and Imperial War Museum Archives in London, the Biblioteca y Centro de Documentación at the Museo Nacional Centro de Arte Reina Sofía and the Biblioteca Nacional de España in Madrid, and the Centro Documental de la Memoria Histórica in Salamanca. Myron Momryk generously shared his own archival research with me. And thanks to Patricia Pedroza González and Samantha Ash for helping me with translations.

My research would have been impossible without funding and time. Early support came from Penn State's English Department, the Institute for the Arts and Humanities, the Africana Research Center, the Center for American Literary Studies, and the Research and Graduate Studies Office. I am also thankful to the Social Sciences and Humanities Research Council of Canada and the Editing Modernism in Canada Project for their crucial assistance. Support for this project has also come from Keene State's Early Career Summer Research Seed Funding and an Arts and Humanities Course Reassignment Grant as well as from a Keene State College Faculty Development Grant.

The editorial team at the University of Toronto Press has championed and improved this book; I am truly thankful to editors Siobhan McMenemy, Mark Thompson, and Frances Mundy, copy editor Matthew Kudelka, and the two insightful and generous anonymous readers of the manuscript.

My academic career has taken me far away from many of my family and friends, and I am grateful for their stalwart love and cheerleading, often from afar. My thanks to Greg Bowley, Tobin LeBlanc Haley, Nic Cotton, Jay Nathwani, Katie Wylde, and Rodolfo Novak. I cherish the memory of Renaissance man and dear friend Andrew Prince ז"ל. It is impossible to put into words the depth of my appreciation for Samantha Ash and Cara Zacks, whose friendship never ends. Colleen, Mike, and the New family have been unceasingly optimistic. My brothers, Ben and Sam, and their partners, Ardith and Jenni, remain the very finest partners-in-crime. My parents, Ricki and Steven, gave me my love of learning and reading. I dedicate this book to them in gratitude for their incredible dedication to me, to my work, and to our family. My grandparents have all been incredible role models and sources of unconditional love. I am in constant awe of my grandmother Gloria Robins, her cosmopolitanism, and her keen aesthetic sensibilities. I feel the recent losses of my grandmother Helen Sharpe ז"ל and my grandfather Sydney Robins ז"ל especially profoundly. Bubie Helen read many of these works along with me, often providing running commentary in our weekly chats. I treasure our correspondence, which has been an enormously gratifying aspect of this project. My Grampy Sydney was both my cheerleader and debate partner; I am forever inspired by the clarity and elegance of his writing and thinking. Their memories, and the memory of my grandfather Sydney Sharpe ז"ל, are truly a blessing.

Finally, I am deeply, happily forever indebted to the brilliant and kind Michael New, for being my partner, my most careful reader, my home, and my sunshine.

Many writers, their families, and their publishers generously granted me permission to use copyrighted works, translations, interviews, and archival documents. I am extremely grateful to George Elliott Clarke and Pottersfield Press and Guernica Editions, Stephen Collis, Brian Dedora and Book*hug, Mark Frutkin, Sylvia Tait Grier and the Estate of Eldon Grier, Susan Holbrook and Coach House Books, Maureen Hynes and Pedlar Press, Jay Stewart and the Estate of Dorothy Livesay, Seymour Mayne, Myron Momryk, Jim Nason and Frontenac House, Nicola Vulpe and Guernica Editions, Jonathan Waddington and the Estate of Miriam Waddington, J.A. Wainwright, Terrence Rundle West, the Writer's Trust and the Estate of George Woodcock, and Uli Rushby-Smith for the Ilsa Barea translation of Lorca's "Balada de la placeta." "Lorca Lives," "Take This Waltz," and "The Traitor" by Leonard Cohen. Copyright © 1979, 1988, and 2006 by Leonard Cohen, used by permission of The Wylie Agency LLC. "Lorca Lives" by Leonard Cohen, copyright 2006, HarperCollins Publishers. "Letter from Spain," and "Song of Spain" from *The Collected Poems of Langston Hughes* by Langston Hughes, edited by Arnold Rampersad with David Roessel, Associate Editor, copyright © 1994 by the Estate of Langston Hughes. Used by permission of Alfred A. Knopf, an imprint of the Knopf Doubleday Publishing Group, a division of Penguin Random House LLC. All rights reserved. Reprinted by permission of Harold Ober Associates. Copyright 1994 by the Langston Hughes Estate. "Of Castles in Spain" by A.M. Klein, as published in *Complete Poems, Part 2,* © University of Toronto Press 1990. Reprinted with permission of the publisher. Quotations from the archival writings of Salaria Kea and Frances Patai appear courtesy of the Tamiment Library, New York University. Excerpts from "Little Viennese Waltz" from *Collected Poems* by Federico García Lorca. Originally published in *Poet in New York* by Federico García Lorca. Translation copyright © 1988 by The Estate of Federico García Lorca, and Greg Simon and Steven F. White. Reprinted by permission of Farrar, Straus and Giroux. Edna St. Vincent Millay, excerpt from "Say that We Saw Spain Die" from *Collected Poems* (HarperCollins Publishers). Copyright 1939, © 1967 by Edna St. Vincent Millay and Norma Millay Ellis. Reprinted with the permission of The Permissions Company, Inc., on behalf of Holly Peppe, Literary Executor, The Edna St. Vincent Millay Society. www.millay.org. Every effort was made to find and contact the estates of Patrick Anderson, Louis Dudek, John Murray Gibbon, H.T. Munro, Ernest Neumann, and Henri Sevilla, but they could not be reached.

Parts of this book have appeared in sections of previously published essays. I am thankful for my editors' and anonymous readers' insights and for permission to incorporate portions of them here. Part of chapter 1 originally appeared as Emily Robins Sharpe, "Traitors in Love: The Spanish Civil War Romance Novel in Jewish North America" in *Studies in Jewish American Literature*, vol. 35, no. 2, 2016, pp. 147–64, Copyright © 2016 the Pennsylvania State University Press. This article is used by permission of The Pennsylvania State University Press. Part of that chapter also appeared in Emily Robins Sharpe, "Jewish Novels of the Spanish Civil War" in *The Edinburgh Companion to Modern Jewish Fiction*, ed. David Brauner and Axel Stähler, Edinburgh University Press, 2015, pp. 355–66, reproduced with permission of The Licensor through PLSclear. Part of chapter 2 originally appeared in Emily Robins Sharpe, "Tracing Morocco: Postcolonialism and Spanish Civil War Literature" in *ariel*, vol. 49, issue 2–3, 2018, pp. 89–117, copyright © 2018 Johns Hopkins University Press and the University of Calgary. Parts of chapter 3 originally appeared as "Salaria Kea's Spanish Memoirs" in *The Volunteer*, December 2011, vol. 28, issue 4; and "'The heart above the ruins': Miriam Waddington's Poetry, the Spanish Civil War, and Jewish Canadian Literature" in *Canadian Jewish Studies*, issue 26, 2018, pp. 56–74.

MOSAIC FICTIONS

Writing Identity in the Spanish Civil War

Introduction
A Better Earth: Looking at Spain, Envisioning Canada

"In Spain we would learn to know ourselves; we would find ourselves."
Ted Allan, *This Time a Better Earth*

Knowing Ourselves, Finding Ourselves: Canadians in Spain

Spain was where Canadians were supposed to learn to be Canadians. Nearly 1,700 Canadians volunteered in the Spanish Civil War (1936–9), joining a transnational, polyglot community of thousands, all connected through a shared conviction that defeating Franco would prevent the spread of European fascism. But for the Canadian volunteers, the war meant something more. As the protagonist of Montreal writer and former volunteer Ted Allan's novel *This Time a Better Earth* (1939) predicts, hopes, or perhaps retrospectively reflects of his fellow Canadian volunteers, travelling to Spain was how they would "learn to know" themselves. This conviction – that fighting in Spain would facilitate the discovery of a new Canadian identity – was more than a literary trope of young men made wise by their time on a battlefield; it was also a shared belief among Canadians, that independent participation in an international war would clarify their country's place in the world.

Just a few years earlier, in 1931, two critical, unconnected events had transpired across the world from each other: Spain abandoned monarchy for democracy, and, as a result of the United Kingdom's ratification of the Statute of Westminster, Canada gained near-complete legal independence. In Spain, the democratically elected leftist government of the Second Spanish Republic weakened the political power of the nobility and clergy and reduced the size of the military. It introduced new rights for its citizens, expanded the franchise, and improved access to education. The government also grappled with various leftist and independent factions over issues such as workers' rights and Catalan independence. A series of workers' revolutions across the country threatened the new democracy's equilibrium. The ongoing social revolutions that resulted brought about a new coalition government, the Popular Front. Meanwhile, having been assigned to a faraway command in the Canary Islands, General Francisco Franco harnessed Moroccans' antipathy toward their colonizer to support his fascist invasion. With the military support of fascist Italy and Nazi Germany, Franco's insurgent forces attacked Spain in July 1936.[1] After European and North American governments pledged they would not intervene, the Republicans' only support (and it was weak) came from the governments of Mexico and the Soviet Union, as well as from 35,000 international volunteers who journeyed to Spain to support the Republican loyalists as soldiers, medics, ambulance drivers, and social workers. Most of the international volunteers served in the communist International Brigades; some joined other parties to the Popular Front coalition, such as the anarchist Confederación Nacional del Trabajo (National Confederation of Labour) and the Trotskyist Partido Obrero de Unificación Marxista (Workers' Party of Marxist Unification).

Spain's struggles as a newly democratic nation resounded across the Atlantic in Canada's own troubles. In Canada, the Great Depression was a time of rampant poverty and unemployment, harsh restrictions on immigration, mistreatment of Indigenous populations, and nationwide debates over who in the Dominion counted as authentic Canadians. Furthermore, Canada's population lacked a legal framework, at least in terms of a Canadian identity: many may have personally identified as Canadian, but it was not until the 1947 Canadian Citizenship Act that Canadians actually held Canadian citizenship instead of British (although they remained both Canadian citizens and British subjects until as recently as the early 1980s).[2] For recent arrivals, xenophobic policies, anti-immigrant violence, and rampant antisemitism belied the title "new Canadians" with which they had been welcomed into the country. Irving Abella writes that Canadian antisemitism grew in the years leading up to the First World War as the "Anglicized, comfortable, integrated community" of Jewish Canadians gave way to "Yiddish-speaking, Orthodox, penurious immigrants" (103).[3] As the Nazis gained power in Germany, and despite widely sympathetic media coverage of the plight of Europe's Jews, Canada's Jews faced widespread discrimination. Anti-immigrant sentiments and antisemitism often intersected, as in Canada's refusal to accept almost any Jewish refugees from Nazi Germany between 1930 and 1939. What's more, as James Walker explains of this era, "exclusion did not just relate to keeping out Jewish refugees from Europe. In Canada itself, Jews were excluded from or restricted within certain occupations, university programs, summer resorts, beaches and hotels, residential districts, and social and recreational clubs" (218). The 1933 anti-Jewish riots in Toronto's Christie Pits neighbourhood were another violent manifestation of these Canadian forms of antisemitism. Around this same time, the Canadian government's plainly inadequate response to the early years of the Depression saw single, unemployed men consigned to work camps, where they performed manual labour for pennies a day. Many rightly identified all of this as part of a rising tide of authoritarian, right-wing ethnic nationalism.

Franco's attempted coup and the ensuing civil war that erupted in Spain in 1936 riveted many in anglophone Canada. Though there was little immigration from Spain to Canada, and the language barrier was high, Canadian activists, writers, and artists were drawn to what they saw as a struggle for postcolonial identity very similar to their own, albeit more violent.[4] The murder of Federico García Lorca, an internationally acclaimed writer and a non-combatant, by Franco's forces further galvanized support for the Spanish left among Canada's artistic community. For recent immigrants, the image of a fledgling democracy threatened by monarchy-backed fascism recalled the oppressive conditions they had only recently escaped. Many on the left were convinced that after Italy's invasion of Ethiopia (a fellow League of Nations member), and with Hitler gaining power in Germany, and now with a civil war having broken out in Spain, fascism would be certain to spread if it was not actively countered. Yet the Canadian government – like the governments of the United States, England, France, and most other countries – had pledged not to intervene in Spain.

Despite their government's unwillingness to intercede, many in Canada were ready to participate, not only fearful of European fascism's spread but also driven to leave Canada by unemployment, by mounting dissatisfaction with the government's domestic and international policies, and by alienation from the mainstream. Driven too, perhaps, by a burgeoning national pride: the Spanish Civil War would be the first war in which Canadians participated independently of their colonial obligations to Britain. Many of the volunteers lacked military experience, however. Their passports having been stamped "Not Valid for Travel to Spain," these individuals made their way there illegally, to risk their lives for the Spanish Republic and perhaps to be refused re-entry into Canada if they survived.[5] They were joined by Canadian journalists, including Myrtle Eugenia Jean "Jim" Watts and Ted Allan, as well as by volunteer nurses and doctors, the most famous of them being Norman Bethune, who would pioneer his blood transfusion technique on the battlefields of Spain.[6]

Most of the Canadians who participated in the Spanish Civil War did not fit the national ideal of Canadianness and were far removed from the archetype of white, Anglo-Saxon Protestant Canadian manhood. Most of the volunteers had immigrated to Canada in the decade before the war broke out; between thirty-eight and fifty-two of them identified as Jewish.[7] In other words, these Canadians did not always see themselves as fully Canadian, nor did other Canadians see them as that, either socially or (in some cases) legally. But at the same time, they had first-hand experience of the poverty and discrimination they hoped to fight against in Spain.[8]

Canadian support for Spain did not come just in the form of 1,700 volunteers, or of activists back home raising funds for the Spanish Republic's struggle. Canadian artists were captivated by the conflict. Anglophone writers took up the Spanish Civil War, with the result that it became one of the most extensively documented events in Canadian history. From poetry to fiction to reportage, Canadian authors – many of them now well-known for their other, canonical writings, including Hugh Garner, Dorothy Livesay, and Hugh MacLennan – depicted what happened in Spain for a Canadian audience. In this, they joined a global literary outpouring – one that has been widely recognized in the United States, England, Ireland, and Spain and that is beginning to receive attention in Canada.[9]

Canadian Spanish Civil War literature provides an important perspective on the burgeoning anglophone Canadian literary canon with its twinned emphases on transnational issues and an emergent Canadian national settler colonial identity. Even before the Spanish Civil War broke out, Canadian modernist literature frequently took up the formation of a national character as a prominent theme. Canadianness needed to separate itself from British colonial subjecthood, estranged French heritage, and the creeping cultural influence of the United States. It was also, in this construction, separate from Indigenous identity.[10] The many little magazines and other non-mainstream periodicals that flourished during the 1920s, '30s, and '40s demonstrate widespread literary innovation and experimentation, including alternating fascinations with and rejections of what were perceived to be British or American styles, from social realism to Imagism. For instance, as I will discuss in chapter 4 regarding the Montreal little magazines *First Statement* and *Preview*, the editors of the former often cast the latter as overly influenced by British Victorianism and therefore colonial, effeminate, and antiquated, while representing the writing in *First Statement* as, by contrast, American, independent, masculine, and robust. The conflation of colonialism with gender, sexuality, and literary innovation is also a part of the period's politics.

The Canadian modernist scene was a leftist one, with all the permutations and party affiliations that suggests, and the writers I will discuss, broadly speaking, were themselves leftists. At the same time, within this broad leftism, beginning in the 1920s, "women's issues were being subordinated to class struggle and then, with the rise of European fascism in the early 1930s, fighting racism and anti-Semitism at home and overseas" (Rifkind, *Comrades* 11). While their print runs were small, Canada's little magazines and leftist periodicals were influential: many of the poems, essays, and works of fiction I will analyse here first found an audience in *First Statement, Preview, New Frontier, Canadian Forum,* or the *Daily Clarion.* For authors depicting the Spanish Civil War – and its relationship to fascism and Nazism and the inherent sexism of both – the stakes of constituting this national character mounted.

It is perhaps no coincidence then that so many of the Canadian authors who wrote about Spain were themselves members of marginalized groups – groups often excluded from the still-imaginary notion of Canadian citizenship because of their gender, race, religion, ethnicity, sexuality, or immigration status. Some of the writers grappling with the stakes of national belonging were Jewish immigrants or their descendants, who had escaped Eastern European antisemitic violence to settle in the New World. Whether they were religious or secular, devout or atheist, openly Jewish or passing as gentiles, the period's politics rendered that identity salient. What's more, the Spanish Civil War coincided with an outpouring of Canadian Jewish literature. As Ruth Panofsky notes, "the flowering of Canadian Jewish writing in English dates from the mid-1940s" ("Guest Editor's" 139). Rebecca Margolis explains that Jewish authors writing in English emerged from the Yiddish-speaking immigrant literary community – a community that "looked to European and US models for their writing" (433). These Yiddish writers were part of the modernist avant-garde as a result of their contact with a transnational Yiddish literary canon, one that was not available in Canada in translation (Margolis 435).

This period saw the publication of writers I will discuss in this book, including Miriam Waddington, Leonard Cohen, Mordecai Richler, and A.M. Klein. Michael Greenstein credits Klein as the founder of Jewish Canadian literature (3), and Norman Ravvin further cites him as "the first non-Anglo, non-francophone ethnic voice to gain an important foothold in the Canadian canon" ("The War and Before" 185). Klein's poem "Of Castles in Spain" (1938) was just one of many to voice support for the Spanish Republic in the midst of the war. James Doyle writes that Klein's 1930s poetry was often explicitly socialist, a turn Doyle connects to the influence of socialist Yiddish literature (142). In the section "To One Gone to the Wars," Klein's speaker regretfully justifies his non-enlistment and offers this "non-liturgic prayer":

> For that your aim be sure,
> Your bullet swift

Unperilous your air, your trenches dry,
Your courage unattainted by defeat,
Your courage high. (473, 19–24)

Klein dedicates this section to "S.H.A.," his friend the volunteer Samuel H. Abramson. Klein's poem *imagines* combat, while many other authors had first-hand experience. Ted Allan, who writes about "learn[ing] to know ourselves ... [to] find ourselves," was a Jewish author passing as a gentile (8). A member of the Communist Party of Canada, Allan went to Spain as a journalist to cover the war for the communist *Daily Clarion.* In addition to his writing for the *Daily Clarion* and *New Frontier*, he volunteered with the Canadian doctor Norman Bethune and his mobile blood transfusion service as political commissar. Upon returning to Canada, Allan published *This Time a Better Earth.* His Spanish Civil War novel depicts a multicultural cast of North Americans and Europeans who collectively belie his idealistic reference to a Canadian "we": the protagonist is a gentile Torontonian, but he volunteers with characters whom he perceives as distinct from himself. They are African American, Québécois, working-class Albertan, and Jewish American. This character falls in love with a leftist German woman, works for a Spanish man, and encounters a female Moroccan sex worker. In this (perhaps tokenist) assemblage, Allan signals many of the groups who saw the Spanish Civil War's very personal repercussions for themselves. He also invokes some of the regional distinctions of national belonging: amid the linguistic, cultural, and religious clashes in Quebec, for instance, Jewish identity signifies differently than in anglophone Protestant Toronto.

The internationalism that Allan and many other Canadian authors portray (however problematically) suggests that Canada, the United States, and Spain could be reimagined as part of a specific global continuum. At the same time, in imagining the linkages between Spaniards, Americans, and Canadians, Allan carefully specifies that it is the variously marginalized North Americans who form this patriotic, internationalist community. In other words, Allan, like so many of the Jewish Canadian writers I will discuss, envisions a Canadian citizenry composed primarily of a pan-provincial group of settler Canadians, reliant on marginalized Americans too for their emerging concept of pluralist democracy.

Yet many constituencies remain absent from Allan's selective representation of North American men. Despite the trailblazing roles that women played in the Spanish Civil War, for instance, the representation of the female love interest – a German photojournalist based on the combat photographer Gerda Taro – emphasizes her romantic role over her work. Nor does *This Time a Better Earth* depict the participation of

Indigenous and immigrant Canadians. The novel was published in the United States and England (Bart Vautour notes the "remote possibility" that a Canadian edition exists) but received widespread, positive attention in Canada as well (Vautour, Introduction xxvi). Allan's emphasis on American diversity, then, may have been motivated by market concerns. But despite his limited representation of Canadians, I suggest that Allan's novel invites readers to picture Canada as diverse and inclusive and that it amplifies this diversity by incorporating non-white (or not-quite-white) Americans and by showing them on the battlefields of Spain.

The Mosaic: Picturing Canadians

Allan's character Lisa, a photojournalist, perhaps provides a clue to this image of Canadians. The Spanish Civil War was the first conflict to be documented by hand-held cameras – a detail that allowed for the war's combatants and carnage to be seen around the world, and one that challenged viewers to rethink their understanding of the kinds of truths photographs could communicate. For instance, Hungarian British journalist Arthur Koestler includes page after page of Spanish destruction in the appendix to his book of reportage *L'Espagne ensanglantée: Un livre noir sur l'Espagne* (*Bloody Spain: A Black Book on Spain*; 1937), including a section titled "Photographies documentaires de la barbarie fasciste en Espagne" (Documentary Photographs of Fascist Barbarity in Spain), while Virginia Woolf's *Three Guineas* instructs the reader in a method for interpreting photographs for these types of images of carnage.[11] We might additionally see visual and textual representations of Spain fostering new directions in a developing Canadian identity. At the same time that photographic documentation inspired support of the Spanish Republic and feelings of fellowship with Spaniards, it helped normalize the presence of individuals outside the mainstream within a broadened vision of citizenship.

Allan represents Jewish and Black populations of another nation: these characters are explicitly from the United States, not Canada (although, as I will argue in the following chapter, the novel's protagonist and his love interest are also coded as Jewish). The distancing gesture of *This Time a Better Earth*, and of other Canadian literature about the Spanish Civil War, can perhaps be understood in the context of a more explicit exploration of Canada's immigrant populations, including Jewish immigrants, that had been published just a year before. The early years of the twentieth century saw a variety of tracts written about the influx of new Canadians, including John Murray Gibbon's *Canadian Mosaic: The Making of a Northern Nation* (1938) – which was published while the Spanish Civil War was still raging and had an explicit and visual focus on Jewish immigration.[12] Through photographs and illustrations of "Hebrews" and other immigrant groups, Gibbon argues for sympathy toward white ethnic immigrants as a way of facilitating their assimilation into British Canadian society. With its limited European focus and explicitly nationalist project, *Canadian Mosaic* demonstrates a distancing gesture and documentary function (both evident in Allan's *This Time a Better Earth*) that I see as emblematic of Canada's many self-consciously multiethnic representations of the Spanish Civil War.

The use of the term "mosaic" to describe Canadian multiculturalism is often attributed to Gibbon's *Canadian Mosaic*, although Gibbon himself credits the American writer Victoria Hayward in *Romantic Canada* (1922), followed by Kate A. Foster's *Our Canadian Mosaic* (1926; Gibbon ix). It is a metaphor for a Canada composed of peacefully coexisting, distinct yet connected cultures that fit together like decorative tiles: a representation that proves integral to how many marginalized Canadian writers would envision Canada via Spain. (Canadian Jewish writer Miriam Waddington refers to a "scarred mosaic" in her poetic book of photography *Call Them Canadians*, 15). While Gibbon invokes a now outmoded metaphor for Canadian society, my own book's title makes use of the term "mosaic" to challenge this idea of Canadian multiculturalism composed of discrete communities, and to invoke the Mosaic – that is, Jewish – writers who promulgated this metaphor as they strove to write their communities into that very society.[13]

Canadian Mosaic relies on cultural stereotyping as well as a limited white-ish perspective on who counts as potentially Canadian. The immigrant groups highlighted are restricted to American, French, English, Scottish, Irish, Welsh, German, Dutch, Belgian, Scandinavian, Eastern Baltic, Polish, Ukrainian, Czechoslovakian, Balkan, Hungarian, Russian, Italian, Spanish, and finally "Hebrew" immigrants – a reminder that in mid-century North America, Jews remained a racial Other.[14] Antonia Smith has argued that Gibbon's book was a response to what was widely perceived as a threat to British Canadians. To safeguard against cultural dilution, they "attempt[ed] simultaneously to consolidate white, British-Canadian identity, perform it as stable both for themselves and for their immigrant audience, and in so doing cause it to function as a model for successful assimilation into 'Canadian culture'" (38). Gibbon suggests that new citizens should be allowed to maintain what he sees as certain minor cultural differences – food, for instance, or costume – while taming what he represents as their more extreme dissimilarities so that they can fit into Canadian society. He seems hopeful that established citizens might overcome their antipathy toward the white ethnic immigrants entering their country and even grow to accept them as fellow countrymen.[15]

In *Canadian Mosaic*, Jewish immigrants are the only group categorized by race or religion rather than nationality. Indeed, in his chapter on

"Hebrews," Gibbon includes Jews from many of the countries he discusses earlier in the book. He comments, too, on Jews' particular resistance to assimilation (406), yet his exploration of the history of Jews in Canada (he includes Jewish converts to Christianity in the chapter) highlights their many contributions to the military, science, medicine, and the arts, as well as their tendency to organize to take care of new immigrants, thus "avoid[ing] overcrowding in the larger cities by encouraging Hebrew immigrants to settle in the smaller communities" (422). This emphasis on Jewish immigrants' self-directed dispersion within Canada is reinforced by Gibbon's extensive use of secondary materials – interviews and images – to positively showcase Jews' attempts to join the mainstream. He quotes at length from a *Winnipeg Tribune* interview with a first-generation Canadian Jew, a lawyer, who attempts to explain how Jews view the nation:

> Certainly we can give to Canada our first loyalty. We have no conflicting loyalty – nothing that we must withhold ... I think that if we are permitted to identify ourselves wholly with the life of this country, we will be able to repay with a generous bonus any kindness and consideration that is extended to us here.
>
> What I want most – my greatest desire – is this: I don't ask anything except the opportunity to participate as an equal in the communal life of this country ... I want to have the inner feeling and the inner assurance that I am one with this people – that they acknowledge that I have as great a stake in this country's future as they have. (qtd in Gibbon 410)

This anonymous, articulate plea for inclusion is one of the book's only first-person representations of a contemporary, adult Jew living in Canada (the others are an anonymous farmer, 405, and [in a single sentence] Rabbi Maurice N. Eisendrath, 411). Gibbon also includes a series of photographs of Jews and one sketch of a pretty, dark-haired woman representing the "Hebrew-Canadian type." (He illustrates each section of the book in this way.) The photographs he includes – intended, like the text, to emphasize positive Jewish contributions to Canada – underscore the book's often patronizing, infantilizing, feminizing perspective even as Gibbon attempts to historicize the long-standing presence of Jews in Canada. The captions he provides for his photographs of Jews read as follows: "Tevel Finkelstein, first Hebrew settler in Manitoba"; "Aaron Hart, prominent merchant in Québec after the British occupation of 1760"; "Dinner time in the Jewish Orphanage at Winnipeg"; "Twenty-nine racial groups are represented in Ogden Public School, Toronto"; "Twenty-one races are represented in this group from Aberdeen School, Winnipeg, which distinguished itself on account of fine diction in the Manitoba Competitive Musical Festival of 1938" (figures 1–3).

Tevel Finkelstein, first Hebrew settler in Manitoba.

Aaron Hart, prominent merchant in Quebec after the British occupation of 1760.

Dinner time in the Jewish Orphanage at Winnipeg.

Twenty-nine racial groups are represented in Ogden Public School, Toronto.

Twenty-one races are represented in this group from Aberdeen School, Winnipeg, which distinguished itself on account of fine diction in the Manitoba Competitive Musical Festival of 1938.

(above and opposite) Images from John Murray Gibbon's *Canadian Mosaic: The Making of a Northern Nation*, McClelland and Stewart, 1938.

"Hebrew-Canadian Type" by Ernest Neumann, from John Murray Gibbon's *Canadian Mosaic: The Making of a Northern Nation*, McClelland and Stewart, 1938.

The only visual representations of adult Jews are taken from early in Canadian history; the orphans, and the unidentified public school students (who may or may not be Jewish), are all children. Gibbon also avoids the usual photos of immigrants disembarking from ships at Halifax's Pier 21 or New York's Ellis Island or working in sweatshops. In the visual emphasis on children – and despite textual assertions of the prominent roles played by Jews in Canadian society and in founding community organizations – Gibbon's book exemplifies the patriarchal perspective that casts immigrants as children in need of guidance and teaching so that they will learn to be full members of the community.[16]

However, the disjuncture between pictures and text also leaves open the possibility that adult Jewish Canadians look like all other Canadians – that they might be assimilated, at least visually, while maintaining the Jewish values Gibbon is at pains to emphasize. The immigrant groups profiled in *Canadian Mosaic* are all future potential insiders to Canada, but it's also clear that Jewish immigrants are the most outside: what Eric L. Goldstein has referred to in the American context as "unstable members of America's racial culture" (189). At the same time, Gibbon's invocations of the benefits of Mosaic culture – and of the Mosaic religion's benefits to Canada – argue for selective sympathy and inclusion. He mostly avoids discussing the stakes of this inclusion – alluding only briefly to Nazi racial laws, he offers the tragic understatement that "recently through the Anti-Semitic policy of the Nazis, a number of German Jews have sought refuge in Canada" (409). Gibbon's *Canadian Mosaic* also envisions an end to Jews' racialized difference and their gaining of a certain amount of white privilege.

The metaphor of the pluralist Canadian "mosaic" is often contrasted with the American melting pot, in which immigrants ostensibly shed their differences in order to become full Americans. Epitomized in the play *The Melting-Pot* (1905) by the Jewish British author Israel Zangwill (himself married to a gentile woman), melting pot assimilation also emphasized strengthening the nation through white ethnic intermarriage as means to address the large number of European immigrants entering the country. The ideals of the melting pot and the mosaic could not, of course, legitimate the anti-miscegenation laws that remained in place in the United States or the paternalistic policies of the many Canadian Indian Acts, which were designed to curtail intermarriage and to segregate populations – certainly, Gibbon's book and Zangwill's play take little notice of the people who lived in North America before European colonization. These metaphors remain lacking. But Gibbon's book is useful for contextualizing how Canadian Jews were being represented – both positively and negatively, as effeminate and infantile, hardworking and adaptable – and how they in turn represented themselves. The omissions and oversights in *Canadian Mosaic* speak to the larger shortcomings of the Canadian mosaic – of the empty and interstitial spaces that the writers I will discuss sought to fill by articulating a Canadian mosaic of their own.

Looking at Spain: War and Cosmopolitanism

Both *Canadian Mosaic* and *The Melting-Pot* underscore the larger question of Jewish identity in North America – the ways in which Jews have been racialized, sexualized and desexualized, gendered, and othered by a white, Christian dominant culture. As I will discuss in the following chapters, Jewish identity remains nebulous in literature of this period – is it a race, an ethnicity, a religion, a sexuality, a gender, a nation? Given this broader cultural confusion around Jews and Jewishness, I am interested in both Jewish authors' depictions of the Spanish Civil War and, more broadly, depictions of Jewish participation in the context of a multicultural community. These texts shed light on the connection between Jewishness and other categories of identity. As Jonathan Freedman notes, fictions around Jews can disrupt categories of otherness – of ethnicity, immigration, race, gender, and sexuality. More importantly, he argues, Jews, Jewishness, and Judaism "do this in such a way as to reveal what was at stake in the making of those categories in the first place" (15). In both Canadian and international Spanish Civil War literature, representations of Jews are always connected to larger questions of identity, complicating racial, ethnic, sexual, and gender divisions by suggesting the ease with which these designations can be circumvented or transcended. This fixation on the Jewish presence, and on the Jewish stake in Spain's war, suggests a reliance on narratives of outsiders' inclusion in order to understand the larger questions of mobility and human rights at play in the Spanish conflict.[17] Jews were connected to non-normativity – racial and religious difference, male effeminacy and female masculinity, queerness, foreignness – so tracing the role of Jewish characters helps us better understand the ongoing negotiation of the margins and the centre, the discourse around outsiders and their difference.

Given the connections between Jewishness and outsider status, it is also significant that Ted Allan invokes Jewish American identity through the inclusion of a heroic Jewish American secondary character. Despite important distinctions between Canadian and American cultures (and within each country's cultures), these early twentieth-century literary expressions of Jewish Canadian cultural identity were deeply tied to the United States. In writing about the Spanish Civil War, Jewish Canadian authors frequently look to American Jews and Jewish American cultures – even, like Allan, depicting Jewish American volunteer soldiers instead of Jewish Canadians (and emphasizing American racial diversity far more than Canadian).

There are many possible reasons for this hemispheric perspective. In addition to the market concerns I mentioned regarding the publication of Allan's novel, coming to Canada was an incidental choice for many immigrants, who often intended to settle later in the United States. In this context, the predominantly Ashkenazi, immigrant Jewish American narrative trumps the nascent Canadian identity as experienced by Jewish immigrants. This cultural porousness was reinforced by many elements of the specific Spanish context: Canadian Jews were a comparatively small presence in the Spanish Civil War, whereas American Jews comprised up to 40 per cent of the country's volunteers, filling many high-ranking positions. Jewish American soldiers were highly visible to North Americans in a way that Jewish Canadians were not. Moreover, Jewish American soldiers served alongside many Canadians because the International Brigades battalions were divided by language or nationality. Until the Canadian Mackenzie-Papineau Battalion was established in 1937, Canadians were typically assigned to the American Abraham Lincoln Brigade (along with Cuban and Irish volunteers). That year also saw the creation of the Yiddish-speaking Botwin Company, which united Jewish volunteers from around the world, including those from England, across Europe, and Mandatory Palestine.[18] On the battlefields of Spain – and in writers' imaginings of those battlefields – American Jews, and Jews from other countries, themselves became part of a Canadian mosaic.

As Jewish Canadian authors focus on American participation, they also think through their own connections to Spain: while it remains a metaphor with powerful patriotic baggage in Canada, the mosaic is not regionally specific. Actual mosaics are a frequent decoration in Spain, too – a reminder of the country's Muslim heritage before the Spanish Inquisition almost entirely rid the country of Jewish and Muslim Spaniards. Spain has its own mosaics, and its own Mosaic fiction as well – that is, it has long refused to acknowledge its Jewish heritage. Franco certainly played on the country's pre-expulsion Muslim heritage to pull Moroccan support to his side; that aside, Spain was an emphatically Catholic nation, with the Church playing an outsized role in the country's governance from before the Inquisition until the Second Spanish Republic. Franco was willing to self-servingly praise Spain's Muslim heritage, but he did not acknowledge Spain's third major religion. In thinking about the multiple resonances of the mosaic, then, I suggest the possibility that for some volunteers, Spain was a possible site of reclamation – an earlier location of expulsion and dispersion for Jews and Muslims.[19]

In multiple and sometimes unexpected ways, the war generated cosmopolitan sympathy. These connections – between Canadian and international Jewish volunteers, between Canadian artists and a Spanish poet-playwright, between Jewish volunteers and Spain, and between Jewish Canadians and members of other minority and subaltern groups – are just a few examples of the complex and intersecting motivations behind the unprecedented international solidarity with the Spanish Republic. In analysing First World War poetry, Jahan Ramazani argues that "war can be, paradoxically, a catalyst for meaningful cross-cultural encounters and reflections" (856).[20] I suggest that in Spanish Civil War literature from just a few years later, these encounters and reflections become an occasion to foment sorely needed social change.

Some of these cross-cultural encounters took place in person; many more, however, were imagined, as most Canadian writers did not participate directly in the Spanish Civil War. Instead, their sympathy for the Republic was based in imagined depictions of Spain and an appreciation of Spanish literature in translation. Nicola Vulpe suggests that Canadian poets "writ[e] at once about the Spanish War but only rarely about Spain" ("This Issue" 31).[21] On the other hand, Candida Rifkind suggests that Canadian writers did not differentiate between experience abroad and back home, and characterizes Canadian Spanish Civil War literature as "an imaginative participation" because of the transnational empathy the Popular Front encouraged, the belief that "the people are a living entity, that a wound to one part is an injury to the whole" (Rifkind, *Comrades* 93–4). Canadian writers' often imagined sympathy can veer toward an Orientalizing gaze, or lead to a Canada-centric emphasis.

Whether instrumentalizing or sincere, altruistic or self-serving, Canadian literature about the Spanish Civil War imagines transnational solidarity as a force that is ultimately locally and globally beneficial – a vision of Canada that inverts and expands the centre and peripheries of the country depicted in Gibbon's *Canadian Mosaic*. Canadian sympathy for Spanish citizens – imagined though this connection may have been – is articulated as a cosmopolitan as well as patriotic value. Philosophical cosmopolitanism insists that human sympathy exceeds, and must take precedence over, national, racial, linguistic, or religious boundaries. Canadian writers depict Canadian identity as inherently cosmopolitan. For those invested in the Spanish cause, a newly imagined nationalism called for a decolonized identity intimately tied to inclusion in the new nation – not necessarily what immigrants and other marginalized groups experienced in Canada, but certainly the hoped-for outcome of Canadian autonomy. This cosmopolitan vision of Canadian national identity is articulated from the margins of Canadian society. For these authors, cosmopolitan nationalism entails a conceptual broadening of national community to include individuals from different backgrounds and with different migration histories.[22]

The imagined Canadian cosmopolitanism cultivated in the moment of the Spanish Civil War at once claims that everyone is a citizen of the world and that everyone can, or at least might, be a citizen of Canada. In justifying their participation in an international political cause, Canadians envision their own country as a diverse, independent nation rather than a homogeneous colony of subjects. National citizenship becomes a broad, flexible, inclusive category that is ethically constituted – that is, a category based on action and political affiliation, not birth country, gender, race, or religion. Marginalized writers recast international crises as Canadian problems.

In arguing for both the international stake in Spain's war and their own suitability for Canadian inclusion, the writers I discuss promote the importance of forging permanent links within a stable, if idealized, national community. The widening circle of community and sympathy that characterizes Canadian Spanish Civil War literature demonstrates how cosmopolitan sympathy inspired by the war may at times lead, somewhat paradoxically, *toward* patriotism rather than away from it, in a version of what Kwame Anthony Appiah has characterized as rooted cosmopolitanism.[23] Will Kymlicka and Kathryn Walker specifically note that "the idea that 'being Canadian' includes or entails 'being a good citizen of the world' has a long history in Canadian public debate and academic discourse, and is underpinned by several structural features of Canada's internal political dynamics and its position in the world" (1). Even as the very possibility of "rootedness" remains a founding fiction of proto-patriotic narrative, unavailable to most marginalized groups including those indigenous to the region, the Canadian cosmopolitan patriotism I identify in Spanish Civil War literature takes up established tropes of geographical rootedness – images of Canada's preindustrial landscape integral to the literature and visual art of the late nineteenth and early twentieth centuries – and populates them with multiracial, multiethnic, multilingual inhabitants.[24] This patriotism is insistent on inclusive citizenship, based in an appreciation for the contours of national belonging – a patriotism defined by residents rather than by the state. Canadian cosmopolitanism disentangles ethnicity from nationality, in other words, and replaces it with an ethical imperative to wider inclusiveness. In this way, what Glenn Willmott terms Canada's "anticipatory nationalism" (3) – an imagined community attempting to forge a communal imagination – encodes an obligation toward not just shared identification and community, but international involvement and responsibility.

In writing Canadians into an international community, Jewish Canadian writers often adopt a purposefully detached narrative perspective, implicitly comparing experiences of marginalization as a way of discussing Canadian issues at a remove: the inclusion of minoritized American characters within a Canadian community in *This Time a Better Earth* is just one example. Some writers assume gentile pseudonyms and create gentile narrators, thereby producing a textual disinterestedness through which to stage Jewish characters' intense attachments to their new communities. In a parallel gesture, white authors may use African American characters to vocalize the connections between Spanish fascism and American racism. These poses of detachment are created in the midst of intense, violent global engagement in the Spanish Civil War. Writers demonstrate simultaneous detachment from and attachment to different cultures – even as the pretense of detachment or objectivity is always aspirational and, in many cases, risks appropriation. Both the cosmopolitan patriotism forged in Canada and the cosmopolitan communities produced in Spain inevitably regulate identities even as they seem to support a more diverse membership.

The paradoxical arrangement of representing or performing detachment to demonstrate a seemingly objective perspective on attachments speaks to the deep ambivalence many felt toward the prospects and parameters of citizenship.[25] At the same time, these versions of nationalism provide a counterpoint to the exclusionary nationalisms created by fascist ideologies. Canadian modernists alternately glorified and derided cosmopolitan literature in contrast to the supposedly provincial, while in Spain, so-called cosmopolitans were denigrated by the Spanish Republic's opposing side.[26] "Cosmopolitan" has long been a euphemistic epithet for "Jew." And as many Spanish Civil War historians have noted, Franco's supporters expanded that particular usage to include anyone associated with modernity. Helen Graham stipulates that among their fellow Spaniards, fascist antagonism extended to "progressive teachers, intellectuals, self-educated workers, 'new' women … the socially, culturally, and sexually different" (29). This antipathy included those from outside the country as well: the insurgents frequently characterized Spain and the West as dominated by Jews.[27]

Canadian cosmopolitanism strives to connect experiences of diaspora with both Canada's decolonization and Spain's international communities. In writing Canadian national identity into existence, marginalized authors chart the intersections between the cosmopolitanisms forged by necessary, often involuntary travel (for instance, the transatlantic slave trade, the need to flee Eastern European antisemitism or British and Irish poverty for the promise of land in the New World) and the privileges of choice in mobility (even in the decision to fight in Spain, as dangerous and immediate a choice as that seemed). However, in attempting to encompass multiple experiences, there are unavoidable misapprehensions, silences, and disparities. Cosmopolitanism's omissions and missteps, then, demonstrate that even in representing diversity and tolerance as guiding national principles, any community's constitutive multiplicity precludes a single unifying force.

Jewish Literatures and Minority Literatures

In this book I situate Jewish Canadian literature in a comparative context as my route into discussing larger issues around the Spanish Civil War and identity. By placing Jewish Canadian literature in conversation with overlapping categories of Canadian, Jewish American, African American, feminist, and queer literatures, I demonstrate the possibilities of expanding our understanding of anglophone Spanish Civil War literature. Decentring those texts that have become canonical – Ernest Hemingway's *For Whom the Bell Tolls* and George Orwell's *Homage to Catalonia* among them – provides a more complex, nuanced understanding of the war's stakes for individuals who were themselves at the margins.

In this approach and in my particular focus on occasional (often polemic) literature, I also aim to highlight how both centring a minority literature and studying it comparatively can help us interrogate that literature's broader cultural context.[28] Norman Ravvin's analysis of Jewish North American writings calls for what he terms a "transcultural drama," one that acknowledges how Jewish writers participate simultaneously in multiple literary and social cultures (*A House of Words* 158). In my particular project, the social-political situation sees Jewish writers attempting to participate in or join the dominant culture – which in Canada at that time meant anglophone and gentile – while simultaneously trying to define that same mainstream as one that would include them; these writers were both involved in leftism and unavoidably marked as other by the era's ambient antisemitism.

These social conditions call for an expansive understanding of Jewish literature. It is perhaps a commonplace to state that Jewish literature isn't always written by Jews, nor does it need to showcase Jewish characters. Further, as Benjamin Schreier argues, we cannot interpret Jewish literature as a mirror of Jewish experience: instead of seeing Jewish literature as somehow representational of Jewish identity, we must understand the category of Jewish literature "in terms of a history of the desire for a representational concept of The Jew rather than as part of the history of the representation of Jews" (Schreier 22). Not only is it helpful to an analysis of Spanish Civil War literature to think about how the conflict has been depicted alongside authorial attempts to represent Jews, but literature about this particular world historical event can be usefully interpreted in terms of what Michael P. Kramer calls "ethnic metonymy" (347) – that is, non-religious identity markers, such as cultural practices or political involvement. Similarly, in analysing Jewish American Second World War novels, Leah Garrett argues for the inclusion of Jewish authors, texts about Jewish characters, and texts displaying what she calls "family resemblances": "in which works that fall under the rubric of 'Jewish American' share certain traits, including in many instances the aim to hide the Jewish aspects in the clothing of universalism" (Garrett 220). For Garrett, the Second World War novels she analyses are Jewish in their related responses to wartime, and American in their attempts to translate the Jewish experience for a broader mainstream audience (222). Similarly, I focus in this project on how marginalized authors translate experiences of marginalization for a mainstream Canadian audience.

Even in looking to authors who avoided openly self-identifying as Jewish – as many depicting the Spanish Civil War, including Ted Allan, did[29] – and even in studying writings by and about Jews who placed little importance on their Judaism or their connection to the diaspora, as their leftist political beliefs superseded any other belief system, I follow David A. Hollinger in suggesting that "surely there is still something Jewish here to be studied" (164). My approach to Jewish literature allows cosmopolitan hybridity to coexist with chosen and coerced affiliations – for example, Allan's adoption of a gentile pseudonym was a protective measure while he reported on Canadian Nazism, not necessarily an eschewal of his identity.

What I am calling mainstream Canada is also a construct, the country's borders a colonial fiction in which Jewish immigrants participated and from which they benefited. While my own study remains grounded in North America and limited to anglophone sources, transnational and multilingual perspectives on Jewish Spanish Civil War literature offer possibilities for future study. Lital Levy and Allison Schachter's recent call for a transnational, comparative approach to Jewish literature, one that thinks beyond the texts themselves to their "production, reception, and circulation in relation to Jewish audiences and larger literary systems," offers one method (105n11). Levy and Schachter emphasize that dominant understandings of Jewish literature often overlook "the circuit of modern Jewish-language literatures, composed of multiple centers in Asia, Africa, Europe, and North America" (93). As the authors point out, many scholars of Jewish literature – including those who are trying to define it – begin from an established canon, primarily constituted of Jewish American authors. Their point resonates with Michael Greenstein's reading of Jewish Canadian literature, which he characterizes as multiply marginalized – Jewish Canadian authors write from outside the Canadian mainstream, outside both American and Jewish American literary cultures, and outside of the Europe from which they and their families come (12; more recent scholarship also highlights a broader cross-section of Jewish Canadian writers of Sephardic and Mizrahi descent as well). Thus, Greenstein argues that many works of fiction centre on quests: "the quests of anti-heroes, orphans, adolescents, and immigrants for their parents, their homeland, and a meaningful tradition" (7). In Jewish Canadian writing about the Spanish Civil War, we might see that undertaking not as a narrative of return, but as a commitment to making a home of Canada through engagement abroad, thus reversing the direction of that return.

What happens to our understanding of Spanish Civil War literature and of Jewish Canadian literature when we start somewhere else? I mean this "somewhere else" quite literally – looking to Canadian writers in addition to American, and to literature frequently set not just in metonyms for Jewish populations like those of New York's Lower East Side and Montreal's Mile End, but in a country whose population underwent forced conversions from Islam and Judaism a few centuries earlier, so that each Spanish character carries the possibility of shared Jewish ancestry. I also mean this "somewhere else" in terms of the texts themselves, as I emphasize out-of-print and even unpublished writings – literary texts from archives and little magazines, rather than an established canon. These texts may have been written for a wider readership, but that doesn't mean they found it. And finally, "somewhere else" also suggests that we should look beyond the signifiers of Jewishness – yoked, as they so often are, to familial and communal regionalisms – and consider the more stigmatized aspects of Jewishness. In this book, I try to follow Jewishness where it went for those who identified as Jews, for those who were fascinated by them, and for those who hated them: to consider what happens if we think about Jews as a race or ethnicity, since so many in the 1930s did; to think of the category's gendered and sexualized dimensions, as so many antisemites did in representing Jewish bodies – especially Jewish male bodies – as other, effeminate, and queer; and finally to think about Jewishness as changing over time and across geographies.

Looking to Canadian and American writers, and to writers from different backgrounds, helps reposition how we understand what "Jewish" might mean to different people in different social contexts, as the markers of Jewishness bump into nationality and immigration status, religion, race and ethnicity, gender, and sexuality.[30] Mine is, in other words, an intersectional, comparative approach to understanding what Jewishness meant and what authors were trying to do with it within writings about a uniquely polemical topic: the "last great cause" (cf. Weintraub). The literature I analyse speaks at once to the need to support the Spanish Republic and stop European fascism, and simultaneously to the necessity of reframing citizenship in North America to include immigrants, Jews, and other marginalized groups.[31]

Reading Identity in Spanish Civil War Literature

In highlighting intersecting concerns – over race, religion, ethnicity, gender, and sexuality – this book necessarily sacrifices comprehensiveness to a chronological, sometimes cross-border emphasis. As my title suggests, I'm interested in the fictions writers construct. To that end, I look primarily at fictional works but include poetry, memoir, and reportage as well. Scholars such as Bernard Dionne, Gerben Zaagsma, Amelia Glaser, and David Weintraub have done invaluable research to highlight French- and Yiddish-language Spanish Civil War writings from Canada and elsewhere. While my study is limited to texts written in English, there is fertile ground for future study of the interactions between anglophone and francophone Canadian literatures as well as those produced by the polyglot transnational communities that found themselves in Canada, including the robust Yiddish-speaking literary community. My study also omits drama, unfortunately – I look forward to future study of Spanish Civil War plays, including those by Canadian playwrights Harold Griffin (*Underground*, 1936; *Hostage*, 1937), George Luscombe, Mac Reynolds, and Larry Cox (*The Mac Paps*, 1980), and Tara Beagan (*Jesus Chrysler*, 2011). Further work on Canadian Spanish Civil War literature's relationship to other national literatures remains an important future project. In bringing together Canadian Spanish Civil War literature and cosmopolitan discourses of affiliation, this project is one attempt to study the formation of literary nationalism: an entrance into examining the interactive effects of global crisis on the literary aesthetics of a newly decolonized nation, a response to the constitutively international character of both Spanish Civil War literature and Jewish Canadian literature.

In my emphasis on archival and out-of-print texts as well as more established works, I seek to broaden the critical understanding of the breadth of Spanish Civil War literature. Despite the recent publication of a variety of Spanish Civil War literary anthologies, the idea of imagining Spanish Civil War literature as a "canon" is a difficult one to square with that literature's history. It is simply difficult, if not impossible, to parse the limits of this artistic archive in Canada or elsewhere. As Griselda Pollock reminds us, the archive is overdetermined by facts of class, race, gender, sexuality and above all power" (12). In this particular case, all of these forces have conspired to keep many Spanish Civil War texts out of print, particularly those by women, writers of colour, and far leftists.

In Canada, the difficulties of access are compounded by the lack of a designated Spanish Civil War archive. Instead, Canadian-authored materials are scattered among a variety of governmental and academic libraries across North America, England, and Spain, with further Canadian holdings in at least two more Spanish Civil War archives in New York and London (the Abraham Lincoln Brigade Archives and the International Brigade Association Archives, respectively). These and other archives have also been gradually and incompletely accrued: the fall of the Soviet Union led to the dissemination of many previously classified documents. Furthermore, the demonization of former Spanish Civil War volunteers during the McCarthy Era (in Canada as well as the United States) led many former Spanish Republican supporters to rid themselves of texts linking them to the cause – even now, some archival documents have clearly been altered or excised.

The spatial distances and textual gaps in the Spanish Civil War literary archive impose artificial borders on textual interpretation, partly obscuring the comparative perspective so integral to reading literature about an international event. This project attempts to move beyond the enforced categorizations and artificial boundaries imposed by publishing and archival practices. The archive I construct reveals a collective international site, the location of actual violence and imagined community.[32]

To elucidate the multiple, often unexpected intersections between different filiations and affiliations within global leftist participation, *Mosaic Fictions* is organized thematically around shared values, which I trace across literary texts. This approach demonstrates the integral role that overlapping discussions of gender, sexuality, race, religion, and ethnicity play in a developing patriotic cosmopolitanism. Moreover, I see it as responsive to some of the different ways in which Jews were stigmatized in mid-century society, whether they were effeminized or masculinized, romanticized or stereotyped, sexualized or desexualized, racialized or whitened. While, for many writers, political party membership was an additional foundation of their identity, following the Popular Front pan-leftist ideology within which they worked, my study does not separate writers based on this particular axis of affiliation.[33] However, in attempting to attend to the literary and social contexts authors saw for themselves, I do at times bring American literatures into conversation with the Canadian texts that are my focus. Given the randomness with which an immigrant might end up in one or another country, and the ease with which a woman marrying a man might lose her citizenship, and the border's own colonial artifice, for some of the individuals and groups I highlight the distinction between Canada and the United States must be treated as appropriately flexible. As the chapters and the chronology progress, my geographic focus narrows, so that my concluding discussions of Lorca memorials and of contemporary Canadian Spanish Civil War fiction concentrate strictly on Canadian-identified authors. While not every chapter takes on the question of national belonging explicitly, all of the texts I will discuss participate in the broader Canadian project of forging national identity by writing about transnational participation in the Spanish Civil War. These chapters are intended to demonstrate how different authors nuance that patriotic project.

Chapter 1, "Love: Impossible War Romances," examines how race, religion, and gender influence the construction of the patriotic citizen in that most traditional of war literature texts, the wartime romance. Cross-cultural love plots (especially between foreign women and white, Christian, North American men) are central for male writers such as Ernest Hemingway and Upton Sinclair. I argue that stories of failed love affairs reproduce heteronormative imperialism; yet Jewish Canadian authors Ted Allan, Charles Yale Harrison, and Mordecai Richler undercut these romantic tropes, in that they use gentile characters to articulate Jewish masculine heroism, thus subverting that ideal.

Building on the first chapter's exploration of the ambiguous divisions between race, religion, and ethnicity, chapter 2, "Sympathy: Cosmopolitan Combat and Postcolonial Spain," takes on the question of warmaking: how did international volunteers justify their participation in a war fought on behalf of a colonial power? African and Jewish diasporic writers, including Langston Hughes, Mordecai Richler, and John A. Williams, represent African and African American participation in the Spanish conflict – first through the presence of Moroccan mercenaries among Franco's soldiers and African American volunteers in the International Brigades, and then through Francoist Spain's delayed decolonization. These writers connect Spain's and Britain's enduring colonial legacies, insisting on the intersections of race, ethnicity, religion, and nationality in the transnational fight against fascism.

Chapter 3, "Community: Documenting Female Friendship in Spain," approaches questions of race, religion, gender, and belonging in another way, by demonstrating how North American women writers re-envisioned female contributions to wartime. The chapter brings together unpublished, out-of-print, and published works by Salaria Kea, Miriam

Waddington, Martha Gellhorn, and others to argue for their common project of showcasing the women-led communities that sprang up across Spain. Writers – Jewish or not – often analogize their own experiences of the tensions between national and transnational affiliations to Jewish peoples' experiences of antisemitism, instructing their readers in sympathy toward the European victims of war.

Chapter 4, "Inclusion: Elegizing Lorca," examines the Canadian resonances of the fascists' murder of queer Spanish poet and playwright Federico García Lorca. Lorca's enduring power as a symbol of sexual and artistic freedom is evident in writings by a range of Canadian authors, from Patrick Anderson to Leonard Cohen to Brian Dedora – and many more authors internationally. In this sustained elegy project, I argue that Canadian writers participate in an imagined transnational community.

The conclusion, "Remembrance: Envisioning Spain and Canada Now," looks to twenty-first-century fictional depictions of the Spanish Civil War. Where earlier chapters focus on how Canadian authors write around marginalization, these contemporary Canadian works of fiction examine experiences of marginalization unflinchingly and further connect the Spanish Civil War to continuing and emergent local and global crises, including Spanish colonialism, the ongoing oppression of Indigenous peoples, and modern warfare. Together, these novels and short stories demonstrate the Spanish Civil War's continuing literary and political significance as a crucial moment of social critique and cosmopolitan cooperation.

An Ever-Improving Earth

The attempted leftist collaboration of the Popular Front and of individuals from around the world remains a historical touchstone of transnational solidarity and personal sacrifice, notwithstanding the sometimes fatal infighting and suppression among these Popular Front members and the war's disastrous conclusion. The Republic fell in 1939, after it ordered the withdrawal of international troops in the hopes of embarrassing Franco into a similar de-escalation. The manoeuvre failed: Franco captured Madrid and declared himself Caudillo.[34] Thousands of international volunteers were sent to displaced person camps in France; some were allowed to return to their home countries, but others found themselves once again stateless as war spread across Europe. The Second World War's outbreak prompted the mandatory enlistment of many former Spanish Civil War volunteers. In the war and the Holocaust, the Nazis employed the techniques of warfare and mass killing they had practised in Spain.[35]

These horrors proved that the left's intervention in what was never strictly a civil war had been prescient; it also threw its members' visions of affiliation beyond nation into question. Some former volunteers grew disenchanted with their own countries and moved to what was then Mandatory Palestine, directing the cosmopolitanism of the Spanish Republic toward the establishment of a Jewish state. Others found it necessary to moderate their extreme leftism (especially, a couple of decades later, as the McCarthy Era's Red Scare seeped across Canada's borders), espousing liberalism instead. But many supporters of the Spanish Republic continued to represent the Spanish Civil War as the "last great cause." To create an inclusive, ethically constructed nationalism – one that could neutralize its exploitation in fascism's frightening escalation – remains an important project. At the same time, specific threads of this nationalism that found some experimental permutations in Spanish Civil War literature – the threads of feminism, pan-Africanism, anticolonialism, and interfaith solidarity, for example – continue to develop and cohere in their individual force.

In the chapters that follow, I examine what I see as the shared aspirations of the cosmopolitanism that developed in Spain – to truth, to sympathy, to love, to solidarity, and to equality. Even as I chart how these convictions coalesced around Jewish Canadian participation in the Spanish cause, their traces throughout Spanish Civil War literatures by a wide range of writers reveal an imagined community united in its aspiration toward compassion.

1
Love: Impossible War Romances

"So on the battlefields from here to Barcelona, I'm listed with the enemies of love."

Leonard Cohen, "The Traitor"

"He never necked with a girl without wondering, if never daring to ask, O Riva Mandelbaum, O Hanna Steinberg, '*But did thee feel the earth move?*'"

Mordecai Richler, *Joshua Then and Now*

North American Nationalisms, North American Jewishnesses

In Leonard Cohen's Spanish Civil War song "The Traitor," a volunteer soldier's brief flirtation distracts him for a "fatal moment," and the battle is lost. A single dalliance is hardly to blame for Francisco Franco and his fascist forces' victory over the democratic Spanish Republicans and their Popular Front supporters. Yet the trope is pervasive in North American writing about the conflict. An individual soldier's affair with a foreign woman diverts him from fighting; while the romance is born of idealism, it ends, like the war itself, in disaster. Novelistic portrayals of transnational sentiment evoke the stakes of love during wartime, suggesting that, like the ideological factionalism that tore at Popular Front unity, romantic entanglements among leftists were an internal source of corruption that contributed to the Spanish Republic's ultimate defeat.

Why do these novels sacrifice cross-cultural love to the Republic's larger goals? And what happens to these tropes in novels by Jewish Canadian authors? In this chapter I examine a variety of male-authored Jewish Canadian novels written between the 1930s and the 1980s in order to demonstrate how cross-cultural romance plots function as a political allegory. Through the lens of their radical political commitments, Jewish Canadian writers undermine the Spanish Civil War romance's internationalist rhetoric by drawing on tropes of assimilation common to both Jewish and Canadian novels at the turn of the century. Even as their work resonates with the wider canon of war romances, it reveals the absorptive, whitewashing tendencies of patriotic romantic fiction. Specifically, by subverting heteronormative Euro-American depictions of international love as inevitably disastrous, these authors argue for a broader definition of citizenship, one that accounts for religious and ethnic diversity as well as for class-based identification. In response to the rise of totalitarian nationalism in Europe as well as local instability, these novels forecast a radical Canadian nationalism responsive to the fractured identity of a white settler colony, and to antisemitic stereotypes about effeminate, wandering Jewish men. Jewish Canadian authors craft a proto-multicultural discourse of an inclusive, international, fiercely patriotic country even as this vision of Canadian religious, racial, and ethnic tolerance unevenly incorporates female citizens.

For the most part, the novelistic emphasis on failed love contradicts the dominant non-fictional narrative of international volunteers in Spain. Reportage, memoir, and documentaries alike highlight the successful romantic pairings that grew out of international collaboration. These accounts recall the international partnerships of couples like British Cuban writer Mary Low and Cuban Surrealist artist Juan Breá, African American volunteer nurse Salaria Kea and Irish volunteer soldier John O'Reilly, and British doctor Reginald Saxton and Canadian nurse Rosaleen Smythe. While these 1930s narratives of internationalist bliss admittedly have propagandistic purposes, it is curious that novels published at the same time would share nothing of their optimism or, indeed, their sustained romance. Alternatively, as chapter 3 will demonstrate (in part through an analysis of Kea's own representations), female authors' Spanish Civil War writings usually give far less attention to romantic themes than to depictions of working relationships and cross-cultural friendships.

Male-authored Spanish Civil War romance novels are unlike either these real-life stories or traditional war romances, where a soldier might survive combat sustained by memories of his sweetheart back home before eventually returning to her. Instead, the contours of the love affair in Ernest Hemingway's *For Whom the Bell Tolls* (1940) are typical of the genre: the white, gentile North American male protagonist travels to Spain as a volunteer soldier and enters into a relationship with a woman from another country. Their growing romance prevents him from fully committing to his leftist politics, but rather than reject her, he escapes the relationship through a *deus ex machina*: injury (his), death (hers), or some other war-related catastrophe. Freed of his romantic obligations, the male protagonist re-enters the war with renewed commitment to self-sacrifice on behalf of the Republic. This plot parallels the American author John Dos Passos's *Adventures of a Young Man* (1939).[1] In a similar plot, one common to Canadian novels such as Charles Yale Harrison's *Meet Me on the Barricades* (1938), Hugh MacLennan's *The Watch That Ends the Night* (1959), and Hugh Garner's *Cabbagetown* (1968), and in the American novels *No Pasaran!* by Upton Sinclair (1937), *The Un-Americans* by Alvah Bessie (1957), and *Another Hill* by Milton Wolff (1994), the male protagonist leaves his girlfriend or wife behind in North America so that he can support the Spanish Republicans, implicitly choosing direct political engagement and the homosocial, international atmosphere of the battlefield over local politics and a stable family life.

In either case, such novels usually conclude with the protagonist's arrival on the battlefield, where he is joyfully reunited with male comrades, ready to commit to the Spanish cause by engaging in the (remarkably non-violent) trappings of war – the sharing of trenches and anecdotes, the travel, and the escape from desk jobs or unemployment. This celebratory conclusion relies, too, on a readership willing to suspend its knowledge of the war's outcome: many of these novels, like *For Whom the Bell Tolls*, were published after the Popular Front's political fracturing and the war's catastrophic conclusion. Shortly thereafter, the Second World War commenced. The failed international relationship seems to stand in for – and perhaps even sublate – the story of the international community's larger failure to prevent another world war.

The disjuncture between non-fiction and fiction representations of love in Spanish Civil War novels suggests a masculinist scepticism toward other cultures and countries, a scepticism coloured by – and invested in – gender-based notions of belonging. In contrast, star-crossed romances typical of other civil wars celebrate the successful struggle to coalesce around a new, unified national identity. Romances written in the postbellum United States, in the wake of Third World decolonization, or in the midst of efforts to bridge post-Confederation cultures of anglophone and francophone Canada suggest that that most traditional of structures – a procreative, heterosexual marriage – will produce a hopeful future for the newly established nation. Hugh MacLennan's novel *Two Solitudes* (1945) is perhaps the most famous Canadian example of the genre. The novel traces the life of a young boy, the son of an Irish immigrant to Canada and a Québécois man. While Paul is socially, linguistically, and geographically mobile, it is his decision to enlist in the Second World War that concludes the novel, suggesting love, travel, and violence as potential routes to overcome the English–French binary. The title of critic Michael Greenstein's foundational *Third Solitudes: Tradition and Discontinuity in Jewish-Canadian Literature* contains a criticism of reunification romance narratives of this kind – that such stories boil down complex, interrelated communities into binaries, each represented by an individual character. Caren Irr likewise points out that MacLennan's unification narrative gestures to each character's multiple affiliations (the mother is an Irish immigrant, both anglophone and Catholic, the father strongly Québécois but also fluent in English), even as it not only reduces Canada to just two groups but also elides Indigenous peoples along with minority and immigrant groups (72). At the same time, the ultimate, if reductive, message of so many of these stories seems to be that cooperation on the smallest level – that of the family – is capable of transforming a state into a nation.[2]

In contrast to romances of union or reunion, cooperation across borders or battle lines isn't ultimately necessary for Hemingway's Spanish Civil War protagonist, or for Sinclair's. Put another way, male-authored Spanish Civil War novels undermine their own internationalism with the death of foreign love interests, implicitly reaffirming the power of national classifications and of masculine patriotism. Such portrayals of doomed cross-cultural romance between gentile anglophone North American men and white ethnic or foreign women re-enact a colonial history in which sex is tantamount to dominion, reinforcing the male protagonist and his home country's stable identity, especially against the backdrop of Spain's shifting social structures and unpredictable future. Female characters are depicted as too radical or too conservative; they represent both the regression to traditional family structures and the attraction of having one's country be "the whole world," as Virginia Woolf terms women's lack of stable citizenship in her pacifist Spanish Civil War treatise *Three Guineas* (1938). While conventional unification romances aim to unite divided factions, Spanish Civil War romance novels construct – and inevitably undercut – a deterritorialized internationalist community: the female character's demise short-circuits the long-term implications of transnational love.

As MacLennan's novel *Two Solitudes* illustrates, nascent ideas of Canadian identity are tied to tropes of masculinity and violence. Yet early Jewish articulations of national belonging additionally insert Jewish men into a broadened idea of masculinity as a route to mainstream inclusion. During this period, Canada continued to struggle not only with its solitudes but also with alternating confusion, hostility, and hospitality toward ethnic and religious minorities. Jewish authors' invocations of Canadian identity amount to early attempts to constitute an empty category chiefly defined by what it was not: not British, not French, and not American.

This new identity is also, significantly, neither geographically Canadian nor ethnically or religiously Jewish. Authors rehearse national reunification narratives displaced onto another nation: a gentile protagonist meets individuals from across North America once he has ventured to Spain, and from this distanced perspective he can better understand how they all contribute to a unified nation. Many of the novels that feature culturally savvy, brave, masculine North American protagonists were composed by Jewish writers – members of a wider community desperately trying to attain social acceptance in North America. In the American context, Alan M. Wald has argued that the Spanish Civil War provided the opportunity for Jewish American volunteers-turned-writers to demonstrate Jewish bravery and masculinity – not only to their fellow volunteers at the front, but also to Americans back home – by writing fictionalized accounts that "challenge the popular idea that twentieth-century Jewish American culture primarily carries forward the 'ethic of mentshlekhkayt'" (Wald, *Trinity* 44), that is, the notion that Jewish American culture is constituted by honourable yet physically passive men. The novels Wald discusses – by Spanish Civil War veterans Milton Wolff, Alvah Bessie, and William Herrick – use Jewish protagonists "backed by the authority of the Popular Front, who bludgeon and in some cases kill" (Wald, *Trinity* 44).[3]

Instead of emphasizing violence, Jewish Canadian literature about the war constructs a specifically Canadian masculinity contingent on transnational sympathy and selflessness. Furthermore, these narratives of interfaith romance complicate the dominant narrative trope of Jewish American novels focused on what Frederic Cople Jaher has termed the "quest for the ultimate *shiksa*" – that is, the common plot of a Jewish male protagonist assimilating through romance and marriage with an American Christian female character (518; italics in the original). Much like the trope of Canada as two solitudes, this plot represents broader social concerns, "becom[ing] microcosmic representations of momentous issues of group and self survival and betrayal, of balancing anxieties and ambitions, of reconciling religious and national loyalties, and of bridging the past and the present" (Jaher 519). For Jaher, female characters are instrumentalized as Jewish male characters strive for entry into the mainstream – a literary project of assimilation and (conditional) acceptance that resonates with many Jewish Canadian authors' Spanish Civil War novels.[4] These novels' ultimate dispatching of female characters is not, then, a rejection of assimilation through marriage – an escape from "the threat of death, of the loss of identity" (Fiedler 33). Rather, Spanish Civil War novels craft a broader vision of insider status responsive to provincial distinctions, but reject women's inclusion.

However, by adopting and undermining the rhetoric of colonial masculine dominance and American assimilation, Jewish Canadian writers displace the country (to Spain) and the narrative voice (to a culturally savvy, masculine, gentile Canadian) to articulate Jewish heroism and interracial solidarity. In venerating a Canadian's ability to share his nationalism through travel, these narratives suggest the merits of diasporic heritage and the potential for personal growth inherent in cross-cultural contact, at the same time that they espouse the inclusion of Jewish men in a widened definition of national belonging. Jewish – or Jew-*ish* – characters display a set of unstable identity markers, always connected to larger questions of affiliation. They complicate racial and ethnic designations by suggesting the ease of circumventing or transcending them. In other words, in writing Jewish characters into pan–North American scenes, Jewish authors actually obfuscate the very designation "Jewish," by untying it from biology, religion, ethnicity, or a Zionist nationality.

Civilized Masculinity and Jewish Bravery: *This Time a Better Earth*

As I began to discuss in the introduction to this book, Ted Allan's novel *This Time a Better Earth* (1939) is an integral text for my understanding of how Spanish Civil War literature articulates inclusion. The novel is at once a genre-establishing Spanish Civil War romance novel and something of a Trojan horse, in that it uses the trappings of romance to espouse hemispheric American racial and religious acceptance. Allan, born Alan Herman, was a prolific Jewish journalist and author. He adopted the pseudonym "Ted Allan" in order to report undercover on fascist organizations in Quebec, keeping the pseudonym for the rest of his life and hiding his Judaism from his readers until the publication of the autobiographical *Lies My Father Told Me* (1949). Allan was a Communist Party of Canada member, a *Daily Clarion* and *New Frontier* journalist in Spain, and the political commissar of Bethune's mobile blood transfusion service. After returning from the war, he published *This Time a Better Earth*, a transnational romance novel with extensive, if mostly sublimated, Jewish content.

At first glance, the plot of *This Time a Better Earth* is straightforward: the narrator, journalist Bob Curtis, travels to Spain to volunteer with the International Brigades. After sustaining injuries in a bombing, he is unable to fight. While convalescing, he begins an affair with a German photographer named Lisa Kammerer. They plan to marry and leave Spain, but before they can, Lisa is killed in the war. Bob briefly mourns before returning to the front to reunite with his fellow North American volunteers. (Before publishing *This Time a Better Earth*, Allan published a short story, "Lisa," in *Harper's* that recounts a very similar section of the narrative. Lisa Poirer, a war photographer, is killed in an aerial bombardment at the front. In this earlier version, neither the narrator nor Lisa's nationality is specified.)

The novel's romantic plot owes much to Allan's real-life relationship with the photographer Gerda Taro. Taro, born Gerta Pohorylle, and her companion Robert Capa, born André Friedmann, rose to fame as war photographers. Both were European Jews who selected American-sounding pseudonyms (in reference, they claimed, to Greta Garbo and Frank Capra, although Cápa, Hungarian for *shark*, was also his childhood nickname) in an attempt to gain credibility. Capa is best known for the image "Loyalist Militiaman at the Moment of Death, Cerro Muriano, September 5, 1936," often called "The Falling Soldier." Taro and Allan travelled together in Spain, and Allan was with her when she fell off a car's running board while retreating from an offensive. Her legs were run over by a tank, and she died that evening in a hospital. She is widely considered the first female photojournalist to cover a war, and the first to die in action.[5]

This Time a Better Earth passes as mainstream on a variety of levels. Allan effaces characters' Jewish connections in favour of normative whiteness. Allan himself was a Jewish author from Montreal writing under a gentile pseudonym, and his novel adapts the story of Taro – another Jew who adopted an assimilated name – using a narrator from Toronto. Allan avoids narrating the linguistic and religious conflicts of Quebec, and he expunges the potential Jewishness of his characters' and his own personal histories and names. Instead of explicitly articulating Jewish bravery, Allan ventriloquizes Jewish masculinity, hewing to the same standards of gentile wartime bravery and heterosexual prowess as his Jewish American counterparts, but using gentile characters to commend Jewish valour. If, as the bellicose protagonist states, "a man must experience more than love to be a man" (135), then the narrative allows a variety of Jewish and Jewish-passing characters to achieve this sexist construct of North American masculinity.

Allan's authorial gesture toward gentile normativity is a diversion tactic. By distancing himself from the implied author of the novel, Allan both partakes in and subverts the tropes of Spanish Civil War novels and the nationalist narratives they allegorize. Jewish characters are generally minor in Spanish Civil War novels; for his part, Allan never mentions individual characters' religions, relying instead on markers such as Jewish-sounding names and Yiddish-inflected diction. Characters' identities are clarified only when they differ from that of the protagonist racially or linguistically, as is the case with the African American and

Québécois characters. Allan constructs the narrator, Bob, as a sort of North American Everyman: he is working class, white, gentile, and from central Ontario rather than the Prairies, the Maritimes, or Quebec. He is also intensely patriotic, brought nearly to tears when he sings Canada's proto–National Anthem, "The Maple Leaf Forever." Over the novel's course, Bob abandons this patriotism for a class-based North American identity, eventually proclaiming, "My so-called youth is almost a general biography of the youth of America – my background, that is" (86). This statement elides distinctions of nation and region; indeed, following Vautour's reading that Bob is a fictionalized version of Allan, this "general biography" suggests that what unifies North American youth is class struggle, not religious belief (Vautour, Introduction xix). As Irr notes, Allan, like many leftist authors writing about Toronto, locates difference in class rather than ethnicity. For her, Allan's novel perpetuates white English Canadian hegemony by espousing a pan-ethnic, pan-Canadian communism whose "purportedly unmarked language of the 'center' … becomes a vacant placelessness, rather than the expansive universality that was intended" (156).

Rather than read the novel as an assimilation narrative – an interpretation that elucidates the political flaws of Allan's proletarian novel, but takes Allan's protagonist at face value – I understand Allan's gestures toward minority assimilation as potentially subversive. Allan's novel takes up what Daniel Coleman has characterized as the common Canadian allegory of the "maturing colonial son," in which the nascent nation demonstrates its maturity (and its superiority to the United States) through its ability to civilize "less-fortunate people, whether world-weary immigrants needing a peaceful new home, even more weary Aboriginals, who were believed to be fast approaching extinction, or francophone adopted brothers" (Coleman 6). Instead, in *This Time a Better Earth*, Bob and his multicultural American and Canadian comrades learn how to be good soldiers and citizens from one of the novel's only Jewish characters, Milton Schwartz. Milty's rise requires him to subsume his sexual appetites and abandon his Yiddishized English to speak American. The novel shows a group of North Americans learning battlefield masculinity from an American Jew. Milty's eventual ascension to sergeant over a group of Canadians suggests that Canada includes – and might even need to be led by – Jewish America (especially at the novel's conclusion, when all the other American characters have been killed or wounded).

In contrast to the novel's representations of strong North American male friendships, Allan portrays heterosexual romance as inherently unstable. One volunteer has a wife and children back home, but is killed in battle. Doug, the lone African American volunteer, falls in love with his nurse after he is blinded by shrapnel; although he becomes "unable to see color" (Irr 160), it is unclear whether the nurse is colour-blind as well. One of the few Spanish women included in the narrative is a "Moorish" sex worker named Mercedes, who bites a foreign journalist (the same character – and the same unfortunate anecdote – makes an appearance in Hemingway's Spanish Civil War play, *The Fifth Column*, published the previous year). Most significantly for this study, the novel's two primary romantic narratives – Bob's earnest relationship with the German photographer Lisa, and Milty's infatuation with the local sex worker Maria – distract the male characters from their political convictions.

Bob and Milty are foils: Milty's detachment from national identification (he sarcastically introduces himself as "Milton Schwartz of the Brooklyn Schwartzes what came over on the *Berengaria*" [17, italics in the original]) appears in sharp contrast to Bob's intense patriotism. And while Bob's profound commitment – indeed, that of all the other volunteers – to the Spanish Republican cause is never questioned, Milty's brazen sexuality initially leads other characters to doubt the authenticity of his leftism. He is the one who initially finds the men a "swell brothel, government-inspected" (36), and when he is absent during a bombing, the other characters wrongly assume that rather than help rescue the injured, he is "probably drunk or in some brothel" – in fact, he is trying to save children buried under rubble (45). Milty's vigorous energy, when channelled toward the Spanish cause, eventually propels him to military greatness, while Bob's alternating passionate and placating relationship with Lisa leaves him doubting his leftist convictions. Lisa's intelligence and sensitivity to global conflict make Bob aware of his own personal shortcomings – an awareness made more acute by his leave from the front after sustaining an injury. He continually frets that their relationship means more to him than it does to her, telling her early on, "if I lose you I'll die" (90). Her death pays for Bob's deficiencies. He returns to the front as a soldier, where he learns masculine bravery from Milty, along with the ability to compartmentalize his domestic, intellectual, and political lives. His friendship with Milty serves as a corrective to whatever he might have absorbed of Lisa's egalitarian beliefs.

Milty and Lisa's dedication to the Spanish cause is continually doubted, as those around them transpose both characters' presumed histories of international rootlessness onto their political convictions. And Lisa's talents, like Milty's, exceed those of the people around her – her very name, Kammerer, suggests, as Irr points out, her propensity toward photography. Lisa is an outspoken supporter of the Spanish Republic, a career photojournalist who convinces her editor to send her – and not her male colleague – to the war zone. She boycotts German products (except for her Leica camera) and refuses the moniker "lady comrade" (97) or to be shielded, because of her gender, from the sights and experiences of war. She is also deeply sensitive to the paradox of doing her work well, describing the experience of photographing dead fascist soldiers: "I got good pictures ... wonderful pictures ... But, Bob, it was terrible. Their bodies strewn over the ground like garbage. A hand here. A head there ... They were so young, young Italian boys" (83). While this particular military success is represented as a potential turning point for the Spanish Republic, Lisa's description of it is a reminder of the fascist soldiers' youth and humanity – young men are dying on both sides, and photographing their bodies is, for Lisa, both a way to publicize the Spanish conflict and an ethically questionable way to make a living.

Bob follows her to the front, where Lisa continually reminds him that she does not want to take him away from the war. At first she cautions him, "Do not try to tell yourself it is love ... It's the war. You need a woman. I need a man" (88). Bob's response – "Goddamn it, I love you. I can't help that" (89) – suggests that she is much more in control of her feelings than he is. In a novel that prizes pragmatism, such statements suggest her strength. Yet other characters perceive her yearnings for the war to end and, eventually, for marriage to Bob as a lack of dedication to the Spanish cause. The narrative swerves between emphasizing the importance of personal relationships during crisis, and voicing Bob's critiques of Lisa for that very desire: "Go to hell," he rebuffs her when she expresses concern over his war-induced anxieties (90); and later, when he complains that the suffering he has witnessed "makes him sick," her attempt to both console and prepare him for what he has yet to see prompts Bob to chide her, "It is I who should be telling you ... I mean a man should comfort a woman about such things, not a woman a man ..." (121; ellipses in the original). Lisa's response – that she "can't understand [Bob's] English ... Maybe, that is because [he] speak[s] American" (121) – rejects his gendered assumptions of the roles they should play: she has been in Spain longer, witnessed more of the conflict, and, importantly, witnessed it from the front while he has been sidelined by his injury. What Lisa calls his "American" amounts to a flawed, short-sighted articulation of gender divisions. Her emphasis on care undercuts Bob's masculinist aspiration toward self-sufficiency. Yet the narrative simultaneously indicts Lisa for contravening these gender stereotypes.

Lisa is unique in her ability to remember both the global unrest beyond Spain's borders and the individual stakes of the war for those living within those borders. Her role in the narrative exemplifies the function of female characters in Spanish Civil War romance novels more generally: they remind male characters of life outside war, and by extension, the possibility of social relationships that transcend national difference. In this transcendence, female characters threaten war's exigence. Lisa's musings on the title's "better earth" alternately validate Bob's commitment to the Spanish cause and infuriate him. Furthermore, her perceived weaknesses lead to disaster: after she reflects that she would like to have a baby, she and Bob are trapped during a bombing with a traumatized infant (which leads her to recant); after each of her requests for a romantic vacation away from Spain someday after the war's end, the Republicans experience a crisis. Lisa's last entreaty for a vacation in Paris – while she is bravely photographing an air raid from the front lines – is immediately followed by the accident that causes her death. Lisa's connections to communities within the war zone ultimately estrange her from Bob.

With Lisa's death, the narrative shifts its focus from heterosexual romance to Bob's return to the homosocial sphere of the battlefield, which is presided over by Sergeant Milty Schwartz, who is now lecturing "like a college professor" (161). James Doyle reads the novel's conclusion as evidence that "in times of political crisis people must be prepared to sacrifice personal to political commitment" (123), an assertion that overlooks Lisa's own political commitments, commitments that far exceeded Bob's. While the novel's end certainly evinces the need to continue fighting against fascism, it cannot imagine that women might partake in this fight. Allan's conclusion demonstrates Warren Hoffman's suggestion that Jewish immigrants had to pass not only along ethnic and racial lines but also along sexual lines in order to gain acceptance into mainstream North American culture. Hoffman contends that Jews asserted their whiteness by adopting heteronormative American sexual and gender identities, essentially cross-dressing in the pursuit of demonstrating their ethnic and national inclusion (9).[6] *This Time a Better Earth* concludes with Milty's vow to share his dugout and to teach Bob marksmanship: "I'll teach you how to shoot a gun good," he promises in the same American that Lisa claimed she could not understand (162). The two characters walk arm-in-arm under the Spanish sun. This final, vividly rendered image – in contrast to the vaguely described romantic scenes between Bob and Lisa – reflects the equality in their pairing: Bob and Milty are approximately the same age, from working-class roots, and they walk side by side. Together, they will live under the Spanish earth, putting down roots (but not in North America), and *practising* their gun skills (but seemingly not with the intent to kill), while warfare remains safely offstage.[7] Wartime North American homosociability mediates stereotypical Jewish effeminacy, establishing its own "invisible, carefully blurred, always-already-crossed line from being 'interested in men'" (Sedgwick 89).

In *This Time a Better Earth*, the process of joining a North American community requires learning the trappings of wartime masculinity. These manly pursuits are also represented as the appropriate expression of the sexual energy that initially garners Milty so much criticism. Allan thus reconfigures antisemitic stereotypes of the weak, castrated Jewish male and contemporary, contradictory concerns over Jewish men as sexual predators by showing how both Bob and Milty learn to balance virility and wartime honour. Parallels between the character Bob and the novel's Jewish author, and between Lisa and Gerda Taro, open up important questions about ethnic and gender identity within the novel, questions that, depending on the degree to which Allan and his novel succeed at passing, have politically charged implications. If, as Catherine Rottenberg argues, passing narratives can allow for new entries into discussions of identity, then the male Canadian identity constructed by *This Time a Better Earth* relies upon interfaith friendship – not heterosexual love – as the route into a leftist community.[8] In the war's context, this particular assimilation narrative is one of masculinization and nationalist acceptance – yet one that continues to exclude women. The egalitarian cosmopolitanism that Lisa espouses simultaneously threatens the homosocial geography of the battlefield.

This Time a Better Earth departs from the traditional Spanish Civil War romance plot by asserting an inherently internationalist, multiethnic version of antifascist nationalism. The novel ultimately leverages male minority characters into an imagined Canadian community by way of their American nationality. Yet, it leaves women behind in this transaction – instead, the death of the cosmopolitan, unpatriotic woman facilitates male bonding. Even as the novel attempts to rehabilitate the cosmopolitan ideal of multiple loyalties (within and surpassing gender, religion, and local community), female and Jewish characters are repeatedly asked to prove their allegiance to Spain and, by extension, to any country or cause. In the end, only the Jewish American character transcends doubts about his authenticity. Lisa, the stateless European woman, remains the narrator's main distraction from fighting the war.

Yet this outcome also overlooks one of the war's main provocations: women's rights. *This Time a Better Earth* and many American Spanish Civil War romance novels represent an idealized version of violent conflict leading to better government, happier citizens, and definitive North American nationalism. This idealization inherently rejects or misunderstands the concurrent nascent feminist movements in Spain, as I will discuss in chapter 3. These novels may be predicated upon internationalist ethics, but they ultimately suggest that cross-cultural contact actually reinforces national definitions. Fictional international friendships might bolster the characters' sense of rootedness in their home countries, while international romantic relationships threaten characters with deracination.

The binary these romance novels construct – between romantic international love, and love of internationalism – elides women's integral role in the Spanish Republic's struggle, as well as the Republic's early attempts to institutionalize women's equality. The actual presence of women on the Spanish battlefields – not only in the typically feminine role of nurses, but also as soldiers, ambulance drivers, journalists, and political leaders – may, perhaps, have ruined a certain type of fictional war romance, one reliant on longing, nostalgia, and women's idealization. No matter how Spanish and international female volunteers might risk their lives and demonstrate their dedication to the Spanish government and its citizens, in novels about the conflict female characters always divert men from their political beliefs.

Modernizing Spain and North America: *Meet Me on the Barricades*

One way in which masculinist novels about the Spanish Civil War undercut the cause they ostensibly espouse is by misrepresenting women's roles. Another is unquestionably adhering to party dogma. Charles Yale Harrison's Spanish Civil War novel *Meet Me on the Barricades* (1938) levels a more explicit critique at the white, masculinist norms of North American leftist novels than Ted Allan's more subtly Jewish text, in large part by undermining the strict gender roles upon which war novels tend to rely. A Jewish journalist born in Philadelphia and raised in Montreal, Harrison changed his political affiliations as often as his address, a confirmed fellow traveller.[9] He was a founding member of the John Reed Clubs and a staff member of the American Marxist magazine *New Masses*, a position that ended in a falling out with fellow leftist activist Michael Gold. Harrison knew the horrors of war first-hand, having served in the First World War – combat he describes in gruesome detail in the novel *Generals Die in Bed* (1930). When the Spanish Civil War broke out, Harrison was politically unaffiliated but staunchly leftist, writing at once in support of the Spanish Republic and against its war. Published by Charles Scribner's Sons in the United States in 1938, *Meet Me on the Barricades* uses a fantastical modernist narrative to restructure the traditional gender roles of the war romance trope. The novel, published a year before James Thurber's well-known short story "The Secret Life of Walter Mitty," uses a similarly socially detached, imaginative protagonist to suggest the shortcomings of transnational leftism and the hypocrisy of waging a war for peace. Harrison exposes the fissures within the Popular

Front; he also turns a critical eye on North American leftists' investment in gendered notions of belonging and fears of a world without borders. The novel struck a chord in North America: while it did not garner the polyglot readership of his earlier novels, it was widely and mostly positively reviewed in the English and Yiddish press.[10]

The high modernist form of *Meet Me on the Barricades* satirizes bellicose politics as overcompensation for sexual inadequacy, representing characters' declining physicality as a symptom of their vacant political convictions.[11] Harrison represents heterosexual romantic relationships as oppressive, unfulfilling, and – even when imaginary – anticlimactic. The antihero P. Herbert Simpson is a New York oboe player whose heart problems thwart his attempts to engage with those around him. His vivid imagination allows him to imagine an escape from his unrewarding marriage with a prudish, domineering wife into a passionate fantasy of a Russian girlfriend, and from a dull symphony practice to the front lines of the Spanish Civil War. Yet despite Simpson's excitement at imagining himself on the battlefields of Spain, the narrator explains: "The war in China, however, did not greatly move [Simpson], for while he could easily picture himself as a Spaniard or a German, he simply refused to imagine himself as a Chinese" (12). Simpson's imaginary glorification of the Spanish conflict is premised on a racist sense of shared whiteness; it is also imbued with a violent sexuality, as he imagines his exploits upon the Spanish Republic's triumph: "we shall celebrate with wine, song and lusty fascist wenches ... sexual intercourse is more or less pardonable, particularly in time of war" (13). His aggressive contempt for women coalesces around Spain, where Simpson can imagine himself doing what he cannot do in real life. He wants to prove his masculinity by fighting in a war or sleeping with his wife, at the same time that he is physically unable, since his heart condition means he "must control [him]self" sexually, socially, and intellectually (27). The novel's title highlights his constant shortcomings – Simpson cannot meet anyone on the battlefield, or anywhere else: while his imagined persona, the Spanish loyalist Captain Pedro, dies a martyr's death on the war's front lines, Simpson himself dies in bed at the novel's conclusion, his heart pushed past its limit by the excitement of imagined military engagement.

Simpson's failures of nerve and of conviction are closely tied to his outsider status. His obsession with national distinctions reinforces this alienation: even after five years playing with the orchestra "he still had little in common with the polyglot groupings which went to make up the ensemble ... Being the only Anglo-Saxon in the entire orchestra, Simpson soon developed a feeling of inferiority as though he were an unwanted alien" (9). Whereas many Spanish Civil War novels, including *This Time a Better Earth*, use similarly positioned narrators – white, gentile men who are friendly with a cast of multiethnic, transnational characters – to espouse unity and empathy, Harrison's construction of Simpson instead points to his failed cosmopolitanism. Simpson foresees the Spanish Civil War's loss precipitating fascism's global rise, yet he remains unable to empathize with those who would suffer for it.

Where Allan's novel foregrounds (and inverts) Jewish characters' process of mainstream acculturation, in *Meet Me on the Barricades* Harrison directly criticizes what he represents as the Communist Party's instrumentalization of working-class Jewish experience. When the socially oblivious Simpson claims that Gold's *Jews Without Money* (1930) "goes to show that there are poor Jews, too," his more politically astute friend replies, "Ghetto tripe. [The novel is a] proletarian Cook's tour for gaping *goyim*" (76; italics in the original). Through this inconclusive exchange, in which Gold's novel is both mocked and lauded, Harrison gestures to the problematic nature of North American assimilation narratives – narratives that Gold's novel similarly problematizes.

Yet this "proletarian Cook's tour" might also be seen as characterizing many Spanish Civil War novels, with their vicarious representations of foreign love affairs and battlefield bravado for armchair leftists. That is, Harrison suggests that to fictionalize the Spanish cause is to romanticize it, an act as socially irresponsible as the false empathy *Jews Without Money* might have inspired. In this broader critique of leftist literature, Harrison's surreal satire repudiates the possibility of wartime romance and refuses the Canadian literary project of inserting minority characters into a broadened idea of masculinity as a route to citizenship. *Meet Me on the Barricades* instead interrogates the cultural anxieties that brought individuals to those barricades – whether in person or in fantasy.

Simpson's Spanish acquaintances eventually disabuse him of his problematic idealism around the Spanish cause, and his dawning understanding of the country's political realities results in some clarity about North America. In a chapter modelled on the Nighttown episode of *Ulysses*, Simpson hallucinates a series of political figures and writers, from a Mike Gold-esque "East Side Novelist" to Gertrude Stein. Simpson – as Leopold Bloom – interacts with these imagined characters and begins to hallucinate an America enthralled with modernist prose innovation. Stage directions explain:

> *A hundred people are injured outside Madison Square Garden in a vain attempt to gain admission to hear a debate between Joyce and the literary editor of "The Daily Worker" on "Is Stream of Consciousness Superior to the Simple Declarative Sentence as a Revolutionary Literary Device?" Riots break out in a score of American cities. Bloodshed.* (79; italics in the original)

But even in a fantasy world, this notion of America cannot hold; the country is torn apart as "*Anti-war meetings are broken up. Aliens are deported. Civil liberties are trampled upon by the authorities ... The country experiences another cataclysmic economic crisis. The suicide rate mounts*" (82–3; italics in the original). These imagined sequences of literary and political upheavals elicit comparable social responses, thereby insisting on their interplay. Simpson can no longer deny the factionalism within the Popular Front, nor can he deny his own cross-cultural failings.

Both Allan's subversion and Harrison's parody of the traditional war romance demonstrate the International Brigades' ethos of global harmony, while simultaneously undermining the static identity categories on which this global harmony relies. The displacement of Jewish identity becomes a commentary on interfaith allegiance and the signifiers of difference. This constructed binary of Judaism and Marxism, or of Judaism and relative personal security and employment, encodes a more complex negotiation between religious affiliation and politics.

Together, Allan's and Harrison's novels suggest that Canadians and Americans are not born, but made – that the values of citizenship and belonging can be learned and demonstrated. Furthermore, these novels imply that even the cosmopolitan communities produced in Spain inevitably regulated the identities of a more diverse constituency. The authors allude to the possibility of colonial conquest inherent in the cross-cultural romance trope – spreading leftist North American values by seducing foreign women in the name of the Spanish cause – and undermine the teleological narrative of Jewish immigrant progress toward white gentility. In the process, Harrison and Allan challenge the hierarchy of whiteness and ethnicity, suggesting the universal capacity for North American or Canadian identification, but *especially* for those outside the British–French paradigm. In subverting this hierarchy, these authors also – to varying extents – reject the traditional image of easily assimilated, feminized minorities, which itself could be said to anticipate the stereotype of the passive, weak Holocaust victim.[12]

Only a few years after the Spanish Civil War's devastating conclusion, the global revelation of the Holocaust's horrors would radically alter public discourse around Jewish immigration and integration. And shortly thereafter, the so-called premature antifascists who volunteered in Spain, hoping in vain to prevent another world war, would again face scrutiny and discrimination during the Cold War and the North American Red Scare. Published in the midst of the late-1930s European tumult, Harrison's and Allan's novels thus mark a specific moment of both panic and optimism. They also forecast, in their emphasis on battlefield bravado, the significant contributions of Jewish North American authors to war fiction – particularly the growing universalism of Jewish protagonists, and these novels' pluralist message.[13]

Criticism of the Last Great Cause: *The Acrobats*

By the 1950s, the concerns that brought Canadians to the Spanish Civil War had been overshadowed by other local and global issues, new waves of immigration, new laws, and new wars. Yet, the Spanish Civil War continued to play a significant role in the Canadian literary imaginary. Hugh MacLennan's novel *The Watch That Ends the Night* (1959) utilizes many of the tropes around violence and gender of his earlier unification romance, underscoring the Spanish conflict's significance to Canada through a fictionalized narrative of the pioneering Montreal blood transfusion doctor Norman Bethune. MacLennan depicts the romantic and political fissures between the doctor character – an orphan – and his wife, a terminally ill upper-class anglophone Montreal woman. Their boundary-crossing marriage – of cultures, classes, and physical abilities – results in one child, Sally. As in so many earlier Spanish Civil War romances, the male protagonist chooses to serve the international community rather than his family, which is connected to a retrograde, failing society weakened by capitalism and fascism. He is seduced by a radical communist nurse and leaves his family to serve with her in Spain, eventually abandoning her too and then serving in the Korean conflict. Too late, he chooses the stability of his domestic life over the excitement of political engagement.

The novel's hero, if there is one, is Sally. Sally is capable of transcending what she comes to characterize as her father's naive idealism and her mother's self-doubt and weakness, especially through her study of psychology. It is this academic path that suggests the next generation's growing understanding of the intersections between the personal and the political. At the novel's conclusion, with her mother's death, her father's re-disappearance, and her upcoming marriage to a fellow McGill student who has been parented by a kind, generous Jewish stepfather, Sally seems poised to create a (slightly more diverse) new Canadian generation.

Like *Two Solitudes*, this later MacLennan novel represents Canadian identity through a synthesis of regionally representative citizens; however, this novel also inserts the possibility of white ethnic heritage into this Canadian child's make-up. Sally represents the union of her mother's deteriorating anglophone class privilege and her father's vibrant yet raw political and social convictions, as well as the triumph of a Canadian upbringing over her parents' hereditary faults and personal follies. MacLennan also highlights the influence of non-biological family, as adoptive parents and stepparents often hold greater moral sway over their children, recalling John Murray Gibbon's assertion in *Canadian Mosaic*, discussed in my introduction, that white ethnic immigrants can learn to be Canadian. Along with *Two Solitudes*, then, *The Watch That Ends the Night* points to a necessary generational shift, as characters move away from worrying over their personal migration histories and begin to recognize their inexorable ties to Canada, defining themselves through their connection to the land.

While MacLennan's novel earnestly invokes the Spanish Civil War as a way of juxtaposing women's traditional and radical roles in Canada and Spain, another novel of the 1950s more explicitly and directly treats the ongoing entanglements between Spain and North America. Jewish Montreal author Mordecai Richler's novel *The Acrobats* (1954) is set on Francoist Spanish soil. In it, and in his ongoing textual treatment of the Spanish Civil War, Richler directly addresses Jewish participation, Canadian identity, and gender roles. Linking these issues becomes an implicit critique of the antisemitic feminization of Jews that the earlier novels by Harrison and Allan more problematically gesture toward. Furthermore, Richler avoids instrumentalizing the Spanish people's struggle as a way of clarifying, from a distance, Canada's own evolving notion of citizenship. In both *The Acrobats* and *Joshua Then and Now* (1980), Richler presents a variety of cross-cultural relationships, ultimately constructing an unidealized, geographically rooted cosmopolitanism.

Richler's satirical, critical writing relentlessly questions received ideas and ideals regarding what makes a country, a Jew, or a Canadian. His novelistic interrogation is amplified by his frequent use of his hometown as a setting – a location of tensions between francophones and anglophones as well as virulent antisemitism. This antisemitism included legal and political challenges and was reflected in antisemitic and anti-immigration articles and speeches from religious leaders and politicians like Lionel Groulx and Adrien Arcand (Walker 220–2). Here, I want to highlight how Richler's interrogation of Canadian and Jewish identity intersects with his treatment of the Spanish conflict. Throughout his writing career, Richler returned to the Spanish Civil War (biographer Reinhold Kramer additionally notes that Richler's unpublished memoir was titled "Back to Ibiza").[14] The conflict inspired *The Acrobats*, his earliest novel, part of which he composed while living in Ibiza. *The Acrobats* was published in Britain by André Deutsch, and then the following year by Putnam in the United States, retitled and marketed as a pulp called *Wicked We Love*. If, as I will discuss, Richler uses the war as a means to analyse the significance of ideological conviction for characters often unable to take action, that does not necessarily mean that the Spanish cause was Richler's cause: while many of the authors discussed in this study (including Richler's friend Ted Allan) were personally invested in what they perceived as the values at the conflict's core, throughout his life Richler seems to have veered away from extreme political convictions, renouncing Zionism after joining the leftist Labour-Zionist group Habonim in high school, for instance, while also eschewing Canadian nationalism. Richler's distrust of Canadian nationalism ran parallel with his criticism of mid-century Québécois nationalism, which he saw as tainted by antisemitism and racism.[15] At the same time, as Melina Baum Singer has convincingly argued, his protagonist Duddy Kravitz's obsession with owning Canadian land suggests a deep understanding of the fraught parameters of mainstream Canadian acceptance, based as it is on adopting a settler-colonial mentality.[16] For Richler's characters, purchasing Canadian land and travelling to Spain – whether to fight or to vacation – are egotistic, self-serving projects, attempts to claim something unclaimable.

Where *Meet Me on the Barricades* satirizes the investments some had in the Spanish cause and *The Watch That Ends the Night* sees these investments as inevitably Canadian-centric, *The Acrobats* and (later) *Joshua Then and Now* lampoon subsequent generations' erasure of these transnational political stakes. Often, Richler suggests, these cultural misconceptions emerge around cross-cultural romantic relationships. In *The Acrobats*, Spain is a postwar wasteland where expatriates and tourists try, and fail, to hide from past experiences of antisemitism, sexual abuse, homophobia, and other violent trauma. This early text introduces Richler's satirical critique of Hemingway and all that *For Whom the Bell Tolls* connotes about violent American masculinity and disinterested international participation.[17] *The Acrobats* begins with Canadian protagonist André's explanation that he has come to Spain "to study life in its entirety. One day I hope to write a book about it. You know, like that *Who Do the Bells Toll For*" (10). But this "entirety" is, of course, missing from Hemingway's controversial narrative of the solitary, womanizing soldier Robert Jordan. For Richler, notions of masculinity and belonging must always be understood in terms of relationships and personal connections – not in spite of them.

In *The Acrobats*, Richler sets up a series of unhappy relationships through which he suggests that differences of religion, nationality, and sexuality are not the cause of conflict, but the empty markers to which we assign blame. The novel presents the loveless marriage between an American Jew and his gentile wife; the romantic struggles of her brother Derek, an International Brigades veteran and closeted gay man, and his Spanish lover; the complicated relationship between André and his Spanish girlfriend, Toni, a sex worker who finds herself pregnant after being assaulted by a Nazi; and the thwarted desires for a family of Chaim, an Ashkenazi Jew living in Spain and dreaming of making *aliyah*. As I will discuss further in chapter 4, Derek is haunted by memories of the homophobic beatings he endured as a soldier, while his memories of his lover's "dark body" (129) suggest his Orientalized view of Spanish difference. The American husband and wife constantly argue: their relationship is "a degenerated intimacy; an intimacy of smelly socks, after-dinner burping, sleeping noises, soiled underwear, and dental odours" (7). But their primary argument is over the husband's inability to pass as a gentile, even as his failed attempt to do so has cut him off from the rest of his family. Barney's family sat *shiva* for him after he married Jessie, but this personal expulsion does not mitigate his continual identification – in private, at least – as a Jew. And when Jessie is mistaken for a Jew, her response is one of horror and anger, as she disgustedly calls her husband a "Yid" (90).

All of these unhappy relationships serve as metaphors for Spain's failed postwar reunification and for North America's lukewarm, botched attempts at multicultural inclusion. *The Acrobats* ironizes the distance between Spain's imagined future as a place where democracy and internationalism could flourish, and the realities of fascist rule. The novel likewise undercuts any other location where anyone might be safe: as he will do in *Joshua Then and Now*, Richler depicts how Jewish characters do not quite feel at home in North America *or* Spain, yet prefer to send money to Israel rather than try the promise of what Chaim hopefully calls "Our land! A place where a Jew can go if he's in trouble and be sure to find friends. Love, too, if that's what he needs" (115). But nowhere is truly welcoming for any of the characters: at the novel's conclusion, Jessie and Barney are on the verge of divorce, and André has been murdered, leaving Toni to build a new life reliant on Chaim's paternal protection. Other characters have committed suicide or likewise fled Spain. Spain remains an unlivable location, and no romantic connection has endured. The novel's last line has Chaim promising that "[t]here is always hope," yet there is little evidence of where or when it might be found (209).

Even as Richler's novel critiques the hollowness of Spain's promise, and of Israel's, as well as the blindnesses of 1930s leftism and the ongoing North American ignorance of Spanish politics, like *The Watch That Ends the Night* it avoids an extensive study of what Spanish Civil War participation signifies politically back in North America.[18] *The Acrobats* further reframes the Spanish Civil War's ongoing significance in Canada by foregrounding the many personal and political losses that its conclusion presaged. Richler re-examines these losses at a further chronological remove in his later novel. *Joshua Then and Now* covers much of the same geographical territory after Franco's death and Spain's halting return to democracy, but it is also more firmly located in Canada and more optimistic about the possibilities of cross-cultural love.

Nostalgia for the Last Great Cause: *Joshua Then and Now*

Richler's later novel *Joshua Then and Now* (1980) takes a humorous perspective on Spain's enduring place in the Jewish Canadian imaginary. The novel's eponymous protagonist is obsessed with the Spanish Civil War he was born too late to fight in. Through Joshua's fascination with the conflict – and fixation on a Hemingwayesque construction of international participation – the novel undermines Spanish Civil War novelistic tropes, departing from earnest invocations of comradely emotion to expose the disjunction between espousing leftist beliefs and being a leftist, and the political and social fissures within Canada's Jewish population.

The nervous breakdown and disappearance of Joshua's gentile wife Pauline inverts the typical Spanish Civil War novel narrative of the male character abandoning his lover in the name of a supposedly universal cause. In this way, Richler exposes these cross-cultural relationships as necessary underpinnings – not hindrances – to political engagement.[19] Pauline's impact on Joshua's dawning understanding of social responsibility accentuates Joshua's own fixation on demonstrating Jewish masculinity. Richler suggests that this fixation, above all, explains why the Spanish struggle is so important to Jewish Canadian men. Joshua and his friends can mock their own marginalized status amid Canada's legacy of religious intolerance. For instance, the annual meeting of their William Lyon Mackenzie King Memorial Society includes a rendition of "Safe in the Arms of Jesus" sung in Yiddish, discussion of the former prime minister's friendship with Hitler, and a hockey game. However, at the same time, the Spanish Civil War and Hemingway's writings about it remain their gauge of manliness. Spain – understood through American gentile masculinity – becomes their way into the Canadian mainstream. Joshua's friend Seymour reflects: "I wanted to fight on the Ebro. Come back with a wound, maybe. Nothing serious. I mean, not like Jake Barnes. But enough so that people would point me out even now. Sure he's in knitwear, but you know that limp, he got it in Spain. Do you understand?" (*Joshua* 178).

Richler's characters understand this sentiment and indeed transform it into a new concept of Canadian identity. In synthesizing American and Canadian cultural tropes with their own subverted and subversive Jewish customs, Richler's characters humorously exemplify Marie Vautier's concept of the "new myth," that is, narratives that undermine received (often colonial) tropes of traditional history and that in so doing "undermine the assumptions contained in the liberal humanist ideal of an established national literature with equally established literary and historical myths" (Vautier 25). However, Joshua's hybrid creations are not intended as new, authentically multicultural Canadian texts – put another way, "Safe in the Arms of Jesus" was, arguably, never intended for widespread performance after Richler's characters translated it into Yiddish. Rather, Richler's purposeful, comic misinterpretations point to the inevitable gaps, mistranslations, and confusions both within and across cultures: the permeability of cultural distinctions.

In *Joshua Then and Now,* these misunderstandings are frequently gendered. In both Canada and Spain, female gentile characters connect Joshua's Jewishness to his sexual and intellectual prowess. During Joshua's first visit to Spain as a young man, he is convinced that his Spanish-French mistress Monique is attracted to his handsome semitic features: "You had such big ears. And your nose! My God!" (337). Upon her discovery that his large facial features are not indicative of other physical characteristics, Monique's affection for Joshua is quickly revealed to be little more than mutually projected exoticism: Monique hopes that Joshua's stereotypically Jewish features might translate to sexual gratification, and Joshua uses Monique's attraction to prove his masculinity to himself – if only temporarily. The notion of his international appeal helps him imagine that members of his own race, religion, and class are also exceptionally masculine.

Joshua's wife Pauline similarly explains that her initial attraction to him stemmed from what she perceived as Jewish men's "appetite" (209), along with his ability to shock her friends and family. Joshua consciously allows himself to be misread as much as he misreads others. The fling with Monique becomes not only his sexual initiation, but also a necessary aspect of his romanticization of the Spanish cause – an opportunity to become the Hemingway hero he had dreamed of while growing up in Montreal:

> [H]e never necked with a girl without wondering, if never daring to ask, O Riva Mandelbaum, O Hanna Steinberg, "*But did thee feel the earth move?*"
> "*Yes. As I died. Put thy arm around me, please.*"
> "*No. I have thy hand. Thy hand is enough.*" (115; italics in the original)

By imagining himself in a Jewish version of Robert Jordan's Spanish seduction, Joshua suggests the disconnect between his romantic life and that of Hemingway's hypermasculine gentile protagonist even while he mocks this version of sexual prowess. In sending up Joshua's youthful affairs, Richler also undermines the same stereotypes of the effeminate Jewish man that earlier Spanish Civil War novels similarly seek to dispel. In *Joshua Then and Now*, the Spanish struggle remains an important cause for Jewish Canadian men: not only a political call-to-arms but also an opportunity for them to break away from their exoticized role as physically stigmatized, socially ghettoized objects of scorn and attraction.

However, the novel does not just reverse stereotypes, as Allan's novel does, by depicting Jewish bravery. *Joshua Then and Now* posits a successful long-term interfaith romance, imagining a Jewish Canadian character in Spain and alternative, powerful roles for women in building and rebuilding Spanish and Canadian society. More broadly, the novel criticizes the dominant culture to which this desire to fight is a reaction. By satirizing historical memory, Richler interrogates Anglo-American masculinity, Canadian religious intolerance, and antisemitic stereotypes of male effeminacy that compel violence and war. The novel mocks the Spanish Civil War cross-cultural romance in which Republicans triumph over fascist forces but individual male characters must always choose politics over love. Joshua's longing to be a genuine hero of the International Brigades throws into sharp relief the society that produces such an ideal.

Joshua's tangential participation in the Spanish conflict ultimately gains him little; likewise, his belief that a Spanish romance will somehow sexually legitimize him. His conviction that Monique's attraction to him signifies Jewish success is also quickly proven wrong. Instead, he finds that his time in Spain has reinforced the identity he already knew he had: "Damn. Making Ibiza his base, he had come to Spain to look at battlefields, talk to survivors, learn what he could about the Spanish Civil War. Instead, he was discovering that he was Jewish. Something anybody could have told him" (221). Having recognized the problematic nature of his Spanish fixation, he commits to remaining in Montreal, choosing local community – and especially family – over an imagined transnational collective. By relentlessly, explicitly inserting Jewish Canadians into a historical moment during which religious affiliations were often occluded, Richler critiques the gentile masculinity represented in so many Spanish Civil War novels.

In this critique of political unity, however, Richler's satire also explodes the possibility of a cohesive Jewish Canadian – or even Canadian, or Jewish – national identity. Instead, *Joshua Then and Now* proposes voluntary personal affiliation as an alternative to prescribed identity categories. The novel concludes with Pauline and Joshua's tentative reunion in the yard of their home, where he has been trying without success to tend the garden. Such a conclusion reiterates the fixation on territory – on becoming rooted – so important to earlier Canadian texts about the Spanish Civil War and to Richler's oeuvre, but this time emphasizing the couple's future. With what is, as Zailig Pollock points out, "a sentimental picture of a woman literally supporting her man" (127), the novel's conclusion emphasizes Richler's "unfashionable view of women's role" of providing "*unconditional* love and support" (127; italics in the original). In other words, the conclusion becomes a traditional romance of reconciliation even while subverting the genre's gendered assumptions. At the same time, Richler refuses to imply that the interfaith couple's reconciliation provides some sort of promise for a new, stable Canadian identity. *Joshua Then and Now* constructs the same unrelenting, oversimplified dualities common to many fictions of assimilation and multiculturalism. But in parodying the hollowness of received Canadian, Spanish, and Jewish histories, Richler also illustrates that the identity categories the characters work so hard to fit into are themselves fantasies of belonging – that the categories "Canadian" and "Jew" may actually be vacant, constituted by those also struggling for inclusion. *Joshua Then and Now* eschews wholeness and stability entirely, showing the complications and shortcomings inherent in the binary thinking encouraged by assimilationism and anti-assimilationism alike.[20]

All of the novels I have discussed so far attempt to articulate a cosmopolitan approach to belonging. They insist that human sympathy extends beyond national, religious, ethnic, and racial distinctions, allowing for multiple affiliations. However, earlier novels often share an older, idealist form of cosmopolitanism, one that is predicated on its cultural prestige, and not – with European fascism's rise – its necessary correlative of sympathy and sanctuary for those whose identity has rendered them unwelcome in their own communities. Earlier novels do undercut – or satirize – these same identity categories, challenging traditional approaches to citizenship and internationalism through the potentially subversive presence of characters of unclear origins. While the international romance is almost always between a male North American character and a foreign female character, additional characters with less obvious affiliations – because they themselves do not know their parentage, or because the narrative itself obscures their nationality – allude to the possibility of broadened citizenship.

Richler extends these gestures toward acceptance by presenting sympathetic Spanish, Canadian, and American citizens – and even former Nazis – while connecting the struggles of different non-normative couples – non-normative because they are international, interfaith, or queer. Similarly, whereas earlier Spanish Civil War romances laud the male protagonist's decision to leave his girlfriend or wife behind, Richler imagines the reverse situation – the woman's leaving – and finds it equally traumatizing, if not more so: Pauline suffers a nervous breakdown from which she recuperates, but without his wife, not only Joshua but the natural world is shaken, and even the vegetables in their garden cannot grow. Joshua and Pauline's reunion emphasizes the impossibility of distinguishing between the personal and the political. The fictional relationships Richler creates implicitly critique previous novels' unquestioning belief in the Spanish cause, or in the rightness of Hemingway's masculine constructions, or in the possibility of international connection unmediated by eroticized preconceptions, or in the establishment of a harmonious Jewish community: these early absolutist convictions are ultimately revealed to be – like Monique's amateur attempts at physiognomy – disappointingly false.

The Spanish Civil War Romance Novel's Political Projects

By complicating and expanding the Spanish cause's implications, Richler's *Joshua Then and Now* compels a re-evaluation of North American involvement. The novel's focus on the complexities of gender, religion, and ethnicity in Spain and Canada are focalized through a Jewish male protagonist who is increasingly sensitized to female characters' experiences. But even as Richler critiques this chain of personal fictions, the Spanish battlefields his characters visualize affect women, albeit without directly including them: *Joshua Then and Now* connects sexism and antisemitism but fails to imagine the social roles female characters might envision for themselves, as it does for Jewish Canadian men. In this way, *Joshua Then and Now* represents an important shift in fictional representations of the Spanish Civil War, toward an increasingly intersectional perspective. The earlier novels by Allan, Harrison, and Richler conceptualize the Spanish conflict's global implications. In their North American focus, their novels mediate between fears over international war and fears of internationalism, striving for a vocabulary of proto-multicultural acceptance while still exposing (and sometimes reinscribing) gendered associations of race, ethnicity, and religion. In their responses to a very particular moment – of Canadian, North American, and Spanish political flux and of Jewish migration – these early Jewish Canadian novels about the Spanish Civil War attempt to articulate a national identity that is at once patriotic and cosmopolitan. Richler's later novel, then, challenges the motivations of this earlier cosmopolitanism, underscoring its problematically gendered approach to leveraging Jewish men – but not women – into the mainstream.

If the Spanish Civil War romance's narrative prizes battlefield success over romance, then *Joshua Then and Now* reyokes the false binary. The novel suggests the importance of citizenship rights and social equality, yet it does so by emphasizing the extent to which the Spanish conflict exists in an imaginary realm of fantasized masculinity. Jewish characters' dreams of wartime bravado are, of course, reactive to gentile characters' own illusions. In leveraging (or aspiring to leverage) marginalized individuals into a dominant culture, these novels remind us of those so often left behind: women and people of colour.

2
Sympathy: Cosmopolitan Combat and Postcolonial Spain

"An oppressed colonial people of color being used by fascism to make a colony of Spain."

Langston Hughes, "Negroes in Spain"

Race and Diaspora in Spain

As the previous chapter suggests, Jewish authors' attempts to define the parameters of identity are intractably yoked to ideals of gentile masculinity: to leverage themselves into mainstream whiteness, authors both enact and undermine narratives of wartime romance and white ethnic assimilation. For the characters they depict, assimilation into the dominant culture – whether Canadian, American, or Spanish – remains contingent on their being recognized as white, heterosexual, and male. Only as masculine white men are these characters acknowledged as national subjects.

Passing as white Christians in a North American context is one thing; passing as white Christians in a country with a centuries-long history of Jewish and Muslim persecution and ongoing colonial strongholds in Africa and the Americas is quite another. Spain's long-held colonial empire and history of forced conversions and expulsions brought international volunteers face to face with often uncomfortable ambiguities about the country's history and future. In literary depictions, then, Jewish characters' hard-won proximity to whiteness and masculinity – to power and privilege – is rendered even more tenuous by the complexities of race, gender, nationality, and religion that Spain presents.

For some volunteers, supporting a country with a long and ongoing history of colonialism inspired a deep ambivalence toward the Popular Front's project – even as the international volunteers themselves were often motivated by idealistic visions of a society free of discrimination and imperialism. This chapter examines how literary depictions of the war configure supporters' antiracist, anticolonial beliefs within a colonial war's framework. Given the concurrent North American fixation on immigrants' relative whiteness as well as a long-standing fascination, on the part of Black intellectuals, with Spain, this chapter also asks how writers imagine race in a Spanish context. What happens when categories of race, ethnicity, religion, and nationality – already complex in a Canadian or American context – collide with other nations' understandings of these categories? How do North American writers recognize groups whose collective identity complicates or transcends easy distinctions, such as North American Jews, women, or Moroccan "Moors" – a term with multiple referents related to religion and ethnicity?

I approach these questions in two ways. The first half of the chapter examines how North American writers who participated in the Spanish Civil War depict Black people's participation in that war. Perhaps best known in this regard is Langston Hughes, whose journalism and poetry from Spain highlight the ironies of the participation of Moroccans on the fascist side, and of African Americans on the loyalist side. The second half looks to two postwar authors who have returned repeatedly to the Spanish Civil War in their fiction to complicate developing 1970s and '80s discourses of multiculturalism and pan-Africanism: the African American novelist John A. Williams and the Jewish Canadian writer Mordecai Richler, whose novel concluded my previous chapter. Together, these complementary halves demonstrate the evolving stakes of crafting a narrative of Spanish Civil War volunteerism.

During the war, and over the following decades, Spain's history of colonial subjugation in the New World and in North Africa provided an uncomfortable backdrop for otherwise triumphal narratives of North American antiracist and antifascist activism. Read together, the depictions and erasures of African diasporic contact across political lines reveal the underlying contradictions and tenuous logics used to construct categories of racial, national, and religious difference – categories used as rallying cries on both sides of the battle line. Especially when placed alongside narratives by white and white ethnic writers, Williams's retrospection and Hughes's war poetry portray the war in political terms – as a struggle to end European fascism, establish a new kind of radical society, and maintain a nascent democracy – and in historical ones, as a continuation of the global and historical struggles that gave rise to modernity itself: colonization and the slave trade.

Furthermore, literary representations of African and African American characters are frequently linked to Jewish characters' portrayals.

Such connections are not uncommon in twentieth-century literature, but the interrelations between diasporized communities in Spanish Civil War literature suggest the continuing importance of involuntary filiations in the midst of a burgeoning cosmopolitan leftism. Richler's writing connects Spain's enduring colonial presence in Morocco and Latin America to Britain's colonial legacies in Canada, the United States, and Mandatory Palestine. In so doing, it also highlights the collapsing categories of race, ethnicity, and religion that undergird the Second Spanish Republic's supposed egalitarianism.

Colonial Spain

When Francisco Franco's attempted coup led to the Spanish Civil War's outbreak in 1936, Spain's colonial holdings in Africa were all that remained of *el imperio en el que nunca se pone el sol* – the empire on which the sun never set. Spain's colonial history, particularly its then recent colonization efforts in North Africa, contributed to and confused the country's civil war, which was fought against the backdrop of a decade-long global economic crisis and the escalation of European fascism.

The transnational collaborations the Spanish Civil War occasioned were inextricably linked to Spain's colonial history. The Mexican government accepted Spanish Republican refugees and exiles. Many of the thousands of international volunteers in Spain came from the country's former colonies, travelling from Mexico and Cuba to the former centre of empire. Spain's own former colonial subjects were joined by members of other marginalized groups who identified with the antifascist cause and who understood the stakes of the struggle. Among them, a small but significant segment of the American volunteers – approximately one hundred – were African Americans. Many African American volunteers in Spain had first tried to volunteer in Ethiopia after fascist Italy's 1935 invasion, but Emperor Haile Selassie rejected international support in an attempt to keep the conflict localized.[1] These volunteers were among the first American citizens to fight in desegregated battalions. They included Oliver Law, the first African American commander of an integrated military force. Together, these participants' diverse motivations show the connections between global struggles, in that they tied Spain's colonial history and current civil war to Ethiopia's 1935 resistance against Mussolini's invasion, and, in the United States, Jim Crow segregation, disenfranchisement, and lynch law. And, as Robert F. Reid-Pharr notes, these African American men quickly became a valuable symbol for the left, "extremely effective emblems of the leftist propaganda machine that developed around the war because their stories fit so neatly the ideological requirements of early twentieth-century radical internationalism" (45).

In several writings both contemporaneous to the conflict and more current, North American literary representations of the war triangulate the Spanish Civil War, the Ethiopian invasion, and American racism. As I will discuss, John A. Williams's novel *Captain Blackman* explicitly connects Spain and the United States, as the eponymous protagonist, an African American man, and his friend Doctorow, a Jewish American, speculate together on what volunteering in Spain might mean globally, "with Blackman concluding that he could fight American lynch law by fighting Spanish fascism; Doctorow concluding that he could fight international anti-Semitism" (153).

Captain Blackman's connection of local and global causes echoes earlier African American fiction and memoir. For instance, the African American veteran Oscar Hunter's short story "700 Calendar Days" contemplates the different effects of volunteering in Spain, Ethiopia, and the United States, directly treating the tensions between individual and group loyalties. Hunter's short story depicts two African American soldiers who discuss the importance of global antiracist work and of serving in integrated battalions "in a place where there ain't a speck of Jim Crow" (300). One character reflects: "I wanted to go to Ethiopia and fight Mussolini. Couldn't get there ... they wasn't running boats from West Street ... I got to Spain. This ain't Ethiopia, but it'll do" (299). This character's resignation to fighting in Spain – "it'll do" – suggests something of the close link, for many, between counteracting fascism in Africa and in Europe, and the way in which social activism, particularly in New York, was mobilized through transnational networks.[2]

Spain would have to do as well for Salaria Kea, the only African American nurse to volunteer in Spain (one of only four African American women to have travelled there), who makes a brief appearance in Williams's novel. As I will further discuss in the following chapter, Kea was a vocal advocate for Ethiopia, for Spain, and for the important roles played by women in activist movements. She wrote extensively about her experiences and lectured across the United States to fundraise for the Spanish cause.[3] A version of her life story was published as a pamphlet by the Negro Committee to Aid Spain. The pamphlet's authorship is of some debate: while typically attributed to Kea, Anne Donlon has presented compelling archival evidence that it was actually authored by another African American volunteer, the social worker Thyra Edwards.[4] This particular iteration of Kea's story is told in the third person and details her political and professional trajectory. It begins by explicitly emphasizing the relationships between the United States, Spain, and Ethiopia through a series of questions: "What have Negroes to do with Spain? What has Spain for us? What about Ethiopia? Why should Negro men be fighting in Spain?" (Kea, "Negro Nurse" 123). These questions are followed by short histories of African American participation in Ethiopia and of Italian fascism in Spain. The pamphlet further connects the African American presence in Spain to a wider African and African diasporic community that had gathered there: "Here in the International Brigade of Volunteers they found other Negroes. From Djibouti, Emperor Haile Selassie's chief mechanic came 'to strike a blow for a free Ethiopia.' From South Africa, from Cuba, from French Senegal, from Haiti, from the Cameroons, Negroes came, stayed and fought" (Kea, "Negro Nurse" 124). And later, in describing the injured soldiers who were her patients, the pamphlet enumerates:

> Czechs from Prague, and from Bohemian villages, Hungarians, French, Finns. Peoples from democratic countries who recognized Italy and Germany's invasion in Spain as a threat to the peace and security of all small countries. Germans and Italians, exiled or escaped from concentration camps and fighting for their freedom here on Spain's battle line. Ethiopians from Djibouti ... Cubans, Mexicans, Russians, Japanese ... There were poor whites and Negroes from the Southern States of the United States. (Kea, "Negro Nurse" 129)

For Kea and others, the Spanish Civil War was an international anticolonial cause, and fascist weaponry did not distinguish by nationality, race, class, or religion. Many authors who depicted Spain likewise offered a roll call of members of the transnational community as a way to highlight their shared values. But even while these authors explicitly connected Ethiopia, Spain, and the United States within an international framework of global fascism, many others resisted making such connections.

Spain's American and Moroccan Wars

Many volunteers readily perceived the network of oppression in Spain, Ethiopia, and the United States. Spain's southern neighbour, Morocco, also became a fraught location within this network, reflecting its confusingly overlapping history of colonization by a succession of European powers. For all the International Brigades supporters' triumphal rhetoric of transnational collaboration, international alliances were not exclusive to the Republican side. Franco enlisted African colonial subjects as soldiers and relied on the support of fascist Italy, Portugal, and Nazi Germany. The Spanish Republic's refusal to decolonize sustained the oppressive conditions that allowed Franco to galvanize Moroccan support.[5]

The roots of Spanish control of Morocco – and Spain's imperial history in the New World – far predated Franco's 1936 uprising. The Spanish-American War of 1898 – frequently referred to in Spain as "the Great Disaster" – destroyed monarchist Spain's empire. The country had begun the twentieth century with bloody independence struggles in Cuba and the Philippines. These losses of land and power precipitated Spain's desire to colonize elsewhere. Supported by the work of *africanistas*, military personnel who led Spain's colonial enterprise, and by the race scientists who provided ideological support for their efforts, Spain looked to Morocco. The Rif Wars of 1909–10 and 1920–6 led to Spain's expansion in North Africa, with Franco as a key leader in these brutal wars.

The Second Spanish Republic's failure to grant Morocco its independence compounded the problem of Morocco's loyalty during the civil war. Even as the newly democratic country instituted many progressive reforms, the government refused to address its colonial presence in Africa, ignoring repeated attempts on the part of Moroccan leaders to negotiate independence – a warning of future turmoil to come. The Spanish Republican government reasoned that maintaining its African colonies would appease Britain and France by not stirring up anticolonial sentiments in Spanish Morocco that could spread to British and French colonies across the African continent.[6]

Meanwhile, assigned to a post in the Canary Islands, Franco harnessed Moroccan poverty and antipathy toward Spain in support of his fascist cause – a cause that already relied on what historian Paul Preston calls "a transference of racial prejudice" (*Spanish Holocaust* 21), in which the Spanish left was characterized as "an inferior race, horrible examples of racial degeneration … sub-human and abnormal" (*Spanish Holocaust* 22). Franco had played an instrumental role in Morocco's colonization by Spain in the first place; yet now, his propaganda was inspiring support from Arab and Berber Muslims by representing his current insurgency as a "reconquest" of Spain. For some, this must have offered a powerful narrative: a long-exiled Muslim population rescues Spain from "Orientals," "Reds," "Jews," and "heathens."[7] Of course, such representations also relied upon a strategic blindness to Spain's own Jewish roots, to say nothing of Franco's prominent role in subjugating the same people he now needed to support his attempt at a coup. Franco promised independence in exchange for Moroccan mercenary support for his assault on Spain proper. And many (but by no means all) Moroccans were prepared to fight in "the Army of Africa" alongside the fascists in the hopes of decolonization or simply out of financial desperation. Franco was being supplied with arms, airplanes, and troops by Nazi Germany and fascist Italy and Portugal, but he would rely heavily on Moroccan soldiers as shock troops on the ground.[8]

A multinational force had made the fascist victory possible; even so, the so-called Nationalists would later downplay the importance of German, Italian, Portuguese, and Moroccan participation. Once he declared himself Caudillo, Franco did not fulfil his promise to grant Morocco its independence until 1956. To this day, the Spanish government holds administrative control over Ceuta, Melilla, and the Canary Islands.

The dictator's debt to Moroccan troops – and before the civil war, his military success in colonizing Morocco – translated into a psychological, even mythological narrative of Spain's origins and future. "My years in Africa live with me with indescribable force," Franco told the journalist Manuel Aznar in 1938. "There was born the possibility of rescuing a great Spain. There was found the idea which today redeems us. Without Africa, I can scarcely explain myself to myself, nor can I explain myself properly to my comrades in arms" (qtd in Rein 197). Franco's own narrative of his and Spain's redemption through Africa relies on a long history of racism and colonization: the Spanish "us" rescued by and remade "great" through Africa remains distinct from an African "them." Racial difference is mobilized to spur reflection about white nationalist alienation in the context of waning colonial power. Franco's confession suggests the interrelations of personal and national identity defined against a Black Other; he is incomprehensible to himself and to his "comrades in arms" without reference to Africa. The continent of Africa becomes a place of spiritual renewal that inspires the future dictator to liberate Spain from a godless, cosmopolitan modernity.

Writing Race and Spain

Franco relied on the Moroccan troops, even while mistreating them, and mythologized Spain's debt to Morocco. As a result of his volatile linking of races, religions, and nations, the issue of race emerged as an ideological battleground in the Spanish Civil War. Leftist writers' invocations of race and nationality had the same impact. As Michael Ugarte notes, "the presence of the black other on both sides of the conflict made for inconsistency on both sides of the ideological divide" (109). International volunteers' responses to the Moroccan soldiers among Franco's ranks alternated between racism and colonial sympathy.[9] Journalistic coverage of Franco's mistreatment of Moroccan soldiers appeared in the North American leftist and Black press, in articles by Black and white authors such as Langston Hughes, Nancy Cunard, Joseph North, Herbert Matthews, Richard Wright, and Thyra Edwards.[10] Other mid-century texts by Black authors argue for Morocco as the root of all that is culturally productive about Spain: travelogues like the Jamaican American author Claude McKay's *A Long Way from Home* (1937) and the African American author Richard Wright's *Pagan Spain* (1957) avoid explicit references to the war or to the two countries' ongoing colonial connection, but their positioning of Morocco as the root of Spanish – even European – culture suggests sympathy for Moroccan citizens as well as immense respect for their country.[11]

Even if – despite these first-hand reports of Morocco's influence on Spain and of the presence of Moroccans in Spain – some North American volunteers and writers remained oblivious to Spain's deep entanglement with North Africa, few could have remained unaware of the role of the "Moro" or "Moor" in the Spanish cultural imaginary. The term itself was elastic, referring to Muslim and Jewish Moroccans, North Africans, Arabs, and many other outsiders, usually non-European and especially of a darker complexion. Notwithstanding the broad historical application of these terms, the most common image of the enemy among International Brigades volunteers was a dark-skinned Moroccan Muslim. This representation was spread in part by Spanish Republican propaganda, in which stereotypical representations of Africans harnessed deeply embedded, internationally recognizable tropes of racism to villainize these soldiers and collapse regional and racial distinctions into a general idea of a Black fascist.[12]

Yet the Spanish and international left took great pride in its progressive attitude toward transnational harmony and racial integration. That attitude also dominates much of the literature by white and white ethnic North American writers, in which characters often comment on the racial equality among the International Brigades. Yet at the same time, such texts often depict the colonial soldiers as updated versions of the archetypal "villains in Spanish fairy stories": Hugh Thomas ascribes such depictions to the role played by "Moors" in the Spanish imaginary (360). This is not to say that writers and volunteers were unaware of Spain's ongoing colonial domination in Morocco or were uncritical of antifascist propaganda – however, even as left-leaning writers explicitly engage race, ethnicity, gender, class, and nationality, some of their better-known depictions of Moroccans are simplistic and negative.

Morocco and Moroccans often play a marginal role in these texts; even so, the relationship between Spain and its North African colony remains relevant to studies of Spanish Civil War literature precisely because of how Moroccan characters so often represent the faceless mob that terrorizes international and Spanish characters. Moroccan characters are, variously, vague and illusory placeholders, scapegoats, terrifying warriors, and occasional objects of pity. Moroccans are "the terrible Moors" (Sinclair 76), who "tortured their prisoners with the most hideous cruelty" and committed "wholesale slaughter of workers, peasants, intellectuals, Protestants" (Sinclair 80). As Upton Sinclair represents them, they "were all Mohammedans, and from the front end of the rifle they were the same; terrible fighters, whose joy in life was to kill Spaniards, and die for the glory of Allah, and go to a heaven full of houris" (Sinclair 84). "If they send Moors to hunt us out," writes Ernest Hemingway in *For Whom the Bell Tolls*, "they will find us" (15). In "The Starched Blue Sky of Spain," Josephine Herbst writes: "You always kept a bullet for yourself if it was the Moors. That was better than to let them get you and cut you up alive" (145). Even Hugh Garner's more sympathetic portrayal of a Moroccan soldier was removed from later editions of his collection of Spanish Civil War short stories. Garner was a former International Brigades volunteer – a British-born Torontonian who served with English, American, and Canadian units in Spain – whose long career as a writer of fiction and autobiography runs the gamut from staunchly antiracist to harshly discriminatory. The original conclusion to his 1938 short story "The Stretcher Bearers" describes a group of Spanish Republican soldiers who torture and then kill a Moroccan prisoner of war: "A small group of Spaniards were taunting a wounded Moor, whom they were slinging across the back of a mule. They were shouting, 'Moro! Moro!' and the Moor was crying, wiping the tears on his sleeve from beneath a dirty bandage around his head" (272n167.3). However, any mention of the Moroccan POW or the narrator's sympathy was excised from the short story upon its reprinting in 1963 (without any other substantive changes).[13]

These representations of Moroccans and "Moors" contrast with the sympathetic portrayals of both African American soldiers and Spanish people – two groups who were also Other to the white North American volunteers and writers. In their flat depictions of Moroccan soldiers, many Euro-American writers obscure the motivations and experiences of Black participants on both sides and the greater promises that a Republican Spain – or a fascist one – represented for oppressed minorities in their own home countries. For instance, though it ostensibly celebrates interracial solidarity, former volunteer Ted Allan's novel *This Time a Better Earth* (1939) explicitly distances the lone African American character from any diasporic history or affiliations that extend beyond his nationality. The character – named "Doug," and possibly based on real-life volunteer Doug Roach – distinguishes himself from the African soldiers on the fascist side: "I am not a Moor. I am an American negro and I am an anti-fascist. And we don't spout the theories of white and black fighting side by side, we live them" (29). The novel thus quickly dispenses with references to the fascists' engagement with Morocco in favour of elucidating the American context of antiracist struggles. The character is then blinded in battle, prompting him to reflect: "Maybe it's because I can't see what's black and what's white now ... I dunno ... but there's no difference" (127; ellipses in the original). The stark distinction that texts like Allan's draw between African Americans and Moroccans, or "Moors," also flattens racial, ethnic, religious, and class differences within Morocco and Spain. If becoming a North American subject requires leaving one's race behind – and becoming ostensibly blind to other volunteers' racial identities too – it does not necessitate a similar colour-blindness toward those who oppose the Popular Front. Furthermore, such simplistic understandings of race and universal whiteness (composed, in the case of Allan, by a Jewish Canadian author passing as a gentile and writing, in part, to leverage Jewish immigrants into mainstream whiteness) pits national affiliation against race, religion, and ethnicity, suggesting the complex calculus of African American soldiers' relationship to Spanish colonization and leftist activism.

Hughes Writing Morocco

Langston Hughes strove to understand and communicate the nuances of Black participation in the Spanish Civil War through his journalism, poetry, and memoir. Hughes went to Spain to cover its civil war for the Black press; his reports for the *Baltimore Afro-American* were intended to inspire American support. In depicting Spain, Hughes wrote extensively about the "Moors" and other people of African descent he encountered there and about how issues around race and colonialism were at the root of the Spanish Civil War. Hughes's political leanings at the time were, according to Anthony Dawahare, "left of the CP on issues of race and nationality" in that he rejected the nationalism of the Communist Party's Black Nation Thesis (which posited giving African American southerners self-determination) in favour of a more international perspective – one he saw in the Spanish cause (95).

For Hughes, the antifascist movement in Spain simultaneously enacted antiracist activism; conversely, he saw racism as an inextricable component of fascism. His texts remain a rare and important consideration of the connections between African American volunteers and Moroccan soldiers. In looking to Hughes's writing, many critics have usefully contextualized his Spanish Civil War poetry in relation to his Spanish Civil War journalism (Thurston, Girón Echevarría), his contact with and writing about the Hispanic world (Enjuto Rangel, May, Mullen, Scaramella, Soto), his poetic intersections with Federico García Lorca (Edwards, Soto), his anti-imperialist internationalism (Dawahare), his and other African American authors' writing about Spain (Kennedy, Nelson, Wald), and his writing about leftist causes more broadly (Maxwell, Shulman, Smethurst). Together, these critical examinations provide vital insights into Hughes's ongoing engagement with global issues of race, class, nationality, and politics. I argue that examining Hughes's writings about Morocco and Spain in the context of other North American literary depictions and erasures of Morocco reveals the postcolonial implications of Spain's civil war – not only in terms of Hughes's position as a far-left, anticolonial Black American writer but also with respect to other North American leftists' attempts to reckon with the intersections of colonialism, race, ethnicity, religion, and nationality in the transnational fight against fascism.

Hughes's 1937 poem "Letter from Spain" (often titled "Dear Brother at Home") encapsulates these fraught intersections and underscores his journalistic purpose as well. The poem, addressed to a "Brother at home" in Alabama, recounts the speaker's experience capturing and conversing with a wounded Moroccan POW. The speaker's optimism about an African anticolonial solidarity is tempered by the POW's death at the poem's conclusion. Hughes composed the poem while visiting the volunteers in Spain and meeting wounded Moroccan POWs; he explains that he wrote the poem to articulate "the irony of the colonial Moors" and to "try to express the feelings of some of the Negro fighting men" (*I Wonder* 353). This irony is writ large across Hughes's writing, which foregrounds interactions between members of the African diaspora. As he states, his obligation in reporting from Spain was

> to write for the colored press. I knew that Spain once belonged to the Moors, a colored people ranging from light dark to dark white. Now the Moors have come again to Spain with the fascist armies as cannon fodder for Franco. But, on the loyalist side there are many colored people of various nationalities in the International Brigades. I want to write about both Moors and colored people. ("Hughes Finds Moors" 106)

Likewise, in this 1937 article, Hughes describes the diverse communities of people of colour on both sides of the conflict and further explains the importance of focusing on this diversity:

> What I sought to find out in Spain was what effect, if any, this bringing of dark troops to Europe had had on the Spanish people in regard to their racial feelings. Had prejudice and hatred been created in a land that did

> not know it before? What had been the treatment of Moorish prisoners by the Loyalists? Are they segregated and ill-treated? Are there any Moors on the government side? (109)

Hughes's attempts to answer these questions form the basis for much of his journalism, as well as his poetry and the memoir *I Wonder as I Wander* (drawn, in part, from this journalism).[14] He emphatically represents Republican Spain as devoid of racism, explaining in his memoir, "I could not find that the enemy's use of these colored troops had brought about any increased feeling of color consciousness on the part of the people of Spain. I was well received everywhere I went, and the Negroes in the International Brigades reported a similar reception" (351). This statement seems to be a response to his earlier questions, if perhaps an incomplete one.[15] Hughes attributes this acceptance to Spain's longstanding Muslim citizenry and cultural influence as well as to postcolonial migration: "Distinct traces of Moorish blood from the days of the Mohammedan conquest remain in the Iberian Peninsula ... There were, too, quite a number of colored Portuguese living in Spain. And in both Valencia and Madrid I saw pure-blooded Negroes from the colonies in Africa, as well as many Cubans who had migrated to Spain" (351). Even in its blanket characterization of Spanish racial acceptance, Hughes's memoir points to a nuanced, transnational understanding of race and nationality.

Hughes's writing on Moroccan participation, when read alongside other North American writers' depictions, highlights the increased personal dangers and global political stakes the war held for Black participants. In looking to Morocco and "the deluded and driven Moors of North Africa" ("Negroes in Spain" 97), Hughes exposes the complexities of what seemed for many to be a clear-cut conflict over fascism. Hughes's representations of Moroccans (and, as Michael Thurston argues, their implied link to the earlier conflict in Ethiopia) call attention to local Spanish and Moroccan contexts as well as to transnational and anticolonial contexts across Africa.[16] These poetic and journalistic depictions of Blackness and colonial subordination as they relate to Spain and Morocco constitute a recursive, multifaceted view of Spain's relationship to the African diaspora.

Placing Hughes's portrayals of Moroccan participation in conversation with other writers' representations of Morocco highlights the colonial situation: specifically, reading Hughes's poem "Letter from Spain" in this broader context suggests that it is, in fact, a poetic recounting of potentially real events. Arnold Rampersad dismisses the poem as "a maudlin dialect poem" (351), but there is subtlety and nuance in the work, not to mention an unsettling commentary on current and future conditions for Black people in Spain. The poem's speaker is the same "Johnny" of "Dear Folks at Home" (called "Postcard from Spain" in the 1995 *Collected Poems of Langston Hughes*) and "Love Letter from Spain" (not included in the collection), as well as countless war and protest anthems. "Letter from Spain" recalls Hughes's article "Negroes in Spain," in which he describes a visit to a hospital where he spoke with Moroccan soldiers and – as in the poem – repeatedly noted their shared skin colour and distinct languages. Yet in the monolingual poem, Johnny's question to the prisoner, "Boy, what you been doin' here / Fightin' against the free?" (201), and his attempt at friendship, "Listen, Moorish prisoner, hell! / Here, shake hands with me!" (202), remain in English, untranslated. But in the context of the poem, an unnamed interlocutor relays the Moroccan soldier's response to both the speaker and the reader. In the translated account of the prisoner:

> They nabbed him in his land
>
> And made him join the fascist army
> And come across to Spain.
> And he said he had a feelin'
> He'd never get back home again.
>
> He said he had a feelin'
> This whole thing wasn't right.
> He said he didn't know
> The folks he had to fight. (201)

Repeating the line "he said he had a feelin'" underscores the prisoner's humanity, giving him intuition and history. The dying soldier's admission that "[t]his whole thing wasn't right" also suggests his uneasiness and perhaps regret over fighting with Franco's forces. His experience in Spain has disconnected him from his family and home in Morocco, revoking the possibility of an easy return. His feeling that "[h]e'd never get back home again" signals both the prisoner's impending death and the disruption of his sense of "home" as an undisputed place of seamless identity. The speaker shares this sense of distance from a homeland, realizing how much he has in common with the Moroccan soldier, as subjugated individuals fighting a war not their own – although they are doing so for very different reasons. As Cecilia Enjuto Rangel suggests, "the difference between the African American soldier and the Moroccan mercenary is one of ideological conviction" (167): while the Moroccan was forced to fight on the front lines, Johnny chose his participation in the Spanish cause, volunteering to fight because he understands his participation as linked to his own experiences in the United States. Hughes's speaker bears witness to the demise of a foe with whom he shares a diasporic kinship and attempts to empathize. As such, the poem problematizes easy wartime narratives of a uniformly evil, dehumanized enemy.

Of the individuals depicted in Hughes's Spanish Civil War poems, the Moroccan soldier stands apart. Not only is the nameless POW more extensively characterized but he is also unique within these poems as the only individuated representative of Franco's forces. Hughes's other references to Franco's soldiers tend to be implicit – they are the unnamed agents of the bombings and violence to which the poems respond. Hughes's poetry asks that we not see the conflict as a simple binary relationship between the loyalists and the fascists. Moreover, by downplaying the presence of Franco's forces in Spain, Hughes foregrounds the fraught relationship between the fascists and their colonized soldiers and between those soldiers and other people of African descent.

The prisoner's claims – that he had no choice but to fight with Franco, and that he understands the war is unjust – corroborate the International Brigades' discourse that Moroccan soldiers would abandon the Army of Africa if given the chance. The poem's speaker, Johnny, listens to a translator explain this soldier's justification for participating in Franco's army, yet that same understanding is unavailable in the reverse: the nameless soldier cannot understand Johnny or express sympathy for his position. Their interaction inspires Johnny to envision Africa's "foundations shakin'" (201) and to predict that a Republican Spain may free the colonies, leading to the end of England and Europe's colonial holdings in Africa. The speaker acknowledges the continent's foundational role in European modernity and states that the foundations of both African and European civilization are shifting. As Brent Hayes Edwards suggests, the speaker "reads the Moor's confusion and homesickness to be auspicious, the burgeoning of an anti-colonial consciousness" ("Langston Hughes" 694). Additionally, by casting the prisoner's participation in the war as the result of a kidnapping ("nabbed ... in his land"), Hughes aligns Moroccan enlistment in Franco's army with the transatlantic slave trade. In its gesture toward English and Italian colonization, the poem indicts the United States' and Europe's continuing dependence on African colonialism, the labour of Black workers, and the lives of Black soldiers as sources of political and economic capital.[17]

Johnny suggests that a shared African heritage might eventually transcend Spain's civil war, as his repeated observation of the two men's common skin colour – the POW is "as dark as [him]" (201, 202) – motivates him to offer the prisoner a handshake. In his optimistic attempts to envision Morocco's future, informed by his own experiences in the International Brigades, Johnny imagines a spreading egalitarian community. Hughes's speaker articulates a developing sense of diasporic kinship by insisting on the inherent connections between Africans and people of African descent. Yet this growing understanding is undercut by the prisoner's loss of understanding and of life. Their conversation is rendered only into English as they communicate via a translator.[18] While Johnny "looked across to Africa / And seed foundations shakin'" (201), enthusing over this inspiring vision, the prisoner's health worsens until eventually he can understand neither the speaker's words nor his gesture of solidarity.

Johnny's optimism for the future of Spain and Africa suggests something of Hughes's "irony of the colonial Moors" – and of the African American volunteers. It may be that Johnny, too, "[doesn't] know / The folks he had to fight" (201) – the subjugated Moroccans who lack the same choice he had when he decided to enlist. Furthermore, notwithstanding Johnny's justifiable pride in his work with the International Brigades, Hughes reminds us of the individual costs of war in the form of the POW's double kidnapping: it is Johnny, after all, who captured this wounded soldier, after the soldier was first "nabbed ... in his [own] land." The letter's first line, "We captured a wounded Moor today," unequivocally inserts the speaker into the soldier's capture yet sidesteps responsibility for the man's wounds. Put another way, while Johnny acknowledges having taken part in imprisoning a Moroccan soldier, he does not implicate himself in the soldier's fatal injury. Johnny's support for the Spanish Republic does not diminish, but the poem underscores the uneven human costs of the war the Spanish Republic must fight.

Johnny's letter describes a failure to forge solidarity, an anecdotal retelling of his personal confrontation with fascism and racism. His physical resemblance to the Moroccan soldier is what ignites his desire for solidarity. But their shared phenotype – their similarity in skin tone – may also heighten the risk that Johnny could be misidentified as a Moroccan soldier. Read alongside other writers' fictional and non-fictional representations of Moroccan participation, the incident depicted in "Letter from Spain" reflects certain anecdotes of Moroccan POWs mistreated and African American volunteers misidentified.

The initial published version of Garner's short story "The Stretcher Bearers," which I referenced earlier, concludes with the abuse and murder of a wounded Moroccan soldier by Spanish Republican soldiers. The story was written in 1938 (a year after Hughes's poem), published in full in 1952, and subsequently republished with the incident excised. This incident is at odds with the dominant journalistic representation of Spanish and international attitudes toward "Franco's Moors." For instance,

Wright's article for the *Daily Worker*, "American Negroes in Key Posts of Spain's Loyalist Forces," includes an extended interview with Louise Thompson, the African American secretary of the English Division of the International Workers Order, about her visit to Spain. Thompson states that the Spanish people understand how the fascists have "misled" the Moroccan, German, and Italian soldiers fighting for them: "So high has become the political consciousness of the civil population that when Italian, German, or Moorish prisoners are brought into towns they are greeted by, 'Long Live the Italian Peoples!' or 'Long Live the German Peoples!' or 'Long Live the Moorish Peoples!'" (121).[19] In contrast to Thompson's glowing report of Spanish and Republican tolerance, Garner, whose story also seems to have been based on first-hand experience, remembers the treatment of Moroccan soldiers differently. In his 1973 memoir, *One Damn Thing after Another*, he recalls watching "[s]ome of the rear-echelon Loyalist Spaniards ... taunting the wounded enemy prisoner, shouting 'Moro! Moro!' and denouncing him for fighting for the Fascists as if he'd had any choice ... I heard the single revolver shot as they killed him ... [T]he captured Moor ... had made me suddenly sick for all mankind" (50). Both Thompson's and Garner's accounts may be true. What I seek to highlight by bringing them together with Hughes's poem are the stakes of Hughes's speaker's interaction with the prisoner. Hughes's speaker, Johnny, and his interpreter spend long minutes trying to converse with the wounded Moroccan – a display of sympathy not unlike Thompson's account. Yet in Garner's depictions, a parallel group of soldiers instead torture and murder the prisoner.

Other fictional incidents also offer real-world parallels and dangerous intimations: as I discussed earlier, Allan's novel *This Time a Better Earth* describes an African American soldier who must explain that he is American but not African. Despite Allan's casual dismissal of bigotry among volunteers and soldiers, similar yet far more worrisome anecdotes appear repeatedly in first-hand accounts from African American volunteers. In an article in the *Afro-American*, Hughes himself recounts how Walter Cobb was mistaken for a Moroccan soldier by Spanish Republicans while driving a captured fascist truck. Luckily, Cobb's language skills allowed him to identify himself. Hughes includes not only Cobb's first-hand account of the incident but also Cobb's observation that people of colour "attrac[t] no attention" in Spain's urban areas and only "friendly" curiosity in more rural areas ("Walter Cobb" 140).[20] Similarly, Robin D.G. Kelley cites Eluard Luchell McDaniel's experience of being shot at by fellow soldiers who mistook him for a "Moor" (32). The experiences of Cobb and McDaniel suggest the very real dangers of volunteering while Black. Both men lived to tell their stories, thanks, it seems, to their ability to explain themselves in several languages. Hughes's speaker and his Moroccan interlocutor are able to verbally communicate only with the help of a translator, up to the point when the injured soldier becomes mute. In all these cases, the Republic's supporters were predisposed to perceive a person of colour as a Moroccan soldier rather than an African American volunteer, unless he could prove or explain otherwise. Read in this broader context, Hughes's Moroccan soldier's situation suggests that anyone who had been wounded, if he were "as dark as [Johnny]," could find himself misidentified. Johnny isn't immune to this risky assumption either: had he encountered the "wounded Moor" a few minutes later, he might have been forced to wonder, forever, whether the POW was literally a "[b]rother [from] home."

A Country and Community of the Imagination

Hughes's writings about Spain celebrate the racial integration of the battalions and commemorate the postcolonial potential that Spain – and Morocco – ultimately lost when Franco won. Together with other writers' portrayals of Moroccan soldiers, "Letter from Spain" reveals the complex affiliations and filiations woven through both sides of the conflict. Comparing African American experiences to fascist imperialism in Ethiopia and across Europe was, for some, a way to frame Spain's war within a mid-century chronicle of transnational violence, oppression, and colonization. Hughes and others demonstrate the complexities of transnational racial connection, the familial (whether biological or chosen) closeness of individuals far apart, and the sometimes futile attempts at intimacy nearby.

The ongoing dominance of race over nationality as an organizational category for identity – or the conflation of race with nationality – is again examined in its evolving role in combat in novels by John A. Williams and Mordecai Richler.[21] Their Spanish Civil War novels rewrite history to include marginalized individuals, underscoring the cultural clashes that arise when selective narratives of history come into conflict with one another. In particular, both authors examine the Spanish Civil War's nostalgic significance for minoritized North American men. However, while both Williams and Richler emphasize the real physical risks of volunteering – as Hughes, too, foregrounds – their retrospective, satirical representations locate this violence within a longer history: of dangers faced by African American soldiers in the country's previous and subsequent wars, in the case of Williams's novel *Captain Blackman*, and of the horrors of the Spanish Inquisition and the Holocaust, in Richler's *Joshua Then and Now.*

Richler's *Joshua Then and Now* (1980), the novel with which I concluded the previous chapter, repeatedly satirizes the self-conscious attention to racial and religious equality in many North American fictional accounts of the war. As I have discussed, Richler's oeuvre reflects the deep ambivalences at the heart of North American involvement, and particularly Jewish support of the Spanish Republic. Here, I want to highlight the moments when *Joshua Then and Now* approaches the intersection of race and religion, to suggest how the novel at once undermines and polices the borders of identity. The novel was published in the midst of the national debates over identity that led to the 1988 passing of the Canadian Multiculturalism Act, which enshrined the country's constitutive diversity (while at the same time reinscribing Canada's populace as split between English and French hegemony, and Indigenous and immigrant minorities, rather than recognizing the country's foundationally heterogeneous composition).[22] Despite his lifelong fascination with the Spanish Civil War, the eponymous protagonist of Richler's novel only ever meets one International Brigades veteran in person, a British friend's uncle. While visiting England from Montreal during the research for a book about the International Brigades, Joshua often accosts the Attlee Battalion veteran. Uncle Willy is willing to continue

> obliging [Joshua] with lies, but only to keep the bitter flowing and maybe touch him for a couple of quid in parting. Uncle Willy's memories of Spain were dim; he was clearly sorry he had ever gone. And now … [w]hat agitated him were the bleeding blacks who seemed to be dropping like monkeys out of every tree in Brixton. (*Joshua* 102)

Richler's use of free indirect discourse here is suggestive: the narrator vocalizes Uncle Willy's vicious racism, yet Joshua himself ignores it. At Uncle Willy's funeral, his nephew insists on reading from W.H. Auden's Spain poems, paying homage to the man's youthful involvement in a cause long since relinquished. Joshua and his friend ignore the actual experiences – and the casual use of racist, dehumanizing language – of the only Spanish Civil War veteran they know in favour of a sustained, romanticized obsession with the country and its civil war.[23]

Explicit references to race are rare in *Joshua Then and Now.* When they do appear, they are part of a persistent fixation on the nature of Jewish affiliation, and specifically how questions of Jewish religious and national identity might compare to those of the African diaspora.[24] Joshua's feelings toward Uncle Willy are reverential and indulgent; the old man's fading memory and xenophobia are apparently mitigated by the fact that he participated in the Spanish cause. Yet Joshua's sympathy does not extend to others interpolated in Spain's mid-century conflicts: upon meeting a Jewish-identified *marrano* (a descendant of the Spaniards forced to convert to Catholicism who continued to practice Judaism in secret) while on a trip to Spain, Joshua's is repulsed by Carlos's appearance and frustrated by his penny-pinching (which is motivated by a lifelong plan to immigrate to Israel). Joshua reflects:

> Carlos came from a family that had ostensibly been practicing Catholics for hundreds of years, but that was beside the point. He was one of those. He was an oily little man, scrawny, his skin walnut-brown, his eyes frightened now, and Joshua's immediate reaction was, You're not my brother, I'm not your keeper. (*Joshua* 193)

Meeting Carlos brings Joshua into personal contact with the Spanish antisemitism he had vividly imagined while walking down streets that once witnessed the Inquisition. Carlos continues to experience discrimination from those around him, who view him as indelibly Jewish; at the same time, his family's ostensible Catholicism, his *marrano* identity, stems from Spain's centuries-old practice of coercing Jews and Muslims to convert. Talking to Carlos and witnessing how others treat him forces Joshua to rethink his understanding of Spain's xenophobic history and present-day strivings for democracy. For Joshua, Carlos's physical characteristics seem indistinguishable from those of the Catholic Spaniards around him; it is his "walnut-brown" skin that differentiates him from Joshua. Joshua feels neither sympathy nor connection, only disgust.

Although Carlos's singing of the *Shema*, the central Jewish prayer, is intensely moving to Joshua, he quickly reverts to racialized sarcasm, echoing Uncle Willy's own complaints about his Black neighbours in Brixton:

> Jews, Jews, Joshua thought, everywhere I go there are other Jews to advise me. Clutching. Claiming. I probably wouldn't even be safe in Senegal. Some big buck, his face reamed with tribal scars, his voice whiny, would drop out of his banana tree to grab my hand and say "Shalom Aleichem." (*Joshua* 195)

In blending antisemitic stereotypes (the Jewish whine) with racist tropes (the "buck" with tribal scars – traditional physical alterations arguably not so far from Jewish customs), Joshua rejects his ties to Carlos and diasporic Jewry. Instead, he adopts the same racist language as his idolized Spanish Civil War veteran. The humour in this imagined scene in Senegal derives from transposing Jewish stereotypes onto a racist African caricature. Joshua's disgust at the "scrawny," "walnut-brown" Spaniard and the imaginary African "reamed with tribal scars" suggests an intense fear of religious affiliation transcending racial distinctions – that is, Joshua's confidence in his own white ethnic North American Jewishness cannot initially abide the transnational religious community that Carlos and the imaginary African represent, to say nothing of the violence and death that drove their ancestors into the diaspora in the first place. What's more, Joshua associates racialized characters with non–North American locations, overlooking the existence of Black North Americans.[25]

Joshua eventually acknowledges that he can no longer idealize the Spanish Civil War. Upon returning to Spain years later, he abandons his previous attitude toward Carlos when he learns that Carlos has been denied his wish to make *aliyah* and immigrate to Israel. Carlos had saved for his planned migration for ten years, never marrying or spending frivolously. Though unambiguously perceived as Jewish within his Spanish Catholic community, he is deemed to be unambiguously Catholic by Israeli immigration officials: "His family hadn't been Jewish for hundreds of years as far as they were concerned. Your rabbis said his mother was officially a Catholic. What they called their law of return didn't apply to him or hundreds of others in Majorca who wanted to go" (*Joshua* 395).[26] Carlos is caught between different communities that repudiate him: he is too Catholic for Israel, too Jewish for Spain. Through him, Joshua is forced to question his own perceived affiliation with Spain as well as his categorization – by others – within Judaism.

Richler's writings often avoid discussions of racism; however, they emphasize discussions of nationality, and particularly issues around how Jewish affiliation undercuts national identity. He repudiates the friendship of a Jewish Spanish character, yet he spends his time in Spain wandering its Jewish quarters, fixating on his feelings of Jewishness and the country's history of antisemitism. He links his irrepressible identity to his foreign national ties:

> Canadian-born, he sometimes felt as if he were condemned to lope slant-shouldered through this world that confused him. One shoulder sloping downwards, groaning under the weight of his Jewish heritage (burnings on the market square, crazed Cossacks on the rampage, gas chambers, as well as Moses, Rabbi Akiba, and Maimonides); the other thrust heavenwards, yearning for an inheritance, any inheritance, weightier than the construction of a transcontinental railway, a reputation for honest trading, good skiing conditions. (*Joshua* 190–1)

The trope of the hyphenated subject alienated from his bifurcated identity is not a new one for Jewish literature. The eventual reconciliation of these two categories is perhaps the expected outcome, but instead, Richler subverts each category's very existence – and particularly the Canadian aspect of Joshua's identity – by relocating the conflict to Spain. In this particular instantiation, Richler's comedic portrayal of the unevenly weighted chips on Joshua's shoulders suggests that Jewish identity is over-full of both oppression and wisdom, whereas Canadian identity is nearly empty. By inscribing Joshua's duelling affiliations onto his body, already a potential site for more antisemitic interpretation, Richler represents Canadian and Jewish affiliations as difficult, maybe impossible, to reconcile.

The "yearning" of Joshua's Canadian side articulates a desire to constitute Canada – a desire that lingered well after the 1930s – in the hopes of giving content to the national pride that, by the novel's publication, had become an integral dimension of the country's identity. Joshua instead undercuts Canada's proud 1980s identity as a multicultural, diverse, peaceful country by emphasizing its history of Nazi collusion. Yet his comparison between his Canadian and Jewish heritage also privileges the emotional weight of the Jews' long history of oppression over more recent Canadian turmoil. In referring to the "transcontinental railway … honest trading, good skiing conditions," Joshua elides not only Canada's pre-Confederation history but also the significance of these Canadian markers, making Canada sound, as Robert M. Crunden puts it, "bland" (240). As his Canadian half yearns "for an inheritance, any inheritance," Joshua suggests that, like Jacob and Esau, Canadianness and Jewishness are related. He also parodies the country's lack of unifying identity even as he glosses over Canada's own history of discrimination: the mistreatment of the Chinese and European immigrants who built the transcontinental railway, and the Indigenous victims of supposedly "honest" traders from England, Scotland, and France. Joshua feels himself to be indelibly Canadian, and at the same time he feels himself to be Jewish – indeed, he is always aware that others almost always perceive him as such – and these two categories are affectively connected around the issue of unsecured belonging. The historic significance of his Canadianness remains unclear, just like the contemporary significance of his Jewishness.

The Canada that Joshua portrays is only bland, however, if we assume that neither Richler nor Joshua sees the larger significance of the railway or the irony of Canada's reputation for honest trading. I argue that in destabilizing the categories underpinning nationalism, Richler illustrates the emptiness of the nomenclature of political identity – of "Canadian," of "Jew," even of "leftist." The characters of Joshua and Carlos disrupt these categories – the two are joined not only by their religion but also by their outsider status. Rather than seeing the novel's project of demystifying hegemony as productive of a new, more stable, inclusive Canadian identity, as Crunden argues – a Canada that includes not only Quebec but also Madrid and Jerusalem – I suggest that Richler is instead pointing toward the impossibility and undesirability of any such national category. *Joshua Then and Now* undercuts the assimilation narrative: the narrative has failed Carlos, who is denied Israeli citizenship and Spanish social acceptance, and it will also, eventually, fail Joshua.

Richler's novel disrupts both the narratives of heroic Spanish Civil War volunteers and the discourses of Canadian multicultural inclusion. The characters bristle at their repeated racialization, turning the ongoing reinscription of their difference by the Québécois and Canadian governments – and of their diasporic (and therefore supposedly derivative, or degraded) Jewishness by the government of Israel – into comedic fodder. Richler rejects the notion that Canadian inclusion is the zenith of multiculturalism. As Kit Dobson points out, however much that notion might reify established social norms and power structures, multicultural literature can (and often does) "demonstrat[e] that belonging is always already transnational, suggesting that the structures of Canada are impermanent, open, and modifiable" (74).[27] Instead of figuring a telos in the geographical move from Old Country, to New Country, to Promised Land, Richler demonstrates how even potentially conflicting nationalist identities can exist in productive tension with one another.

In *Joshua Then and Now*, race and religion are strategic markers that underscore the impossibility of full absorption into an identity. Put another way, the white ethnic Jewish characters in *Joshua Then and Now* only seem white by comparison. Their whiteness is tenuous, predicated on speedy assimilation and the adoption of colonial power. Richler's novel emphasizes, first and foremost, the ways in which Jews and Jewishness become a part of Popular Front discussions of race. Frequently, in the literature I discuss, Jewish characters are included within a supposedly progressive ideal of whiteness – that is, an assumed universality that does not attend to ethnic or racial specificity. But racial and ethnic specificity are unavoidable, and such slippages leave individual characters' status, as national insiders or outsiders, ambivalent. And Richler's protagonist unceasingly refuses pan-ethnic connection in favour of claiming an uncrossable border between white and Black: his revisionary history includes Canadian Jews and Spanish Civil War heroes, but no Jews beyond North American Ashkenazi *Yiddishkeit*, and no Spanish Civil War antiheroes. Significantly, Richler's protagonist repeatedly defines himself against Blackness in a novel preoccupied with untangling the idealized narrative of Spanish Civil War participation, and particularly North American involvement. Even as, in the 1930s, North American supporters of the Spanish Republic were able to see parallels between Jim Crow America and fascist Spain, the character Joshua refuses the kind of antiracist stance that his beloved predecessors might have adopted.

Richler's novel constellates Jewishness in Canada, Spain, Senegal, and Israel. This transnational diaspora echoes another topic of colonial, racial, and religious contention within Spanish Civil War writing, that of the role of Moroccan soldiers in the war. As this chapter argues, literary discussions of minority affiliation are always implicitly predicated on comparisons not only to the white Christian majority, but also to the African non-Christian contingent of Franco's army, and many texts similarly evade the connections – or collapse the distinctions – between religious minorities within the conflict, and between African American volunteers in the International Brigades and Franco's Moroccan mercenaries. But where Richler's protagonist in *Joshua Then and Now* (and in his previous novels too) ultimately rejects the possibility of additional, complementary historical revisions, John A. Williams's protagonist in *Captain Blackman* embraces such intersections, collisions, ambiguities, and impossibilities. In so doing, Williams emphasizes the war's significance – at the time and in retrospect – for multiple political movements and marginalized populations.

Captain Blackman's Postcolonial Spain

Upon arriving in Barcelona to volunteer with the International Brigades in the Spanish Civil War, the eponymous protagonist of John A. Williams's novel *Captain Blackman* senses in the gaze of the Spaniards around him their acknowledgment of a sort of miracle. He imagines them gratefully wondering, "From what place had this huge black man, this moro, this negro, come to aid us?" (154). In this attempt to see himself through Barcelonan eyes, Captain Abraham Blackman adopts the slippery Spanish terminology around nationality, race, ethnicity, and religion. He identifies himself as both "negro" – Spanish for "Black man," along with its American English signification – and "moro," the Spanish term, so often pejorative and with such broad referents. In adopting such loaded terminology, associated in the war's context with Franco's Moroccan mercenaries, Captain Blackman highlights the difficult racial, religious, and colonial politics underpinning the Spanish conflict. Williams's 1972 novel imagines an African American soldier who, wounded in Vietnam, hallucinates that he is a participant in each American war plus two more: the Spanish Civil War and a future anticolonial revolution. *Captain Blackman* constructs a history of American warmaking that highlights Black soldiers' consistently crucial roles. Williams's inclusion of the Spanish Civil War stresses the conflict's significance in American and global history. While the war has frequently been characterized as the first act of the Second World War, its inclusion in *Captain Blackman* also links the African Americans who volunteered in Spain to the war's myriad colonial subtexts.

Writing decades after the Spanish Civil War's tragic conclusion, Williams transforms the conflict's disappointments into incitement for a future anticolonial revolution. Williams's politics evolved from what Matthew Calihman characterizes as a "half-hearted" (147) early involvement in radical politics to, in *Captain Blackman*, a nostalgia for the Popular Front's vision of cultural pluralism that inspired his transnational expansion of Black nationalism. Blackman's decision to volunteer is made with his near constant companion throughout the different wars, a Jewish American character named Robert Doctorow, a fictionalized E.L. Doctorow. Together, they conclude that they can serve their communities through volunteering in Spain, paralleling the many motivations that brought international volunteers to Spain and, as Calihman notes, depicting the beginning of "a multi-ethnic coalition that would include both people of color and white ethnics (as ethnics)" (155). But in tracing their friendship across the wars, Williams also underscores growing affiliative divisions.[28]

Captain Blackman travels to Spain with his friend and anticipates new alliances, yet their time in Spain does not conclude with more attachments – simply a strengthened bond between the two. Abraham Blackman is politicized, at least in part, by the failures of the Spanish Civil War: his depleted faith in the Spanish cause leads to a growing sense of global Black consciousness. Not only does Blackman see himself as a "moro," but the novel's narrator refers to the African American soldiers in the Abraham Lincoln Brigade as the "Moorish Phalanx": "a small black blot among all the International Brigades gathered on the Ebro" (167). And, significantly, this same terminology is applied to Black soldiers on the opposing side, as the "Moorish Phalanx" encounters "numerous Moors on the Rebel side" (167). Captain Blackman's proximity to Moroccan soldiers allows him to see himself in them – just as Langston Hughes's poetic speaker sees himself in the dying Moroccan POW ("Workers, see yourselves as Spain!," Hughes implores in "Song of Spain" [195]). Through this shared descriptor – "Moor" – Blackman takes on the racial and religious ambiguities that float around a term that variously includes Jews, Muslims, and Moroccans of all races. His first name, Abraham, further links him not only to the American Abraham Lincoln Brigade (and its presidential namesake) but also to the patriarch of Islam, Judaism, and Christianity.

But Blackman's ironic double adoption of the title "Moor" reflects a growing cynicism toward transcultural connection that increases as the casualties mount: with the death of (real-life) Lincoln commander Oliver Law, Blackman reflects, "it was going to be black man grieving for black man, Southerner for Southerner, Jew for Jew, Hispanic for Hispanic" (163). I see this grieving – characterized by sometimes overlapping categories of region, race, ethnicity, and religion – as parallel to the distinct personal bond that Hughes's speaker articulates in "Letter from Spain" toward the wounded Moroccan POW. Calihman argues compellingly that this moment in Williams's text is a harbinger of the nationalist "narrow racial politics" that result after Blackman mourns the failures of the Popular Front coalition (157). Furthermore, Williams highlights what so many other works of Spanish Civil War fiction do not: that on both sides of the conflict, members of the African diaspora would mourn one another while Spaniards and former Spanish colonials might mutually mourn one another as well. Yet this mourning does not extend beyond these groups. African Americans might grieve Moroccan deaths, but why shouldn't all volunteers grieve this loss of life? Williams gestures to a post–Popular Front transnationalism while suggesting that it is in death and violence that ethnic, racial, religious, and national boundaries are strengthened, even rebuilt.

Significantly, though, the character Doctorow remains Blackman's close friend: on the personal level, at least, their bond is unbroken. A shared cause, and a shared purpose, cement a relationship that is threatened by filiative conflicts. Their friendship cannot sustain a broader cosmopolitan, multiethnic coalition, but it provides individual comfort, if not collective political efficacy. At the same time, Captain Blackman's acknowledgment of Moroccan soldiers suggests that he recognizes his proximity to, or intimacy with, them. While many texts from the 1930s obscure these connections, *Captain Blackman*, with the advantage of multiple decades' retrospect on the war's disastrous conclusion, gives the Black soldiers on both sides a shared name.

Williams treats nostalgia as a legitimate political imperative, while Richler satirizes nostalgia as sentimentality in the form of a racist, regretful former International Brigades volunteer who is pestered by a nostalgic cosmopolite born too late to fight in Spain.[29] While Richler's novel concludes with his protagonist reaffirming his connection to his interfaith family and his Jewish Canadian identity (even if that category means little to him), Williams's novel commences with Blackman fighting for his manumission and concludes with the protagonist's involvement in a nameless future anticolonial war. Captain Blackman's ongoing activism grows from his recognition of the connections between local and global communities – a recognition generated by his multiple geographical perspectives.[30] His activism is both personal and communal, self-interested and outward-looking, supported by friends and supportive of them too. In contrast to Joshua's renewed dedication to rooting himself and his family in Canada, Captain Blackman's ultimate commitment is to those beyond his immediate circle – to a global community of oppressed, marginalized, colonized people for whose liberation he must risk his own life.

Williams's postwar anticolonial reflections demonstrate how historical comparisons can both clarify and confuse activism. Leftist North American literature about the Spanish Civil War justifiably reveres the international community that cohered in support of the Spanish revolution and the Republic. However, this reverence does not always acknowledge the Spanish Republic's lingering imperialism. Like the interwar Black internationalism of Paris – a location that seemed relatively free of racism, if one were willing to overlook France's violent colonial control in Africa – Republican Spain was publicly represented as a model of progressive social organization. Parisian internationalism remained, in Edwards's words, "characterized by unavoidable misapprehensions and misreadings, persistent blindnesses and solipsisms, self-defeating and abortive collaborations" (*Practice* 5). Nearly a decade later, in Madrid and Barcelona, in Addis Ababa, Rabat, and Tétouan, these colonial implications were still often occluded by a strategic antifascist message.

Representing Race and Religion

Spain seems to have been a crucible for international leftist attitudes toward difference. In representing the war's transnationalism, foreign writers frequently use the conflict as a proxy by playing out debates over immigration and desegregation at a geographic remove. I do not mean to imply that literature about the Spanish Civil War is not about the Spanish Civil War. Rather, I contend that the writers who represent the war bring their own local concerns to it too, with a cosmopolitan emphasis on the parallels and distinctions between individual experiences of oppression. While I focus here on literary representations of Moroccans and "Moors" in the Spanish Civil War, these representations are frequently linked to portrayals of minority, even tokenized, characters – African American and Jewish characters among them – in writing by Garner, Allan, Rukeyser, and others. Such connections between marginalized characters are not uncommon in literature of this era, in which white ethnic individuals gradually attain North American white privilege. However, the relations between various diasporic communities in Spanish Civil War literature suggest an ongoing ambivalence over both given and chosen categories of difference and identity. Hughes, Allan, and others describe Republican Spain's racial and religious tolerance. Yet as Williams's subsequent novel reminds us, race and religion were integral to the conditions that brought so many diasporic Jewish and Muslim soldiers to Spain to fight on opposing sides in a Catholic, colonial war – a war about land, class and race, democracy, communism and fascism, and modernity and tradition. These individuals' hopes of gaining national acceptance and independence played out in a country with a long history of religious discrimination – an originary location of displacement.

Morocco's struggle for independence was perhaps far from the central issue of the Spanish Civil War for most of those involved in the conflict, yet the Moroccan question – the colonial question – echoes in much North American writing about the war. For American and Canadian authors, Spanish egalitarianism could not be represented without reference to North American racism. Yet this familiarity with North American racism would likely have made the overt racism of much anti-Franco visual propaganda clear, even if these authors only rarely wrote about it. There is also the possibility that writers misread or overlooked unfamiliar forms of discrimination: how many authors were fluent enough in Spain's languages to understand the nuances of discriminatory vernacular?[31] Representations of "Moors" by Hughes and his contemporaries highlight how the Spanish conflict provided writers with a new lens on North American intersections of race, ethnicity, gender, and religion. As these texts also suggest, even as African Americans were celebrated among the volunteers as brothers in arms, the same solidarity was unevenly available to people of colour on the opposing side. Individuals who understood that Spain's war was civil in name only could not always extend this perspicacity to understand what drew Moroccan soldiers to its battlefields.

What Hughes termed the "irony of the colonial Moors" was, in some ways, the ultimate irony of the African American soldiers too: they were sometimes misperceived as the fascist enemy, and they were destined to serve – as the Moroccan soldiers had in Spain – in the most dangerous positions on the front lines of the Second World War, the Korean conflict, and the Vietnam War. Williams's *Captain Blackman* depicts not only the large-scale atrocities of the Second World War and the Vietnam War but also the racism and antisemitism directed at African American and Jewish American soldiers within their own battalions as they fought for the United States. Even as Hughes and others publicly represented Spain as both an embattled site of resistance and an egalitarian haven, issues of racial and religious discrimination endured in Spain, Eastern

Europe, and North America. In Hughes's and Williams's vital representations, the Spanish Civil War becomes a crucial juncture in African American history: a war against fascism and an encounter with a postcolonial site of personal and political affiliation. Richler's *Joshua Then and Now,* too, reminds us of the ongoing marginalization and endangerment of Jewish people of colour. Together, these texts demonstrate how Blackness endures as a figuration of difference – even among the most socially aware leftists.

3
Community: Documenting Female Friendship in Spain

"the game gone vulgar, the rules abused"
Edna St Vincent Millay, "Say That We Saw Spain Die"

"Spain cast a ballot, and was outraged, raped
In an Olive Grove, by a Monastery wall"
Dorothy Livesay, "V-J Day"

Gender and War

The American poet Edna St Vincent Millay's 1939 lament for the Spanish Republic imagines the civil war as a traditional Spanish bullfight – a predominantly, if not entirely, masculine arena – with the fascists represented as the bloodthirsty, cruel bullfighter, the Republicans as the foolishly trusting bull. Using only male pronouns to refer to the combatants and to the country, Millay shifts between respect for the Spanish cultural tradition and disgust at the sport's outcome. The war's brutal conclusion becomes the product of a gang of men attacking a male animal, and this emphasis on the conflict's masculinity underscores the gendered conflicts within the war by erasing women from the poem itself – the "vulgar" game is being played entirely by male competitors among whom there is a radical power imbalance.

In a related image, the Canadian poet Dorothy Livesay's "V-J Day" (1947; also published as "In Time of War") also visualizes the Spanish Civil War through a gendered lens, here representing democracy's fall to fascism as the country's rape. Livesay's poem implicitly incriminates the aristocracy and the Catholic Church – the owners of those olive groves and monastery walls, who actively supported the insurgency that led to the war's massive violence. She presents an alternative, nightmarish vision of her frequently romantic poems about the Spanish Civil War; here, the country is the victim of sexual violence – and implicitly so are its female citizens. This image is contrasted to the poem's speaker's memory of getting married as the Spanish Republic perished – she has been able to build a happy, peaceful, loving life; others in Spain cannot. Sexual violence becomes the dark parallel to the speaker's marriage. Livesay concludes with the transnational feeling that "the rubble of Barcelona is this moss under my hand."[1]

The postwar poems of Livesay and Millay are part of a specifically female – and feminist – chorus of literary voices that not only mourn the war's loss but collectively eulogize the unique feminist communities created in Spain during the conflict. Both Livesay and Millay emphasize the conflict's machismo – a machismo that, in "Say That We Saw Spain Die," blinds the participants to the fact that they are not playing a game, but fighting a war; and that in "V-J Day" legitimates sexual violence. This chorus underscores that the move for women's rights in Spain was closely tied to the civil war: as in so many revolutionary conflicts, women there fought for reproductive freedoms, access to education, and political enfranchisement; they enlisted as soldiers (in Spain, with the anarchist group Mujeres Libres [Free Women]); and they pursued leadership positions. Spanish women's public and private emancipation struck a chord with leftist women around the world. Among the thousands of international volunteers were at least seventy North American women working as nurses, and many more who were in Spain to run orphanages and schools, observe as political delegates, and report on and photograph the war (Fyrth 29n1).

In contrast to the violent poems with which I began, this chapter looks to women writers' representations of often-collaborative female wartime work across genres in order to highlight the gendered issues that underpinned the previous two chapters. In the first chapter of this book, I analysed the heavily circumscribed genre of the heterosexual war romance plot; here, I demonstrate female authors' response, which was to decentre romance to focus instead on the blooming of female friendships and pioneering female jobs in the temporary women-led communities that sprang up across Spain in the war's midst. I also complicate the second chapter's discussion of race and religion by further considering gender, taking up the issues of gender and safety suggested by the second chapter's argument that the position of men of African descent was especially fraught within what was essentially a colonial war. As this chapter shows, many female writers depict both women's key wartime roles and the particular risks they confront in wartime. Furthermore, the authors I examine sometimes link the Spanish war to the mounting dangers faced by

European Jews, instructing their audience in sympathy for all victims of patriarchal fascism. Taken together, women's writings about Spain represent a different vision of the truth of the conflict – its stakes and its repercussions.

Most of the writings included here are inspired by direct personal knowledge. North American women visited Spain as nurses, journalists, photographers, social workers, ambulance drivers, and political organizers; among them were Louise Thompson, Jean "Jim" Watts, Martha Gellhorn, Dorothy Parker, Josephine Herbst, Lillian Hellman, Frances Davis, Salaria Kea, Genevieve Taggard, and Muriel Rukeyser. In their subsequent fiction, poetry, and memoir, they focus on different aspects of women's positions in a society at war: some highlight Spanish women's wartime experiences, while others foreground North American women in Spain, who were unevenly accepted for their gender, race, or political leanings. This chapter looks primarily to writings by Jewish authors – Gellhorn, Hellman, Rukeyser, and Miriam Waddington – but brings their depictions into conversation with those of non-Jewish writers, who, like these four, were also marginalized for their sexuality, race, or politics.[2] In this way, I demonstrate their intersectional approaches to wartime feminism as they posit transnational, often transitory, female-dominated communities – of hospitals, orphanages, schools, and hotels – as integral to the war effort.[3]

Representations of transnational contact and transitory spaces are not unique to female writers, to be sure. Yet given women's limited rights – globally, as well as in Spain – writing about female, feminist communities can be a revolutionary act. Female writers with first-hand experience of the Spanish Civil War repeatedly examine the experiences of Spanish and international women – of alienation and inclusion, of exceptionalism, and of community building. In so doing, they implicitly argue against the easy distinction between the battlefield and the home front.[4]

The writers I discuss, as they observe the war's repercussions for women both locally and globally, emphasize the experiences of Jewish participants and foreground especially connections between Spanish fascism and German Nazism. Women's texts about the Spanish Civil War thus represent an important rejoinder to the stereotype of the feminized, infantilized Jewish immigrant, popularized in texts such as *Canadian Mosaic* (discussed in the introduction), as well as to global antisemitism. Read together, these texts articulate radical social shifts in the midst of fluctuating wartime communities while simultaneously commenting on developing notions of patriotism and belonging.[5]

These representations of equality were frequently marginalized as well. As the following analyses highlight, women's depictions of the

Spanish Civil War only rarely gained mainstream awareness because only rarely were leftist women published in the mainstream press. Some writers, like Lillian Hellman and Martha Gellhorn, wrote articles for prominent American publications such as *The New Yorker* and *Collier's*. However, most of the texts I will discuss – especially Canadian texts – were published by leftist little magazines and newspapers such as the *Daily Clarion* and *New Frontier*, or they remained out of print. From Muriel Rukeyser's *Savage Coast* to Salaria Kea's various memoirs to Miriam Waddington's early Spain poems in university newspapers, authors' struggles to get their work in print as well as the economic difficulties of *keeping* it in print have been a barrier to a wider readership. As I will discuss, some of these struggles are ongoing, sustaining to this day some of the gendered, racialized marginalization so many of these authors encountered.

Speaking for Spain

Spanish and international women were integral to the war effort. And the voice of one woman provided the conflict's most enduring rallying cries: the Spanish Republican heroine La Pasionaria, Dolores Ibárruri, whose exhortations "¡No pasarán!" (They shall not pass) and "Más vale morir de pie que vivir de rodillas" (It's better to die on your feet than live on your knees) continue to be emblematic of the Spanish cause.[6]

Writing in 1936 in the Canadian leftist monthly *New Frontier*, Sybil M. Gordon observed of La Pasionaria that "the voice of humanity in Spain and throughout the world is a woman's voice" (9). Yet as Paul Preston points out, Ibárruri was stigmatized by many on the left for her activism – women, even in progressive circles, were not always welcome as political leaders.[7] More recently, anthologies such as *Women's Voices from the Spanish Civil War* (edited by Jim Fyrth and Sally Alexander) and research by scholars like Gina Herrmann, Tabea Alexa Linhard, Shirley Mangini, Paul Preston, and Cary Nelson have illuminated the importance of examining this chorus of women's voices. Nelson, for instance, has described how American leftist poetry about the war exhibits certain patterns necessarily understood within a collective paradigm – which, in the case of Edna St Vincent Millay's poem "Say That We Saw Spain Die," was one of exiled witness (*Revolutionary Memory* 220–4).[8] Broadening this scope, Linhard argues that studying women's writings "should at least partially reveal the implications and intricacies of a conflict that moved far beyond a struggle between fascists and Bolsheviks, even though the respective sides that fought in the war often defined the struggle in those terms" (*Fearless Women* 24). Linhard cautions against simply recuperating Spanish women's accounts without interrogating the forces that have kept these accounts excluded, sidelined, or subsumed into a dominant historical narrative (*Fearless Women* 65). Such caution informs my own approach, which focuses on how North American women wrote about Spain and how these writings have been unevenly received.

Notwithstanding the minimal presence of North American women in Spain (between nine and twelve Canadian women and around sixty American women travelled there), the conflict inspired diverse feminist activism. Women on this other home front – the North American home front – raised funds and awareness and wrote extensively about the Spanish Civil War.[9] Eric S. McDuffie argues that the Spanish Civil War politicized many African American activists, including Claudia Jones and Esther Cooper (92). In discussing the US Communist Party's national and international pronatalism, Paula Rabinowitz comments on the extent to which the Spanish cause drew mothers, in particular, to the cause, "help[ing to] recast mothers into fellow travelers" (*Labor* 57).[10] In Canada, as Larry Hannant notes, women's participation in leftist movements allowed them the kind of direct political work they desired but also – because of the patriarchal structures of the movements themselves – often curtailed the feminist implications of that labour. Candida Rifkind likewise explains that "for women writers on the left, neither the conservative Canadian establishment nor the socialist cultural leadership was particularly interested in re-imagining the female author as a voice of innovation or radicalism" (*Comrades* 10–11), pointing to the "masculinist rhetoric characteristic of Canadian socialism during the Depression" (*Comrades* 11).

Moreover, activist work provided Jewish Canadian women with an escape from their constricted lives, which were limited by the antisemitism that historian Gerald Tulchinsky characterizes as "domestic fascism [that] seemed a greater threat than it was in either the United States or Britain" (*Canada's Jews* 281) as well as by the expectations of Jewish culture, which frequently preserved them as wives, homemakers, and mothers.[11] Participation in leftist movements was an important opportunity for those Jewish women who had been marginalized because of their gender and their religion.

Many of the women who participated in the Spanish conflict in some capacity were taking up roles similar to those they would later adopt during the Second World War. Their involvement was unconventional enough to be controversial, even two decades after the First World War brought a previous generation of women into historically male fields. North American women were drawn to the Spanish war not only as a leftist or democratic cause, but also as a women's cause. North American writers often depict the quotidian experiences of Spanish women in wartime – women who had only recently gained the right to pursue an education, to vote, to control their fertility, or to divorce.[12] All this, in addition to a brief period during which women were even welcomed onto the battlefield – until 1936, when the *milicianas* (militiawomen) were barred from combat roles by the Republican government, although female nurses and cooks were allowed to remain on the battlefront.

The importance of Spanish women's work, even during wartime, is evident in the "women's beat" journalism that Martha Gellhorn and Jean "Jim" Watts were assigned in Spain. Watts – a groundbreaking queer Toronto leftist activist working in male-dominated fields – wrote dispatches that blend accounts of intrepid foreign nurses "who managed to look starched and fresh in spite of everything" ("With Dr. Bethune") and Spanish women – girls, she calls them – who have been "working through all the nerve-racking shelling of the last six months, turning out shells and bullets and hand-grenades ... shirts and uniforms and blankets ... keeping the telephone and telegraph services running ... [having first] fought at the front with those first, hastily-formed militia units" ("Madrid Senoritas [*sic*]"). Such accounts feature tough Spanish women in unconventional gender roles and tough foreign volunteers in more conventional ones.[13] As Nancy Butler suggests, Watts's journalism was "mindful of the daily human cost of the war" (377). And, as Emily Christina Murphy's archival research demonstrates, the Communist Party of Canada's national newspaper the *Daily Clarion* foregrounded Watts's writings in its publication, suggesting that her efforts to disassemble the home front–battlefront binary were supported by the paper.

Those women not directly involved in the war effort were inescapably affected by it. We see something of the importance of representing Spanish women's wartime experiences in a short story by Jewish American writer Lillian Hellman, who travelled to Spain and wrote about the people she encountered. She contributed to the script and raised funds to support the making of the documentary *The Spanish Earth*, and remained a long-term supporter of the Spanish cause, the volunteer soldiers, and Spanish refugees; among other things she helped found the Motion Picture Artists Committee to Aid Republican Spain (Kessler-Harris 119). Her writings, including those about Spain, have been widely criticized as fabrications – by Martha Gellhorn and Ernest Hemingway, and most famously by Mary McCarthy. However, her (at least initially) explicitly fictional story "A Bleached Lady: A Short Story" encapsulates the intersecting issues of the Spanish cause for women locally and internationally as well as the personal traumas that constitute a national tragedy.[14] The story was published in the American Marxist magazine *New Masses* in 1938. Hellman depicts an incident in an American writer's travels around Spain as she and her Spanish chauffeur try to find a meal. The writer narrates the story. She feels intense guilt over her relative privilege and hates the idea of taking food from the impoverished residents of the small town where they finally stop. Invited in by a family, she at first refuses a meal. It is only when their hostess, the titular "bleached lady," "a fat, jolly-looking, youngish woman with very bleached blonde hair," speaks to her in English, to say "[w]e have plenty for a stranger," that the narrator acquiesces ("A Bleached Lady" 21).

The two women begin a conversation about their careers. The Spanish woman was a hairdresser in Madrid before she moved to the country in the vain hope of avoiding bombings. The narrator has difficulties convincing the woman and her family that she is a writer, hindered by her chauffeur's baffling insistence that she is Charlie Chaplin's sister. Yet the fact of the narrator's storytelling is implicit evidence of her career, notwithstanding the family's disbelief. Furthermore, the chauffeur's own lack of credibility is repeatedly – nearly ridiculously – highlighted: in addition to the Chaplin fabrication, he does an elaborate pantomime of the writing act, not trusting the family to understand what a writer does, and more importantly, he is an inept chauffeur, literally falling asleep at the wheel yet refusing to allow the narrator to take over. The disparity between the chauffeur's competence and the narrator's is further thrown into relief by the bleached lady's clear skill as a hairdresser, through her questions about and suggestions for the narrator's hair. The two female characters' professional expertise suggests the drastically different lives they might lead in an egalitarian, peaceful society: the narrator's career success in the United States is undercut by the Spanish characters' doubt, and the hostess's own career has been thwarted by her search for personal safety.

"A Bleached Lady" underscores the tensions between work and family life. In the middle of the visit, the characters watch from the window as another woman – seemingly pregnant – hauls wood out of a bombed-out house, prompting their hostess's concern that the bombs will "make her sick. It is not good to be frightened when a baby is coming" (21). This concern foreshadows the story's ultimate revelation, framed as beauty advice. The hostess, noting the narrator's dark roots, recommends that she visit her cousin, a hairdresser in Madrid. It is this recommendation that carries the intimacy of friendship:

> When you get to Madrid go to a shop called Ninya. Anybody will show you where. It is not open now, but there will be a paper on the door saying where Ninya is. She is a cousin to me and she works good on the hair. Tell her I send you. Tell her I didn't have the baby ... Tell her to put soap in the bleach and do a good job. (21)

In a comment that is ostensibly professional hair advice, the hostess shares a deeply personal story of abortion, miscarriage, or stillbirth caused by the war, entrusting a stranger to communicate family news across a war-torn country. Also encoded in the message is a larger tragic mystery: the bleached lady's unclear status within this childless family. How is she related to the other adults in this home? Is she single or married? Did she lose her partner? Was this a wanted pregnancy? Does she have other children? Can Ninya be found, and is she still alive? Significantly, neither the narrator nor the "bleached lady" is ever named, suggesting the universality of this deeply individual experience. And this story from one anonymous woman is intended to travel, eventually, to "Ninya," a woman whose name is an Anglicization of the Spanish "niña," or girl. Through her name, Ninya stands in for the youth of the story who do not make it to or past childhood.

Hellman's short story's anecdotal, first-person narrative foregrounds one of many personal wartime tragedies. The story's subtitle, "A Short Story," explicitly locates it within the realm of fiction. Its unambiguous fictionalization is significant. As a work of fiction, it can be at once an invention and a collective narrative of the effects of war on a country's women. Recounted by a female American narrator, the story draws implicit connections between women's experiences in both countries, of safety and reproductive health, of professional satisfaction, of mobility, and of independence.

Hellman's biographer Alice Kessler-Harris treats the story as memoir (117); however, the story's basis in Hellman's own experience is better reflected in Hellman's "A Blonde Lady," published as part of a selection of diary entries in the anthology *This Is My Best* (1942) under the title "The Little War." "A Blonde Lady" is nearly identical to "A Bleached Lady: A Short Story" but for certain small details, including the substitution of "Maria's" for "Ninya's" and an additional final paragraph about Hellman's failure to find the hair salon. The same anecdote is included in Hellman's subsequent memoir *An Unfinished Woman* (1969), with slightly different dialogue and additional details about Hellman leaving her shoes for the blonde lady, and discovering upon her return to Madrid that the hair salon was in a neighbourhood razed by bombs (94–100). In "A Blonde Lady," the diary excerpt is dated to 22 October 1937 and located "On the Road to Madrid." In these three versions, Hellman recounts similar events – the incompetent driver, the difficulties of finding food, the kindly family that invites them in. The quick friendship between the narrator and the Madrileña hairdresser is always foregrounded, but the significance of their friendship changes: in Hellman's final permutation of the story, rather than disclose the end of her pregnancy, the blonde lady simply instructs Hellman to convey to her cousin, "Tell her nothing but do good job for my American friend" (*Unfinished Woman* 100). The explicit statement of their friendship replaces the sharing of more personal information. Where the earlier short story focused on the war's devastating personal impact, Hellman's later version uses her hostess to articulate Hellman's own kindness. Hellman's short story speaks for Spanish women by foregrounding the experiences of a single, unnamed professional, whereas her memoir shifts the narrative to centre her own experiences.

The line between memoir and fiction is blurred in Hellman's story, by the author herself as well as by the subsequent denunciations of her autobiographical writings by other American writers. Whether autobiographical or fictional, however, Hellman's narrative sympathetically presents the many losses suffered by women in a war zone – the loss of life and of livelihood, of pregnancy, of family, of sustenance and safety, and of personal mobility.

African Americans in Spain: Salaria Kea's Singular Memoirs

Hellman's truthfulness has been extensively and publicly questioned and derided; other memoir texts from the Spanish Civil War never even made it to the public stage. Volunteer nurse Salaria Kea encountered significant resistance to her writings on Spain – resistance ostensibly spurred by questions of truth and always inflected by racism and sexism. As a result, her narrative of Spanish Civil War participation has been diminished, kept mostly out of print and unremembered, and her own role has been tokenized.[15] Kea, the only African American nurse to volunteer in Spain, began writing prolifically after she came home, as well as collecting others' writings about her – her time in Spain as well as her work on behalf of the Spanish Republic earned her extensive coverage in the Black press. She lectured widely about Spain during the 1930s and 1940s, touring the United States to raise funds for supplies and an ambulance to send to Spain; she also participated in many Spanish Civil War documentary projects into the 1980s.[16] Her memoirs are sometimes first-person, sometimes third-person narratives and were revised repeatedly over the course of nearly fifty years. They were published in one iteration as an anonymous 1938 pamphlet titled "A Negro Nurse in Republican Spain" by the Negro Committee to Aid Spain with the Medical Bureau and North American Committee to Aid Spanish Democracy. As I mentioned in chapter 2, the authorship of this pamphlet has been debated: Anne Donlon convincingly demonstrates that Kea's story may actually have been composed by the African American social worker

Thyra Edwards, a fellow volunteer in Spain who toured the United States with Kea. What's more, Donlon's archival research shows that Kea also assembled articles written about her as she drafted her subsequent writings, often drawing on their words.[17] Another critic, Robert F. Reid-Pharr, sees Kea's later writings as her efforts to expand and put into her own words what had been written about her; in other words, he does not read the 1930s pamphlet as Kea's own writing. For my own part, I am most interested in tracing what Kea was allowed to say or write publicly and what has been suppressed – including the stories about her that could or could not be publicized – through analysing the differences between the pamphlet and her own expanded memoirs.

Kea holds a central place among representations of the International Brigades' tolerance and equality, as evidence – at times, as a token – of American leftists' antiracism. Kea's presence in Spain, and her marriage there to a white Irish soldier, has been foregrounded in popular depictions of the conflict. She features prominently in documentaries (she's even pictured on the cover of *Into the Fire: American Women in the Spanish Civil War*, embracing her husband), and she is mentioned (often in a footnote) in most histories of American participation.[18] As Reid-Pharr suggests, "Kea became a figure for whom meaning trumped presence. Her literally lifesaving work as a nurse was never rendered as more significant than the model of post-racialist cosmopolitanism that her form represented" (59). These depictions of Kea overlook or curtail her own voice – a not uncommon fate for narratives of African Americans in the International Brigades, narratives that, as Robin D.G. Kelley points out, rely on representations rather than first-hand experiences (35). Kea was also not the only African American woman to volunteer in Spain or to document her experiences there: Eslanda Goode Robeson's accounts of meeting African American soldiers while on tour with her husband Paul Robeson, Thyra Edwards's scrapbooks of African American participation, and Louise Thompson's unpublished memoir are all valuable sources of information.[19]

When Kea's own voice *has* been heard, it has been tightly edited: in documentary projects and publications alike, she repeatedly compares antisemitism and Spanish fascism with American racism. Put another way, her narratives point to the connections between different experiences of marginalization and suffering. These comparisons are important because they form a prescient, intersectional articulation of the Second World War Double-V campaign that encouraged African American enlistment in the war against European fascism as a way to overcome Jim Crow racism. However, the editorial erasure of Kea's own descriptions of the racism and sexism she herself experienced is deeply problematic: directors and editors allow her to discuss interracial solidarity but not her own personal experiences of its opposite.[20]

Kea remains a flattened character in the American history of Spanish Civil War involvement. Accounts of that conflict rarely include her writings, and historians and fellow volunteers have censored them. Files in the Tamiment Library's Robert F. Wagner Labor Archives provide numerous examples of the justifications used to repress her writings. These justifications tend to focus on two of Kea's claims that are deemed offensive, exaggerated, or fabricated: that a volunteer doctor refused to eat with her during the voyage to Spain and called her "a nigger wench," and that while in Spain she was captured and imprisoned by fascist soldiers for a number of days before she was rescued. The doctor she accuses was Dr Donald H. Pitts of Elk City, Oklahoma. He was on board the SS *Paris* with Kea as the leader of her volunteer group. Although many have denied her accusation against him, including some of her fellow volunteers on the ship, I can find no evidence that Pitts himself ever contradicted or confirmed their exchange. Any denial of her experience amounts to an assumption that Pitts was a tolerant man and that Kea was unreliable. Nursing historian Frances Patai omitted these incidents from her many writings about volunteer nurses in the Spanish Civil War, concluding that Kea "confused fact with fiction," based on her own assumption that Kea's fellow volunteers would surely have spoken out against racism.[21] Whatever Patai's – and others' – forceful dismissals, historian John Gerassi's interview with volunteer ambulance driver Evelyn Hutchins corroborates Kea's claims. Hutchins explains that this particular doctor caused problems for many volunteers, but especially Kea. Hutchins explains that "he d[id]n't understand why we're fighting and why the Spaniards or why the antifascists all over the world are fighting this war'" (66).[22]

Kea's many archival memoirs provide an incisive perspective on Black women's experiences in the Spanish Civil War. Her accounts challenge dominant narratives of the war, and the ways these accounts were received foreground the political stakes of reconstructing history. In noting the importance of literary recovery work to map Black women's contributions, Donlon highlights the particular stakes of this archival research in the context of the Spanish Civil War as the subsequent Red Scare further contributed to the erasure of Black women: "The many examples of never completed or unpublished life writing of internationalist black women create a gap in the cultural record" ("Thyra Edwards" 103). Each of Kea's accounts of her time in Spain, whether written or spoken, provides a new and very slightly different version of her experiences. However, all of them, from the 1930s and the 1980s, consistently highlight the parallels between Spanish fascism and other types of oppression. In the published version of "A Negro Nurse," for instance, the author observes,

> This was Salaria's first concrete example of discrimination where race was not a factor. Here it was peasantry versus nobility. The peasants had previously accepted the belief that nothing could be done about it just as Harlem nurses had earlier accepted racial discrimination in the hospital dining room. Like the Harlem nurses the peasants were now learning that something could be done about it. One resisted, one fought, liberty could be a reality. There was nothing inviolable about the old prejudices. They could be changed and justice established. (128)

Her memoirs connect American racism to Spanish, Italian, and German fascism. Looking to Black women's participation more broadly, McDuffie suggests that radicals like Kea, Thompson, and Edwards "came to believe that Spanish people, women particularly, shared much in common with black American women ... Additionally, black women radicals understood African American women's destiny as inseparable from those of women in countries under siege by fascism" (108). Kea's writings exemplify this: as time passes, her memoirs further suggest the links between the oppression she witnessed in Spain, McCarthyism, and the Ku Klux Klan threats she and her husband received into the 1970s.[23] As Kea gains distance from the Spanish Civil War, she eventually names the doctor who refused to eat with her, while also acknowledging the many international volunteers who contributed to her safety in Spain. Together, Kea's many memoirs foreground the most important aspects of her experience: the isolation and threats she suffered because of her race, gender, and nationality, and the safety and equality that female-dominated communities in Republican Spain offered her.

Kea's memoirs provide an important perspective on intersectional identity and allyship, as well as on the realities of women's labour in the United States and Spain. She represents the transnational alliances between women – Black and white American women, and Spanish and American women in particular – as being firmly grounded in the difficulties of quotidian work. She highlights the unromantic, difficult labour of nursing and the importance of unified action – even a late memoir ("Hope") emphasizes her education and nursing over details about her family or private life. The pamphlet, her first biographical text, introduces her work in Spain by describing her leadership in New York City to desegregate hospitals and improve conditions for marginalized and minority patients in an overcrowded, diseased maternity ward. In narrating Kea's time in Spain, the author again foregrounds the leadership she and her fellow nurses displayed as they set up a hospital in a former palace, then installed a gas pump, fixed the electricity, and renovated the rooms. All the while, the American nurses tutored local Spanish women in reading and writing so that "[i]n six months Villa Paz had liquidated its illiteracy" ("Negro Nurse" 129). Descriptions like this one emphasize the nurses' united efforts – their labour over "[l]ong hours of work with night indistinguishable from day" ("Negro Nurse" 130).

The early memoir intersperses these more general moments with anecdotes specifically about Kea's own work. The pamphlet relies on the distancing authority of the third person when narrating Kea's own position in the community: "Salaria saw that ... the Negro's efforts must be allied with those of other minorities as the only insurance against an uncertain future. And in Spain [Salaria] worked with freedom. Her services were recognized. For the first time she worked free of racial discrimination or limitations" (129). And in the longer, archival manuscript, Kea elaborates, "Many people visited and remarked on the lone Negro girl serving so diligently yet so far was she from any women of her kind" ("While Passing Through" 26). This comment on Kea's own isolation from other "women of her kind" suggests something of the difficulties of her position – her awareness of her own marginalization as a woman and as an African American. She might be surrounded by fellow members of the working classes, but that camaraderie did not mitigate her own "triple oppression" arising from her race, her gender, and her class.[24]

Kea's allusions to the isolating aspects of her work cohere into a narrative of her own exceptionalism: as McDuffie explains, describing her appointment as head surgical nurse for an American unit: "She supervised white nurses and treated Spanish civilians and wounded volunteers of all nationalities. Her status as an African American woman circumscribed her professional opportunities back home. But in Spain she finally had the chance to realize her talents" (108). For instance, one anecdote from the published memoir recounts her ingenuity in warming a hypothermic, dying soldier by filling hot water bottles with the lunchtime soup. In so doing, the text posits that her nursing training and experience were not, in and of themselves, enough – it was her quick thinking that saved the soldier's life. Her cooperative work is further highlighted in the longer manuscript, which describes how "[t]o Salaria and the staff human life was important whatever rules had to be infracted to save it. They were all dedicated to the same high purposes. So instead of the scolding, transfers and threatened dismissal that may have been her lot at Harlem Hospital here she was praised and cited in government dispatches for 'courage, bravery and ingenuity'" ("While Passing Through" 25). In this later version Kea continues to make use of the distancing objectivity of the third person to comment on her own justifiable pride in her work. But this distancing gesture is not neutral – her reliance on a type of authentication common to slave narratives suggests her keen awareness that her first-person account would not be read with authority.[25]

Reid-Pharr sees the elaboration and added description of "While Passing Through" as Kea's way to "reassert her own individuality" (60) – her own rejoinder to the treatment of her body and her writings. Subsequent historians and critics have done just as she expected: their emphasis on her symbolic role occludes her own accounts of her professional flourishing in a predominantly white, predominantly female community. The resistance she faced while in Spain – from fascists, certainly, but also from Americans – has only been amplified by the ongoing refusal to acknowledge her experiences. And the isolation she experienced while in Spain – even as she worked alongside American women, she was always aware that she was not fully integrated into their vision of America – has, again, been augmented by the isolation of her voice from her body in so many historical accounts of the war. Yet her accounts enrich our understanding of African American transnational feminism. Her depictions of daily life in Republican Spain veer between her unique experiences as a Black woman among primarily white North American and Spanish women, and her sense of community and inclusion among these women as they endeavoured to understand one another's life experiences. Her evolving accounts are a vital record of Spanish Civil War experience and aftermath.

International Communities, International Friendships: Martha Gellhorn's Fiction

Writings by Hellman and Kea evolve over time, connecting women's roles in the Spanish Civil War to more contemporary issues and provoking critical questions around historical truth and feminist perspectives. The fiction writing of Jewish American author and journalist Martha Gellhorn joins these works in examining how women relate to others in a war zone. Where Hellman and Kea focus on how North American women's connections with other women can (partly or temporarily) ease differences of race and language, Gellhorn instead examines friendship in multiple iterations: among North Americans, among men and women, among political allies. And where Kea reflects on the Spanish Civil War's contemporary resonances in the United States, Gellhorn's later writings trace the war's vestiges in personal relationships in Spain and its neighbouring countries. Kea's perspective is transnational and comparative, where Gellhorn's is diachronic.

Gellhorn's writings about Spain span decades as well as genres and include journalism, short fiction, and novellas. Gellhorn reported on Spain for the mainstream American weeklies *Collier's* and *The New Yorker* and collected some of her dispatches in *The Face of War* (1959, 1986) and *The View from the Ground* (1988). The Spanish Civil War also looms over her short and long fiction in pieces published throughout the 1940s and '50s. I focus first on the short story collection *The Heart of Another* (1941), which is permeated by the war. Throughout the collection Gellhorn depicts women working – in official and unofficial capacities – to support those affected by the conflict. While female characters frequently disparage their own labour compared to men's battlefield bravery, the stories themselves undercut this gendered division.[26] The sheer number of stories Gellhorn composed about women in Spain, and her characters' ongoing dedication to Republican Spain and to those traumatized in the course of its defence, demonstrate the often unacknowledged contributions of non-combatants. Furthermore, her stories portray both the conditions of wartime and the war's lingering psychological effects on those who participated, especially as caregivers.

Gellhorn's stories depict a range of homosocial and heterosocial friendships, often in communal settings in which professional skill ostensibly overcomes sexism. In two stories set in Spain in the war's midst, Gellhorn depicts female journalists subsuming their individual needs – even their individual safety – to the communal experiences of journalists and volunteers, with positive and negative outcomes. "Zoo in Madrid" describes a group of journalists on a short break from reporting work, during a pause in airstrikes. The story is remarkable for its nearly completely collective voice – a voice that explicitly speaks for a group of North American journalists whose genders, races, and ages are never revealed. The narrative "we" instead acknowledges the reporters' class privilege in Spain: the story begins "We were sick of the war. We had no right to be ... We were not even especially hungry" (123). Through the kindness of the various park employees, the journalists are able to visit the zoo, and in one of only two individuating moments, the narrator is gifted two camellias by one of the park guards. As they relax, the journalists are able to talk about the war, again in a unified voice: "We did not think any one would believe us when we got home, or understand, or even care ... we said to each other the things we already knew by heart" (126–7). In another moment of individuation, the narrator recalls visiting a hair salon where the bombing of the building's upper floor left the patrons unmoved. This reference to Spanish women's unflappable commitment to beauty is underscored by the story's conclusion, when the narrator observes the "handsome

Spanish girls with peroxided hair" in the bar where the journalists conclude their outing (128). Outside the bar, a bomb has destroyed the sidewalks, leaving the rubble covered in blood. But inside the bar, as in the hair salon and the zoo, life continues. The story's conclusion emphasizes the importance of the transitory communal spaces in a city under siege, as American journalists and Spanish women alike converge on the bar.

In "Zoo in Madrid," Gellhorn depicts the safety and support that group members provide one another in a war zone. In contrast to this communal camaraderie, "A Sense of Direction" focuses on the isolated experience of an American journalist when she visits a battlefield as the guest of an Italian International Brigades commander. Initially grateful for this "professional kindness" (144), the narrator wants to visit with the soldiers and write an article. Instead, the commander propositions her. Even after she rebuffs him, he continues manoeuvring so that they will be alone and then gropes her against her explicit wishes. In the midst of a war zone, the story's tension comes from the danger of sexual assault, not of warfare. At the same time, the narrator repeatedly, guiltily expresses sympathy for the commander. She is "ashamed" when she deflects his advances by asking after his wife, and "sorry for him too" (159), even as she is clearly made more uncomfortable by his presence than by their proximity to the battlefront. Here she echoes the choral voice of the journalists in "Zoo in Madrid" who regret that they are not in the same danger as those on the front lines. And the commander exacerbates this, stating with what the narrator calls "obvious insincerity" that "[w]ar is terrible for a man" even as she characterizes him as "enjoy[ing,] … prosper[ing] and flourish[ing] in it" (147). Alone with the comandante, she is safer from bullets and bombings yet at the same time in unceasing danger of sexual violence.

The paradoxes of the narrator's position are amplified by the language Gellhorn uses. Throughout the story, both the narrator and her fellow journalist Liz repeatedly characterize spaces and experiences as "cosy" that seem anything but: Liz says of the experience of curling up in a hotel room during a shelling, "I've never felt cosier in my life" (143), and the narrator calls one of the places where she and the commander sit together "cosy" as well (158). While the irony is not always apparent, the narrator also dryly characterizes "the romance of war": "waiting around for head wounds with a view of four gray duffle bags whom you once knew by name" (152). Her familiarity with wartime tragedy – and especially her classification of it as "romance" – suggests something of the mental reversals that compound the ambient sexism and rape culture of the 1930s battlefield.

Both "Zoo in Madrid" and "A Sense of Direction" depict the extensive, self-effacing work women must do in the hopes of remaining physically safe and professionally protected during wartime, with the community only sometimes affording security. Many of Gellhorn's other stories about the Spanish Civil War shift their focus to women's postwar security, outside of Spain, as their lives – both professional and personal – remain inextricably yoked to the Republic's failure. The short story collection *The Heart of Another* begins with "Luigi's House," a narrative about spaces of temporary belonging. As the American woman at the story's centre struggles to make a home of a rented Corsican property, the locals first disdain her and then – discovering that she is a fellow antifascist and Spanish Civil War volunteer – embrace her as a resident. The home she seeks to create will be for her husband, who is convalescing in Spain from war wounds until he is well enough to travel. She feels, finally, "safe ... [in] a home for two people, a real place" (16).

However, the protagonist's efforts to improve the rented property unseat and unhinge its current resident, Luigi. So even as she tries to excise the trauma of her time in Spain by finally finding a space of belonging, "her mind ... still tormented with that war and ... what would come next" (2), she visits a corollary strain upon Luigi by gentrifying what is his long-standing home, on land he has farmed for years. Her claim to the land comes through her rental agreement, to be sure, but also through the local community's sense that she and her husband deserve to be welcomed because of their antifascist commitments. Luigi's refusal to share the house and the land with a foreign couple – no matter how impeccable their activist credentials – alienates him from the local community. The protagonist's single-minded focus on caring for her husband and herself by making a home at a time of looming world war comes at the cost of caring for another person with arguably deeper connections to the land. Luigi's connection to the protagonist is as tenuous as hers is to the Spaniards for whom she and her husband have worked. However, with Luigi's suicide at the story's conclusion, she concludes that the house can never be her home: "It was Luigi's house. It was Luigi's house now" (33).

In its depiction of the Spanish Civil War's ongoing reverberations, "Luigi's House" is an important commentary on the transnational communities of care the conflict fostered, both inside and outside Spain. The unnamed protagonist joins a community that wants to support the foreign couple. Yet this same cosmopolitan ideal of belonging is not uniformly accepted, as Luigi's tragic end makes clear – his death is both an echo of the carnage in Spain and a harbinger of the destruction to come across Europe. The American protagonist's efforts to establish a home, to care for her husband, and to join a new community are paralleled in Gellhorn's other stories set outside of Spain and after the war. The novella that concludes *The Heart of Another, Good Will to Men,* is an exhausting account of a former war correspondent's futile efforts to rescue her German friend from a French concentration camp. Like many Spanish and foreign supporters of the Spanish Republic, the character Max has been incarcerated. The correspondent, an American journalist named Elizabeth, spends the week around Christmas – her last days in Europe – visiting everyone in Paris who might be able to free him. Having sustained severe injuries in the Spanish Civil War, Max is at particular risk without medical treatment; as a German communist, he is in further danger: wanted for his support of the Spanish Republic and "in jail as an enemy alien" (209).

Elizabeth's failure to secure Max's safety reveals the extent to which their friends' principles have faltered. As former comrades repeatedly refuse to use their postwar powers to help, her own conviction weakens, sustained only by her belief in friendship. She reflects: "Towards the end I forgot what Max looked like or why I was doing any of this. I had promised, hadn't I? He was my friend" (230). But it seems the only friendship she can offer is to Max's wife, in the form of money and white lies: "how badly she needed hope" (239), Elizabeth concludes. At the same time, her undertaking on Max's behalf – and particularly the ethical shortcomings it exposes among so many of her friends – lead to Elizabeth's own traumatic flashbacks. In the midst of her final and most demoralizing visit, she has a sudden vision of all the Spanish dead she has seen, the bombings and the orphaned children. This abrupt flashback is layered over her earlier recollections of Max's deep loyalty to his wife and best friend in the midst of the war zone – his suffering, and that of the Spanish Republic, now meaningless. In working on behalf of one friend, Elizabeth exposes the duplicity of her other friends, experiencing their betrayal of Max as a simultaneous disloyalty to their political ideals. Like "Luigi's House," the story concludes with the protagonist in relative personal safety but dreading the personal and global conflicts to come.

In a shift from *Good Will to Men*'s ironic allusion to Christian ideals, Gellhorn's later fiction about Spain emphasizes the effects of these global and personal conflicts on Jewish characters and their families. The short story "About Shorty" (1950) examines a German woman's impossible position in the Spanish Civil War, but from the perspective of a female American narrator who speaks on behalf of the volunteer community, seemingly supporting their gendered double standards. Shorty is "a German, as Aryan as can be, married to another German who was a Jew" (120). But while Shorty's absent husband, an International Brigades doctor, gains everyone's respect – "the finest man in Spain" (120) – Shorty's motivations for volunteering are constantly questioned and disparaged, even as she struggles to survive in Madrid. In her husband's absence, Shorty has a series of affairs: the narrator notes that she and her colleagues "did not blame the Russian [paramour], of course; he was only doing what anyone would do" (121). And of her later affair, "all agreed [that Shorty] was on Franco's side, distracting [one man] from his work and destroying [her husband]" (125). The blame they place on Shorty, alongside their indulgent attitude toward her lovers, ignores the ramifications of her husband's volunteering, which leaves her depressed, hungry, and broke. Although she is married to a Jew and volunteering with the Spanish cause, her "Aryan" roots and her many affairs mean, for other characters, that she is little better than a fascist colluder. However, the story concludes by alluding to the lingering repercussions of the Spanish Republic's fall: Shorty abandons her family because of the Nazi occupation of France, knowing that a Jewish ex-husband and a record as an antifascist are tantamount to a death sentence. Her whereabouts remain a mystery to the narrator, who admits that she wishes she could "forget Shorty as I have forgotten her name" (131). Shorty – including the narrator's treatment of her – haunts the story. Gellhorn's refusal to conclude Shorty's own narrative alludes to the unknown fates of many antifascists in Spain and elsewhere.

Likewise, Shorty's uncertain fate hints at the far-reaching impact of Nazi antisemitism. Gellhorn's novella *Till Death Do Us Part* (1958) represents a different postwar role for Jewish characters in its account of the death of a Robert Capa-esque photographer and the emotional aftermath for his New York lover. Where Gellhorn's previous female protagonists unfailingly offer their emotional labour as well as professional advocacy, this narrative instead describes an apolitical, disagreeable, helpless female character, one who – like Shorty – could be accused of distracting politically engaged men from their leftist duties. Helen Richards, a bored New York divorcée, carries on a peripatetic affair with Tim Bara, a photographer who occasionally passes through the city. But for his visits, her existence is vacant, yet she knows little about him – not even his real name. It is only when he dies covering a war that she discovers his traumatic personal history, including the death of his wife (possibly based on Robert Capa's romantic partner and fellow photographer Gerda Taro) in the Spanish Civil War.

The friendship of Tim's close friend is Helen's only solace. Tim's former colleague Paul "Lep" Lepczinski (alluding, perhaps, to the Jewish photographer David "Chim" Seymour) comforts her after Tim's death. His presence inspires her to observe that "[k]nowing Lep, one could not understand why it made any difference if people were Jews or Gentiles" (286). Helen's reflection on Lep's religion is echoed in her own self-reflection, as she repeatedly codes her feelings of social alienation in terms of Jewishness: Helen – a non-Jew – feels guilty about receiving alimony, saying that it makes her feel like "Shylock or a tart" (279). Yet while Helen feels her discomfort in terms of sexuality, religion, and ethnicity – tart or Shylock – she is also drawn to Lep's comfort, so much so that she is convinced she can overlook whatever perceived religious or ethnic differences there are between them. When each of the story's relationships fails, regardless of national, religious, or ethnic similarity, Lep is the heartbroken characters' universal comforter, a cosmopolitan outsider and safe confidant. Lep's thoughts on life after romantic loss bring the story to an optimistic, Zionist – or at least Jewish – conclusion: "What are you doing at that Wailing Wall? The only thing to do, as long as you are alive, is live" (309). In encouraging Helen to cease mourning, Lep reminds her of her own agency in her response to Bara's death as well as in her own unfulfilled life.

Gellhorn's *Till Death Do Us Part* and "About Shorty" foreground romantic relationships alongside friendships – relationships that, by and large, work to the detriment of both parties. In this way, Gellhorn's narratives of disastrous love might seem to parallel the novels I discussed in chapter 1, which suggest that love must always come second to the Spanish Republic's welfare. However, Gellhorn's stories conclude with a deep ambivalence about the female character's role, suggesting that romantic entanglements may have been a protective measure in 1930s leftist society as much as in the mainstream. In their very unpleasantness and instrumentalism, these two female protagonists – Helen and Shorty – demonstrate the difficulties faced by women seemingly abandoned as a result of their male partners' efforts to support the Spanish Republic. Gellhorn's stories serve as a reminder of women's continued marginalization and vulnerability, even amid her own and other feminist writers' efforts to foreground a triumphal narrative of Spanish democracy and egalitarianism.

Wartime Romance: Muriel Rukeyser's Recovered Novel

Yet female-authored romance stories about the Spanish Civil War aren't all doom and gloom. Where Hellman, Kea, and Gellhorn write about personal gains in the midst of massive social loss, the Jewish American author Muriel Rukeyser's recently recovered novel *Savage Coast* (first drafted in 1936) celebrates the transnational community that coheres in Catalonia among the locals and a stopped train full of international athletes and tourists in Spain for the People's Olympiad. Rukeyser's novel only obliquely refers to postwar life, so unlike Gellhorn's fiction, it mostly avoids a consideration of the conflict's long-term impact on relationships. But like Gellhorn, Rukeyser examines and re-examines the Spanish conflict throughout her oeuvre: as Rowena Kennedy-Epstein notes in her introduction to the novel, "In poems, reportage, memoir, essays, and fiction, and more often in experimental forms that combine these genres, she reiterates, re-imagines, and theorizes her experience as a witness to the first days of the war and to her own moment of political, sexual, and poetic awakening" (ix). What's more, Kennedy-Epstein explains, Rukeyser revised the manuscript throughout and after the war (although the specific revision timeline is unclear). Rukeyser was in Spain to report on the Anti-Fascist Olympic Games but ended up witnessing and reporting on the anarchist victory in Barcelona for *New Masses*, the British journal *Life and Letters To-day*, the *New York Times*, and *Esquire* – events that also make it into her better-known poetic works, including *Mediterranean* (1937) and *The Book of the Dead* (1938).[27] After the war, she continued to support Spanish Refugee Aid. Given the dearth of female-authored Spanish Civil War novels, Rukeyser's reimagining of the genre is particularly interesting to my study – hers is, to my knowledge, the only Spanish Civil War novel by a North American woman.[28]

Savage Coast begins with the demoralizing, foreshadowing line, "Everybody knows how that war ended" (7). Despite this beginning, Rukeyser's narrative exists within an optimistic moment, as her protagonist's excitement over attending the People's Olympiad grows into political activism inspired by the political clashes she witnesses and fortified by the community she finds on the train. The novel's young American protagonist is associated with war through her name, Helen. But rather than cause a war, she instead feels at first that she *is* a war: "endless, ragged conflict which tore her open, in her relations with her family, her friends, the people she loved" (12). In Spain, Helen finds this personal conflict externalized and expanded, yet it brings her some measure of internal peace. She establishes friendships with the Catalans and internationals by communicating in English and French. And she eschews the directive of her American cabinmate who demands that they "stick together ... we've got to find the other Americans on the train" (30). Helen easily transitions into a cosmopolitan, temporary community, although her closest friendship grows with another American character, Olive.

Rukeyser repeatedly distinguishes Helen and Olive from the rest of the internationals based on their physical appearance. Olive is racialized in terms suggestive of mixed-race parentage: as her name indicates, she is repeatedly described as "dark," with a face that "missed being Negroid because of the sharp mouth" (44–5), "mulatto" (169), and "profoundly mulatto" (238), and contrasted with Helen's "white face" (170). Likewise, Helen's differences from those around her are unevenly divulged, her whiteness coexisting with her ethnic difference and disability. From the beginning, the narrative returns to her physical disability – an issue with her leg nerves that causes her to limp. Kennedy-Epstein contends that Helen's leg "symbolizes the barrier to action that Helen must overcome" (Introduction xxiv), noting that her bouts of pain disappear by the novel's end. In contrast to Helen's lingering physical pain, it is only toward the novel's end that the reader learns of Helen's Jewishness – this part of her identity seems an aside, revealed only when Helen encounters a more religious Jewish woman and judges her harshly for adhering to the Jewish dietary laws of *kashrut* in a time of food shortages. While this "Semitic-looking girl" is recognized by other characters as Jewish, she is the only one who recognizes Helen as a fellow Jew (201).

The delayed revelation of Helen's Jewishness is key to our understanding of her role within this temporary transnational community. Kennedy-Epstein sees Helen's pained Jewish body recuperated through her relationship with the German athlete Hans, "intimately and erotically restored through sex" (Introduction xxiv).[29] While sex might be, in the novel, the cure for Helen's limp, I am hesitant to see her Jewishness as also cured – rather, her Jewish identity seems more enduringly stigmatized, in the novel, than her physical disability. Helen's inclusion in the community of the stopped train seems contingent on her successful passing as a gentile as well as her willingness to give up the religious practices of Judaism. Olive's inclusion, too, rests on her own racial ambiguity. Yet Olive and Helen are also this community's heroines. Hans quickly declares his love for Helen. The novel concludes in the midst of a political rally, with Olive's hopeful declaration that she wants to have a child with her husband – a child he has long desired – and Hans's plan to fight with the International Brigades. This is at once a traditional conclusion – a mash-up of so many other Spanish Civil War novels that conclude with babies to be born to women left behind – and a far more ambiguous one, with the American characters' plans to stay in Spain or leave unclear, and the novel's depressing introductory reminder of the war's failure unrepeated.

Savage Coast links Helen's and Olive's fates to that of the Spanish Republic. Rukeyser underscores the integral role of women from marginalized communities within the country's struggle – and, what's more, the delayed revelation of Helen's Jewishness, and the ambiguous depictions of her disability and Olive's Blackness, call into question any strict divisions between identity categories. In Spain, American distinctions based on race, ethnicity, and religion break down within a community collaborating to support the Republic – physical disabilities are even inexplicably cured. However, this happy community is also predicated on individual characters abandoning certain connections – Helen does not identify with the Jewish woman, nor Olive with any Black characters. Belonging comes at a cost.

The writers included in this chapter all focus their writings on female characters' experiences of the Spanish Civil War within community: Spanish women, North American women, European women, white women, women of colour, gentile women and Jewish women, disabled women. Whether depicting actual people or fictional characters, Hellman, Kea, Gellhorn, and Rukeyser highlight the tensions between national and transnational affiliations that underpin women's lives as they labour to be recognized as citizens. Many of their texts further examine the intersections of gender identity with race, religion, and ethnicity, even analogizing women's alienation from the masculinist mainstream to the experiences of other marginalized individuals. In Rukeyser's novel, certainly, the tensions over religious, racial, and ethnic identity that permeated North American participation in the Spanish Civil War are writ large. Rukeyser's Helen and Olive do not *do* anything that would mark them as other, but they exist in ethnically ambiguous, feminized, stigmatized bodies. Rukeyser's novel stifles any sense of the struggles that underpin Olive's and Helen's identities beyond the Spanish cause. Similarly, Gellhorn's character Lep is beloved by many gentile characters, but he is beloved *despite* his Jewishness for his willingness to comfort sad gentiles. In contrast, the Jewish doctor in "About Shorty" is explicitly victimized for his religion. Even more unambiguously than these post-Holocaust stories by Gellhorn, Kea's memoirs represent a nascent version of the Double-V campaign, in which the struggles of Black Americans, Jewish Europeans, and working-class Spaniards are connected – struggles that exist precisely because of individuals' Blackness, Jewishness, and working-classness. All three writers inject sympathy toward marginalized characters into their stories – a sympathy that is more explicitly voiced in Miriam Waddington and Dorothy Livesay's later writings.

Looking Back on Spain: Miriam Waddington and Dorothy Livesay

Gellhorn's fiction and Kea's later memoirs were composed after the Spanish Civil War's conclusion, the victory in the Second World War, and the horrors of the Holocaust. Both authors allude to these post–Spanish Civil War horrors in their narratives of Spain, instructing their readers in sympathy toward the victims of xenophobia. Even Rukeyser's novel prefaces its celebratory narrative with a warning of what is to come. With the benefit of even more time, two Canadian writers, Miriam Waddington and Dorothy Livesay, further incorporate the Spanish Civil War into an expanded chronology. Neither writer travelled to Spain, but from the 1930s onward they returned repeatedly to its war. Read alongside the diverse texts I have already discussed in this chapter, Livesay and Waddington's writings extend the Spanish Civil War's resonances, arguing explicitly for the war's relevance to Canadian misogyny, European anti-semitism, and future global unrest.

Through her essays, poetry, and memoirs, Dorothy Livesay deeply influenced how the Spanish Civil War shaped the history of the Canadian left. And as Candida Rifkind, Caren Irr, Dean Irvine, and others have argued, Livesay's self-representations and rewritings continue to shape critical notions of 1930s Canadian leftism – and of her own role in it.[30] A social worker and activist with a long and prolific writing career, Livesay was a member of the Communist Party until the early 1940s, was active in the radical arts groups of the communist-affiliated Progressive Arts Club, and wrote for communist-affiliated publications. Livesay's Spain poem with which I began this chapter is one of many she composed, along with the reports she wrote for the influential Canadian leftist monthly *New Frontier*. What I want to highlight here is how she, like Waddington, sustains her engagement with the Spanish cause in her writing. While Waddington wrote about Spain throughout her career, Livesay further collected many of her own writings – articles and poems, mostly – into *Right Hand Left Hand: A True Life of the Thirties: Paris, Toronto, Montreal, the West and Vancouver. Love, Politics, the Depression and Feminism* (1977). The focus of this "true life" story is her time living across North America (and briefly in Paris) and her participation in a variety of social movements, and not strictly on Spain. Yet Livesay's multitextual depiction of the Spanish Civil War constructs a Canadian community of supporters.

Livesay's use of the term "true life" in her memoir's subtitle underscores an issue related to Salaria Kea's encounters with those who sought to discredit her: Livesay's representation of the Spanish Civil War in *Right Hand Left Hand* draws from multiple sources but *not* Livesay's own first-hand experience of Spain. The chapter "Spain 1936–1939" is, in fact, the book's only section whose title does not reflect Livesay's own travels. In other words, the section is not a memoir of Spain so much as a memoir of the many Canadians who worked on the Spanish people's behalf. The chapter contains article excerpts from *New Frontier*, poetry by Livesay and others, Livesay's reminiscences about the era, her critical commentary on Canadian poetry inspired by the conflict, and film stills from the National Film Board's Spanish Civil War documentary

Los Canadienses (1975). Livesay also uses her poetry as a corrective to other documents' emphasis on male participation. Alongside images of men in combat, Livesay includes a 1936 letter from Norman Bethune, reprinted from *New Frontier*, that mentions the deaths of "thousands of non-combatants, women and children" (243), and that asks for men and women to volunteer as nurses. An interview by Ted Allan with Ernest Hemingway focuses strictly on male combatants. A pamphlet, "Spain's Democracy Talks to Canada," includes quotations from Ibárruri. And Livesay's own essay, "Canadian Poetry and the Spanish Civil War," mentions female poets, including Anne Marriott, Miriam Waddington, and P.K. Page, but emphasizes male poets' writings on Spain.

This chapter about Spain concludes, however, with Livesay's poetry emphasizing women's sexuality and political fervour. For instance, in "Comrade," the speaker remembers a one-night stand with a fellow activist, concluding that even though he is now "a grey man without dreams, / Without a living, or an overcoat" their shared "struggle" connects them more tightly than a love affair ever could (*Right Hand* 262); in "The Lizard: October, 1939," the speaker describes waiting for news of the wars in Spain and China and then "slip[ping] out in pairs, as lovers / Strip ourselves, longing / To see bodies bare and flesh uncloseted, / To hear real voices again, to uphold the song / Of one coming from Madrid, Shanghai or Yenan / Bearers of good news / From the fronts we knew" (268). Livesay also includes her elegy to Lorca, which I will discuss more fully in the following chapter's discussion of queer writers' odes to the murdered poet. Her poetry is ambivalent toward the role of political and romantic action, representing how international conflict – itself constitutively patriarchal – undergirds even the most personal of connections and relationships. The poetry with which Livesay concludes the section on Spain thus expands upon the personal dimension of the conflict, its sexist and homophobic violence and repression, and the real losses behind the bland enumeration of "thousands of non-combatants."

Right Hand Left Hand epitomizes the layered portrayals of Spain that I present in this chapter: in its inclusions and omissions, Livesay represents the Canadian leftist response to Spain – and her own role in raising awareness – by creating a polyvocal collage of writings and images spanning forty years. Her book relies on multiple documents likewise accrued over decades to circle around the truth of the conflict, reminding readers of the overwhelming Canadian response. The section's situation within the work emphasizes Spain's interconnections with the Toronto, Montreal, New Jersey, Canadian West, and Vancouver of Livesay's 1930s. The recontextualization of her poetry within this new framework of contemporaneous and post-1930s writings demonstrates the conflict's continued relevance to ongoing Canadian class struggles.[31]

Where Livesay underscores the relationship between the Spanish cause, 1930s turmoil, and ongoing Canadian unrest, the Jewish Canadian writer, critic, and social worker Miriam Dworkin Waddington highlights the Spanish Civil War's reverberations in subsequent global massacres. Waddington's poetic representations of the Spanish Civil War can be understood as an outgrowth of the polyvocal Yiddish-English socialist, intellectual milieu in which she was raised and educated and in which she worked. Waddington was the child of Jewish Russian immigrants to Winnipeg, a city with a small but active leftist Jewish population. Peter Stevens notes, in his biography of the author, that her home was a hub of art and activism: "The Dworkin home became a centre for many Jewish and Yiddish authors, and, as Isidore Dworkin had left-wing political sympathies, for a number of political activists as well" (1). While I have been unable to find biographical material pointing to specific Spanish Civil War activism, Waddington's sustained community engagement, antifascism, and training in progressive social work are well documented, along with her involvement with the leftist Jewish literary scene in Montreal.[32] Furthermore, along with her prodigious literary output of poetry, short stories, essays, and criticism, Waddington was involved in the Canadian modernist literary magazine *First Statement*, and in bringing Yiddish writers to a wider audience through her translations of Yiddish literature and her editorial work publicizing the writings of A.M. Klein and other Jewish Canadian authors. Her commitment to social activism, her familiarity with the outsider experience, and her interest in representing multiple perspectives and experiences are all evident in her Spanish Civil War poetry.

Waddington's earliest Spanish Civil War poem, "The Exiles: Spain," articulates the strength of a community forged amid chaos and destruction. The poem appears, in fact, to be her earliest published poem, composed while Waddington was a student at the University of Toronto and published in the student newspaper *The Varsity* on 11 December 1936. The poem depicts a group bidding one another their final celebratory farewell before departing to become solitary exiles. It also contrasts love with war, in a deceptively simple representation of the battlefront as a place anathema to human connection. The poem's title is the only clear link between the text and the Spanish Civil War – these exiles exist in the context of a fascist incursion, but the possibility of being exiled, Waddington suggests, exists for all, no matter their citizenship.

While the experience of exile may be universal, the poem refuses to represent these exiles as a dejected, faceless mob of refugees. Instead, "The Exiles: Spain" imagines the strong communal bonds forged among those forced to flee Spain as they allow themselves to enjoy the country's landscape one last time. The poem's first two stanzas begin with the refrain "Come, my friends," as the unnamed speaker implores their companions to join in a final dance on the shore to commemorate their courageous and difficult fight (2, ll. 1, 5). But while the speaker commends their unity after having "fought and so bravely failed," and promises future fortune, since "the ultimate victory [remains] unassailed," it is their surroundings that foreshadow danger (2, ll. 6, 7). These exiles are surrounded by ruins. The natural world is personified and peculiar: Waddington's speaker describes how "the cold sun sets with a distant grief" and then wonders whether the sun will ever rise again (2, l. 2). The "black waves fret" around the shore where the exiles join hands and dance, while "evil frets at [their] hearts" (2, ll. 3, 4). This shared verb, "fret," links the nightly incoming tide to the darkness of impending war. At the same time, however, Waddington gestures to a communal heart unthreatened by evil, a victorious heart that "[r]emains ... above the ruins" (2, ll. 8). The protected victory that "[r]emains in the heart" ends the poem on an indefinite note, one compounded by the speaker's statement that they cannot know whether they will "live through these evil days" (2, l. 10). The dance on the shore represents a final, poignant moment of abandon in a scene itself deeply distraught by the looming war. Paradoxically, it is through the celebration of kinship and national lands that the poem also subtly gestures to the war's mounting threat.

"The Exiles: Spain" also represents this threat in its poetic form. The poem is a Shakespearian sonnet missing its concluding couplet – three rhyming quatrains that lack a final turn or volta. The sonnet form is traditionally associated with declarations of love and friendship, with the final rhyming couplet the culminating statement of amity. Instead, in Waddington's war poem, the curtailed form reproduces the anxiety and uncertainty that mark the poem's message, a message lacking its concluding conviction. We never know whether the speaker's request is met – whether their friends ever "take hands and dance on the shore" – and this unknowing reproduces the speaker's question within the poem's structure, of "whether we [will] live through these evil days" (2, ll. 12, 10). Waddington intimates that there may be more evil days to come, more exiles from more nations, more ruins. Published at the beginning of the Spanish Civil War, "The Exiles: Spain" is unique among Canadian poems about the war in its ambiguous, rather than optimistic, representation of the ongoing Spanish conflict. At the same time, the poem's emphasis on camaraderie is an important commentary on the need for fellowship and community, especially in the midst of violence and exile.[33]

Almost exactly a year later, as the war raged on, Waddington published another poem foregrounding the importance of love and community in the midst of wartime. The free verse poem "Spanish Lovers Seek Respite," published in the University of Toronto's University College magazine *Undergraduate* in fall 1937, imagines how a night without war might facilitate continued allegiance to the cause. As in her previous war poem, Waddington emphasizes the ways in which the natural world both reflects and remains impervious to human conflict. Where the sun was setting in "The Exiles: Spain," here it is the middle of the night, a "menacing night" from which there is only temporary respite (4, l. 17). However, both poems share a belief in the potential comfort of the natural world: the poem's speaker imagines a nightlong escape into the cooling wind of the mountains, explaining, "Up there is peace, dry wind, / And sky clean and dark" ("Spanish Lovers Seek Respite" 4, ll. 19–20).

Echoing "The Exiles: Spain," this poem is also singly voiced by an ungendered speaker appealing for a brief interlude of peace and love before returning to danger and conflict. The speaker of "Spanish Lovers Seek Respite" pleads,

> Let us go away from this:
> No, not forever –
> ...
> We need new strength,
> We need to be with ourselves,
> You with you
> Myself with me,
> And both of us together. (4, ll. 6–7, 10–14)

Solitude, as well as love, will fortify these individuals. Like "The Exiles: Spain," "Spanish Lovers Seek Respite" does not imagine an end to the war, but instead highlights the immediacy of personal relationships. The independence and togetherness that the speaker craves – "Myself with me, / And both of us together" – underscore the individual and collective freedoms that drove support for the Spanish Republic. A brief reprieve from the war will reaffirm the importance of intimacy and of love. Waddington's speaker here insists upon remembering life outside of a war zone. That is, rather than glorifying war, "Spanish Lovers Seek Respite" emphasizes its hoped-for outcome of peace, love, and community.[34]

Taken together, Waddington's early poetic depictions of companionship and solidarity in wartime refuse the comfort of a happy ending.

Both poems end ambivalently, without any indication that their speakers receive what they have requested – a fleeting pause with loved ones – and instead suggest the ongoing, unceasing terror of war. This war impacts everything, tearing apart friendships and families, destroying the natural world, even truncating the sonnet form of "The Exiles: Spain." Community amid destruction is essential yet nearly impossible.

Waddington's early Spanish Civil War poetry emphasizes the importance of protecting community – the vital reason for which the war was fought – from a vantage point simultaneously local and transnational. Waddington's depictions of its exiles and combatants, and of the country's landscape, are all imagined. However, in both poems, Waddington adopts a first-person speaker: a figure who feels intimately the experiences of personal exile and battlefield danger. While neither speaker is gendered, both emphasize the sustaining power of love and friendship. This imagining gives Waddington's poetry a particularly activist bent: she, like many in Canada, perceived the need for Canadians to identify themselves with Spain's communities. If Waddington's upbringing had taught her to view herself as simultaneously belonging to multiple communities and identities within Canada, then in her Spanish Civil War poetry her assumption of participants' voices is an articulation of her sympathy and her sense of community with individuals around the world, especially the exiled and embattled Spanish people, who are threatened by fascism. Ending the war in Spain, and thwarting Franco, Hitler, and Mussolini, becomes a cause not just for Spaniards but for all who are opposed to Nazism and fascism.

Waddington's 1930s poems about Spain maintain some hope, if not for the Spanish Republic then at least for the possibility of sustained community. After the Second World War and the Holocaust, however, the defeat in the Spanish Civil War becomes, for Waddington, an originating moment of all subsequent destruction.[35] It is in Waddington's poem "The Woman in the Hall" (1992) that these personal and communal wounds are most explicitly articulated in an unequivocal statement about the human cost extracted by fascism and Nazism. First published in the leftist Canadian monthly magazine *Canadian Forum* in March 1992 and included in Waddington's collection *The Last Landscape* that same year, this later free-verse poem yokes the carnage of the Spanish Civil War to the Second World War and the Holocaust, to poverty around the world, and to a history of Spanish conquest and warmaking, romanticized in the paintings of Francisco de Goya and suffered by the denizens of Spain's former colonies.

Abandoning the first-person voices of many of her earlier poetic invocations of Spain, "The Woman in the Hall" invites us to examine the volatile titular figure from a narrative distance. She is introduced simply: "There is a woman / in the hall" (768, ll. 1–2). "The Woman in the Hall" is a nondescript, solitary, oracular Everywoman: "she lives alone in / some upstairs room / in a nebulous city" and she may be "birdwoman or / sibyl, farmwife or / fishgutter, or is she / the buttonhole maker" (768, ll. 3–5, 11–14). But her profession is not as important as her history:

> Whoever she is
> she is also Guernica
> and Madrid she is Moscow
> besieged and Dieppe
> betrayed.
> ...
> she is the addled brain
> of the crazy woman who
> survived the camps. (768–9, ll. 20–4, 35–7)

The woman is an accrual of global trauma and "patriarchal injustice," as noted by Judith Brown (269). She is this trauma personified, invisible or repulsive in her daily work yet also a reminder of the recent and not so recent past. The woman's trauma does not spell the end of her attachment to her many communities, however. While solitary, "The Woman in the Hall" is not necessarily alienated from the rest of society; instead, by sharing her deep historical knowledge with others, she rouses their awareness of their own complicity. In her solitude, "sit[ting] out the days on the / shores of the Dead Sea / muttering curses and / incantations" or "in some small / town eking out a life on / a pension," she is the universal confessor: "she hears your messages ... your anger and sorrow" (769–70, ll. 38–41, 68–70, 71–3).

What's more, "The Woman in the Hall" turns this distress into productive change: she is a prophet who, in prophesying, is able to effect transformations in others. The poem concludes,

> she is the ragpicker who
> comes to warn you
> of future Guernicas,
> and she is the woman who
> at last awakens in you
> your broken promises your
> ancient righteousness. (770, ll. 79–85)

"The Woman in the Hall" exists at once within constant global suffering and outside of time. She recalls the Jewish German philosopher Walter Benjamin's "angel of history" in his final essay "On the Concept of History." In contemplating how current progress and past destruction intersect, Benjamin describes *Angelus Novus*, a Paul Klee painting in which the angel appears to be staring at something he is also departing from. The angel's unbroken gaze upon that which he is leaving behind parallels how Benjamin understands the supposed progress of the current moment, which can only be understood in terms of its destructive origins: that "one single catastrophe, which unceasingly piles rubble on top of rubble and hurls it before [its] feet ... That which we call progress, is *this* storm" (italics in the original).[36] Benjamin wrote "On the Concept of History" in 1940, shortly before he committed suicide in Francoist Spain while fleeing the Nazis. Waddington's nameless woman – human, not angelic – invokes a belated, parallel reckoning with fascist antimodernity. "The Woman in the Hall" can see, and make others see, a history of devastation. Furthermore, her humanity allows her to "awaken" them, to inspire them to change.

"The Woman in the Hall" is a poem not about community, but about its absence. Yet although she is friendless, the isolated woman of Waddington's later poem also forges solidarity – offering warnings, and "awaken[ing]" "broken promises" and "ancient righteousness," both of which are essential, even globally protective. In contrast to Waddington's earlier depiction of a desperate final celebratory dance in "The Exiles: Spain" and a moment of passionate abandon in "Spanish Lovers Seek Respite," this later poem calls back to those revolutionary friends, promising both bloodshed and justice to come and affirming the prescience of those early exiles in fearing for future "evil days." Indeed, the poems are further rhetorically linked by the ruins that form the setting for "The Exiles: Spain" and that flow within the blood of "The Woman in the Hall," "her wrists throb[bing] with the / pulse of ruined cities" (770, ll. 74–5). Read alongside Waddington's early poetry about Spain, "The Woman in the Hall" becomes a powerful statement about the foundational role women play in building and rebuilding communities. Whether in Spain, in Canada, or in some "nebulous city," Waddington's poetic speakers underscore the moral duty to work toward a world beyond war.

Writing of Waddington's oeuvre, Ruth Panofsky notes how her poetry yokes Judaism and Jewishness to her diverse communities in Canada. Waddington was the Canadian-born daughter of Jewish immigrants, and in Panofsky's reading, "a gendered social consciousness drove the moral questing for knowledge and understanding that lay at the heart of her poetic practice" (Introduction xiii). In "The Woman in the Hall," Waddington implicitly questions the safety that Canadian nationality ostensibly provides – a safety, as Waddington herself well knew, only unevenly available based on factors such as gender, language, immigration status, and religion. The moral imperative at the core of "The Woman in the Hall" connects Canadian peace to European war and to Jewish and Spanish carnage. As Esther Sánchez-Pardo González argues, Waddington's poetic voice does not stem from "mere sympathy for political minorities or for the 'victims' of society who are isolated in some way, but cannot subscribe to their external reality"; rather, her aesthetic perspective illuminates the social realities that would be easier to ignore (179). Waddington's desperate "Woman in the Hall" tries, in an attempt that may prove futile, to warn those around her of the destruction to come. Despite the ultimate failure of the Spanish communities that Waddington's early poetry depicts, and likewise the international failures to stem the spread of fascism and Nazism, her later poem holds out the promise of a future transnational solidarity. In the face of local and global trauma, there remains, for "The Woman in the Hall," a "heart above the ruins" and the promise of an "ultimate victory." Waddington's poetry is a lesson in sympathy, a warning against complacency, and a stirring of "broken promises" and "ancient righteousness."

Recovering a Chorus of Voices

The poetry, fiction, reportage, and memoirs discussed in this chapter express concerns about women's treatment during war and about the privileging of men's warmaking over women's contributions. These works at times join masculinist novels in eschewing heterosexual relationships in favour of homosocial communities. Yet by inverting and disrupting the telos of heterosexual romance ending in marriage and domesticity – that is, by writing about women's friendships and communities established on the warfront instead of the home front, heterosexual friendships, failed relationships, and strictly sexual relationships – North American women representing the Spanish Civil War also argue for their own entitlement to more comprehensive rights and broader social change at home. In a context of sexist restrictions placed upon them by religious and governmental patriarchy, Popular Front condescension, and internalized sexism alike, these writers represent female participants' strength, bravery, and loyalty.

Women's representations provide a counternarrative of North American women's experiences and of their attempts to foreground Spanish women's contributions. The texts discussed here often expose the Spanish cause's concealed reliance on women's work: on the nurses whose labour literally keeps soldiers in the war, the social organizers who empower Spanish women to lead, the reporters who publicize the horrors of fascism both during and after the war. Furthermore, many of these texts highlight the contributions of additionally marginalized people: Black and Jewish women and men. In discussing gentile British women authors, Maren Tova Linett argues that their inclusion of Jewish characters is a fundamental dimension of their modernism, in which Jews and Jewishness may correspond to women's own outsider status and alienation, or serve as a foil.[37] Antisemitic stereotypes that consistently figure Jews as passive and effeminate (and, as Linett notes, rarely include Jewish women) contribute to this tension between Jewishness and femininity. In Spanish Civil War writings, however, this alternative identification with and against Jews suggests that these marginalized characters do more than serve as foil and mirror; they also serve as a synecdoche for a diversifying community. While, as I have discussed, Jewish male writers sometimes took on gentile pseudonyms, imagining nearly uniformly positive Jewish characters from a place of assumed white privilege, women writers (both Jewish and gentile) write as women, representing characters who are female, Jewish, and Black as, again, almost uniformly positive. This shared emphasis on the multiple races, ethnicities, religions, and nationalities and the intersectional identities represented in Spain is, in part, an inheritance of the International Brigades' conscious rhetoric of global inclusion (and certainly, many works written by white male authors share this emphasis). However, given their shared status as people who might, in Virginia Woolf's words, "have no country" (cf. *Three Guineas*) – but who certainly often wanted one – this effort to bring other marginalized groups together into a broader affiliation demonstrates one productive permutation of cosmopolitan discourse.

The eventual disappointments of the feminist revolutionary movement in Spain foreshadowed both Francoist repression and the frustrations of female volunteers forced to return to their own, often unegalitarian, countries.[38] For North American women, it is as if, upon the return home, the "nation" itself has been transformed into a problematic entity, its gendered contours vividly visible for the first time, while the figure of "the citizen" remains unreflectively male. These frustrations are evident in multiple ways, from Gellhorn's mid-century representations of female characters' ongoing work on behalf of those traumatized by the Spanish Civil War to Waddington's desperate "Woman in the Hall" trying to warn those around her of the destruction to come. Many of these texts are invested in the concept of the nation and in the importance of refiguring the gendered contours of the nation through a more broadly conceived concept of belonging – wartime means further freedoms for otherwise oppressed women, as Woolf observed, but the Spanish Civil War encouraged an expanded philosophical belief in the possibility of establishing an egalitarian nation.

Women's literature about the Spanish Civil War seeks to discern and define alternative modes of community formation as well as broader potential roles for women – and for all citizens. Instead of dispensing with the concept of the nation, or with nationalism, these writers redefine a love of the nation in order to divorce its gendered aspects from what they see as the more positive effects of national affiliation, and implicit within this distinction is an understanding of national identity "as inextricably and ineluctably intertwined with one's gender" (Pierson 41). The war in Spain was, after all, a civil war, in which international volunteers sought to protect what they saw as the rightful government from a fascist, monarchy-supported coup. In fighting for the Spanish Republic – for a nation's right to national boundaries, democratic elections, and efforts at class equalization – foreign volunteers and writers were taking part in a cosmopolitan effort to defend a country's autonomy. For female writers, themselves directly affected by the sexist social structures of their home countries and, once in Spain, by its patriarchal norms as well, the importance of this autonomy – and the implicit contradictions of supporting national self-determination when the nation denies them individual self-determination – is particularly acute.

There was another, tragic dimension to these authors' depictions of nationality, gender, race, and religion, as the threat of Nazism loomed over the Spanish Civil War and its aftermath. Women writers' depictions of Jews – and particularly Jewish women's depictions of Jews – sought to teach sympathy for a group desperately in need of an exit from Europe. Even authors who did not explicitly discuss the dangers of fascism in their fiction were starkly aware of its threat: for instance, Kessler-Harris notes that after Lillian Hellman returned to the United States from Spain in 1938, "she called the *New York Times* (which she described as owned by Jews) to task for not featuring antifascist articles about Spain on its front page. 'It stands to reason,' she wrote, that 'every Jew must be an anti-Fascist to be either a good Jew or a good American'" (142). Writing characters who were both good Jews *and* good Americans (or Canadians) became a moral imperative.

In bringing together different women's voices on the Spanish Civil War, I also want to acknowledge the larger silences. It is perhaps no coincidence that most of the texts I have discussed here are either out of print or archival; in fact, the published works that are in print as I write this – *Savage Coast* and *The Collected Poems of Miriam Waddington* – are available because of the work of feminist literary scholars Rowena Kennedy-Epstein and Ruth Panofsky. While women's participation in the Spanish Civil War is gradually receiving more critical attention, it is only through literary recovery work that the full scope of women's contributions becomes legible.[39] As Linda M. Morra notes in her own study of women's literary archives, "the visibility of female citizens is dependent upon the preservation of their socio-political and cultural traces" (3). These "female citizens" are, in Spanish Civil War literature, legible only in their own self-representations. If, as I argued in chapter 1, Jewish authors depict Jewish soldiers' bravery in order to leverage themselves into an established category of masculinist ideal citizenship, then here, too, we see a series of authors collectively concerned about the security their own countries can offer them.

In women's writings, these leftist voices may diverge, taking on feminist, nationalist, and antiracist projects sometimes elided or avoided within the larger leftist movement. These divergences do not always protect their texts from imperializing or hierarchical articulations of feminism or cosmopolitanism. However, their shared focus on feminist interracial and interfaith solidarity points to an aspiration toward a fuller social equality than is usually articulated in men's fictional representations. Taken together, these texts foreground women's revolutionary capacity to understand the continuities between the domestic sphere and the larger community. Women writers, in other words, create female characters who consistently exceed the paradigms of male representation, representing their own varied and divergent opinions and experiences. The choral, often archived voices of leftist women's writings – voices that repeatedly express the failures of objectivity in articulating the conflicts underpinning the Spanish Republican struggle – are thus communal in voicing their discontent with the status quo for women, arguing, at core, for the value of their multiple experiences.

4
Inclusion: Elegizing Lorca

"Remember Lorca, who died only for being Lorca"
George Woodcock, "Poem for García Lorca"

"His grave is lost but the words remain.
What if it had been the other way round?"
Mark Frutkin, "Death of a Poet"

Lorca, Queerness, and Jewishness

My previous chapters emphasized how different cultural associations with Judaism manifest themselves in Spanish Civil War writings: Are Jews citizens? Are they conventionally masculine or feminine? Are they white, Black, or something else? I have looked to authors' treatments of Jewish masculine bravery and feminist Jewish solidarity, as well as Jewish authors' attempts to propel themselves into whiteness by dissociating themselves from members of the African diaspora, including African Jews. In all of these literary texts, an obsession with attaining mainstream citizen status underscores the depictions of Jewish wartime involvement. In this chapter, I examine another association that seems to stick to Jews – are Jews queer? If so, how is that queerness constructed through varying literary tropes and (mis)translations?

The intersections of Jewishness, queerness, cosmopolitanism, nationality, and modernity are embodied in the Spanish writer Federico García Lorca. This chapter brings together Canadian literary responses to his murder that span the 1930s to the present decade. In so doing, it proposes a literary approach to articulating community distinct from the others I have discussed so far in that it is neither geographically nor chronologically bound. Elegies to Lorca comprise a global literary memorial and community.[1] (While more properly shortened to “García,” the ubiquity of this last name prompted the poet to go by “Lorca,” which is also how most anglophone writers refer to him.) Scholars of American, British, and Hispanophone Spanish Civil War poetry have documented the literary significance of Lorca’s death – not only as a subject for poetry, but also as a galvanizing moment in writers’ support for the Spanish Republic: Lorca’s murder as part of the war demonstrated both the power of artists and the dangers they faced.[2] In this chapter, I focus on the often overlooked role of Canadian writers in this long-standing transnational community as they join the chorus of voices elegizing Lorca and his cosmopolitan, egalitarian values.

What does it mean for Canadian writers to join an international community paying homage to Lorca while simultaneously writing about Canadian national identity? In order to address this question, I first approach Lorca’s own outsider status. For the fascists, Lorca was a traitor to his nation because of his politics, his queerness, and his proximity to racial and religious others. As Jasbir Puar argues, queer people have long been cast as national traitors.[3] If Lorca was viewed as a traitor to many on the right in Spain, he was a hero to many on the left – both in Spain and in Canada. National and sexual communities alike are “discursively produced,” but queerness has the potential to destabilize nationalism, as Peter Dickinson explains (30). Following Dickinson, I want to suggest that we can read Canadian writers depicting Lorca as being in conversation with one another: as creating a community in which national and sexual identities intersect. Canadian writers of the 1930s and 1940s construct a nascent category of national belonging while – through their elegies to Lorca – simultaneously contributing to a transnational project. As I’ve discussed throughout these chapters, Canadian Spanish Civil War literature often represents a more diverse array of citizens than the dominant image of a white, heterosexual, Anglo-Saxon Protestant man. What’s more, these Canadian elegies to Lorca explicitly or implicitly indicate that queerness is an integral part of Canadianness. Lorca is represented as the voice of Spain – a voice violently silenced by fascist aggressors. In continuing to bring Lorca’s legacy to Canada, Canadian writers articulate a Canadian identity while refusing the heteronormalizing forces of what Puar has termed homonationalism. Lorca remains an outsider in Canadian elegies, and this outsiderness becomes a critique of both Spain and Canada. This is to say that I approach national identity – as evinced through writings that aim to construct that category – not as trying to write queerness into an already existing category of Canadianness, but as incorporating queerness and anti-homophobia into a vision of cosmopolitan nationalism that comes to be synonymous with a Canadian identity.

When Federico García Lorca was murdered by fascist militia on 19 August 1936, he was known around the world for his poetry and plays. Deeply connected to his native region of Andalusia and to the Spanish poetic avant-garde collective Generación '27, by the time of the Spanish Civil War's outbreak he had travelled extensively – across Spain and to the United States, Argentina, Uruguay, and Cuba – and had become an outspoken supporter of social justice. On 18 August 1936, he was arrested and then, early the following morning, taken from his cell, shot, and buried in an unmarked grave. Lorca's body has never been recovered, and multiple attempts to excavate it have failed.

Historians and biographers have debated the motives for Lorca's murder – some claim he was killed for his political activism, others suggest he was apolitical, still others contend that his homosexuality and his literary fame threatened the rightist powers.[4] The man who claimed to be Lorca's murderer, the Falangist Black Squad leader Juan Luis Trescastro Medina, boasted the day after Lorca's murder: "We just killed Federico García Lorca. I put two bullets in his arse for being a queer" (qtd in Preston, *Spanish Holocaust* 175).[5] Franco's regime banned Lorca's works until 1953, while Lorca's *Sonnets of Dark Love* remained unpublished until the early 1980s – clearly, Lorca's words, in addition to his very existence, profoundly threatened the fascists.

While I appreciate the common scholarly impulse to delineate Lorca's politics from his queerness as a way to understand Falangist motivations, I'm not convinced that the move to bifurcate the political and the personal is a critically sound gesture. Lorca was murdered for his perceived politics, his perceived sexuality, and his perceived cosmopolitanism: all are inextricable in thinking about his murder – and in understanding the subsequent transnational literary response.

I see the Canadian chorus of responses elegizing Lorca as participating in a Jewish and queer project for a number of reasons. First, and perhaps most obviously, Lorca identified as gay and as ancestrally Jewish. While his queerness is well known (and was at the time of his murder), less widely acknowledged is that Lorca was fascinated by the possibility that he had Jewish *converso* ancestry (*conversos* were Jews who had been forced to convert to Catholicism during the Spanish Inquisition; Gibson, *Federico García Lorca* 11). A visit to the Sephardic synagogue Shearith Israel in New York City prompted Lorca to write to his family "comprendo que en Granada somos casi todos judíos. Era una cosa estupenda ver como parecían todos granadinos" (I understand that in Granada we are almost all Jews. It was an amazing thing to see how much everyone [the Jewish congregants] looked like Granadans; my trans.; qtd in Nordlund 46). This identification shows in his writings: Lorca wrote explicitly about queerness, love, and homophobia, and about Jewish biblical characters, Jewish spaces, and Jewish experiences.

Second, Lorca was murdered for characteristics that the fascists stigmatized for their close association with queerness and Jewishness. The fascists were threatened not only by his sexuality but also by his championing of art; his leftist politics; his populist voice; his compassion for women, "Gitanos," and Black people; his depictions of working-class experience; and his cosmopolitan sympathies. In other words, in considering the motivations for his murder, the specifics of his sexual orientation and his religious and ethnic ancestry are immaterial: he was murdered for being perceived as too queer and too Jewish (or Jew-like), too vocal and too proud.[6]

Third, I follow scholars of queer Jewish studies in wanting to highlight the proximity of Jewishness to queerness (and of homophobia to antisemitism and fascism). The years leading up to Lorca's murder marked the invention of homosexuality as we now understand it, as well as the increasing stigmatization of Jewish people.[7] Much antisemitic discourse of the period represents Jews as gender-fluid and otherwise queer: the men are at once effeminate (even female – think of the mockery of Leopold Bloom in the "Cyclops" episode of *Ulysses*) and sexually predatory, the women masculine in their own excessive sexuality. Jewish identity is queer, in other words, in the sense that it is perceived as resisting mainstream norms of gender performance and sexual mores.

For Canadian writers, Lorca's importance is twofold: by writing about Lorca, they join in a transnational practice of political activism and aesthetic radicalism; and by writing about an author killed for his sexuality and his politics, they examine the queerness of leftism, of the Spanish Republic, and of the imagined transnational communities of Spanish Republican supporters. What's more, in participating in what I have been discussing as a nation-defining literary project, writers who simultaneously invoke Lorca yoke national identity with queerness. Whether all those who wrote about Lorca were aware of his sexuality is unclear; however, his iconic status as a cosmopolitan artist suggests something of the proximities between non-normative art, sexuality, and culture. Canadian authors from the 1930s to the present write about and around Lorca's sexuality as a way of thinking through queerness and Canadianness from a geographic distance. Importantly, their elegies are, like the Canadian Spanish Civil War literature I have discussed thus far, written against the backdrop of different provinces' and regions' geographies and cultures as well as the nation's linguistic and religious solitudes. In their writings they create a queer-Jewish-Canadian discursive community that coheres around antifascist and leftist politics and cosmopolitan values. Published in little magazines as well as leftist newspapers, novels, and poetry books, these authors both remember the poet-playwright and warn of the dangers of fascist, religiously rationalized homophobia.[8]

Lorca's Reception Internationally and in Canada

If Lorca's words threatened the fascists, it was because they were deeply meaningful to many, in Spain and around the world, for their articulation of transcultural solidarities. His writings demonstrate his appreciation for and reimagination of Andalusian literary and musical forms as well as the cultural contributions of Jewish and *gitano* people (the latter term refers, in Spain, to Romani people, although the terms *gitano* and "Gypsy" are often used pejoratively).[9] In addition to representing Jewish and *gitano* cultures in his writings – a not uncommon comparison among cosmopolitan modernists in their fascination with diaspora and outsider identity – beginning with his time in New York Lorca expressed interest in what he saw as the parallels between African American and Spanish *gitano* aesthetic signatures and expressive practices.[10] And just a couple of months before his murder, he bemoaned Spaniards' antagonism toward the so-called Moorish people, lamenting the cultural contributions lost to Spain as a result of their expulsion (Maurer, "Violet Shadow" 23). Lorca's activism and art exemplify the transcultural, cosmopolitan concerns that underscore so much of Spanish Civil War literature.

Lorca's sympathy toward marginalized cultures did not prevent misunderstandings and failures of cultural translation: he was apparently shocked by Argentinian playgoers' negative reactions to his use of the term "Jew" as an epithet in his play *The Shoemaker's Prodigious Wife*:

> Lorca struggled to explain that while the word "Jew" was a traditional term of insult in rural Andalusia, it was not anti-Semitic. "One says 'Jew' contemptuously, yes, but without thinking of actual Jews," he said clumsily, adding that the moment he had realized his play was offensive, he had revised the script to read "hag" instead of "Jew." (Stainton 344)

Lorca's understanding of others' experiences of marginalization may have been uneven, but as Chris Perriam points out, his diverse sympathies contributed to a wide-ranging approach to depicting love and desire in his writings: "Lorca is strong on companionship, on family ties, on spiritual love, on love as commitment to others and to the fight against social injustice as it impacts on Gypsies, women, homosexual men and black people" (152). Perriam's reading of Lorca's approach to writing love suggests one of the many characteristics of his work that made Lorca's oeuvre so meaningful to writers around the world.

In Britain and the United States, Stephen Spender and Langston Hughes laboured to bring translations of Lorca's writings into print. While Canadians did not have a Spender or a Hughes, his writings nonetheless found their way to Canada in English translation, in the form of British and American publications.[11] Most Canadians encountered Lorca through cultural translation as well: for Canadian authors Lorca became their artistic contemporary, a tragic victim representative of what may have seemed a more international, artistic society than their own, who was murdered by a far more repressive government than their own. Such acts of cultural translation always incorporate revision and reimagination, and perhaps nostalgia, romance, and anachronism, as critics studying British and American poetic responses have pointed out. Jonathan Mayhew has demonstrated how many American writers use Lorca as a floating signifier, an icon who means whatever they need him to mean.[12] Similarly, in examining British responses to Lorca, Gayle Rogers argues that Lorca came to stand in for a particular, Andalusian-focused vision of Spain: "Lorca became, in the British afterlife that [Stephen] Spender enabled amid competing readings of him, a symbol not of the Spanish Republic alone, nor of the international communist revolution, as some of the left tried to make him, but of a cosmopolitan Spain that had become European – retroactively, after Franco's victory" (165).[13] To differing extents, then, Canadian writers participate in this particular anglophone tradition of reading Lorca into their nation and allowing his symbolic power to supersede the particulars of his own politics or texts.

Not only did Lorca's writing arrive in Canada, but his murder was important enough to make news, especially among leftists. The Communist Party of Canada's national newspaper the *Daily Clarion* announced Lorca's murder on its front page: an article titled "Fascists Shoot Spanish Author" (15 Sept. 1936) ran nearly a month after Lorca's life ended. It noted that the "brilliant young Spanish writer has been executed at Granada by the fascists" (1). Reflecting its emphasis on radical news as well as literature, the following day, the newspaper ran a poem by H.T. Munro lamenting the silence of the Spanish "Troubadour" but promising that victory for Spain would follow ("To a Guitar" 4).

Lorca and his works also remained in the news. In another article in the *Daily Clarion*, queer Canadian Spanish Civil War correspondent Jean "Jim" Watts reported on the antifascist writer María Teresa León (Rafael Alberti's wife) producing a play by Lorca in Madrid: "Woman First Time Producer of Play: Work of Late García Lorca, Murdered by Fascists" (20 Oct. 1937, 4). Watts suggests one element of Lorca's legacy: the continued life of his writings, now staged in a trailblazing, woman-led production. Watts's article signals to a leftist Canadian audience that

Lorca's words live on, highlighting both art's importance in wartime and women's leadership roles in Spain.

Around the same time, the *Volunteer for Liberty*, the official newspaper of the English-speaking International Brigades volunteers, published an anonymous account of Lorca's murder by an eyewitness, a soldier who had recently escaped from the fascist side to support the Republicans in Granada. The *Volunteer for Liberty* was published in Madrid and Barcelona but distributed in Europe and the United States. In the anonymous article "Death of a Spanish Poet," the soldier recounts how one night Lorca was pulled from his cell by a mob (which included the soldier himself), and driven to a place outside Granada. Alone, Lorca was marched along the road until he turned to address his captors:

> García Lorca spoke. He did not speak feebly, nor did he plead for his life. His powerful words were in defense of the thing he always loved: Liberty. He eulogized the cause of the people, and condemned the barbarity of fascism. (3)

This witness further recounts how Lorca was then assaulted, with bullets and rifle butts, until he could only look silently at his attackers. Finally, their leader, Lieutenant Medina, discharged the final bullets that ended Lorca's life. In this account, Lorca is the victim of a mob of men, a lone antifascist voice against an armed horde. As this belated testimony demonstrates, recounting Lorca's death was an ongoing project that kept the poet's name in regular circulation. Published for a transnational anglophone audience, this article highlights the bravery of Lorca's words – written as well as spoken – and the brutality of the fascists.

True Stories about Lorca

In the context of this leftist Canadian awareness of Lorca's murder, another concurrent publication becomes significant for what it describes, and for what it implies. More than a year after the news of Lorca's murder broke in Canada, in October 1937, "Federico: A True Story" was published in the prominent Canadian leftist monthly *New Frontier*. That story is only obliquely about Lorca, queerness, or Canada. Caren Irr categorizes it as reportage (263n40), but it seems to have mostly escaped scholarly analysis. Its titular claim to truth, "A True Story," might have suggested to some readers that the story would describe the recent murder of Federico García Lorca – surely the most famous Federico known to Canadians. Instead, the narrator describes the first days of another young Federico's enlistment in the Spanish

Civil War, his growing attachment to a fellow soldier named Juan, and his battlefield heroics.

At first, Federico and his fellow troops are unarmed and untrained. After a few days of training, he becomes emboldened and skilled, using rifle practice to drown out the "parrot-cries" of his homesickness (9). Once under a hail of bullets, Federico is, for the first time, described as having friends, as he and his "chosen comrade" Juan flee the bullets only to be captured (9). Juan is shot and killed, but Federico manages to escape before returning to the site of Juan's murder to throw grenades into enemy land, sustaining his own wounds in the process. The story concludes with his return home to convalesce, where he demands that his mother bring him stones that he can throw as practice, in anticipation of further battlefield heroism. Federico's time at the front has made him a man, now able to order his mother around, and excited to rejoin the comrades he "admire[s], revere[s], love[s]" (10). His early, homesick isolation was childish, whereas his strong loyalty to Juan and his other comrades is a part of his maturation.

"Federico: A True Story" is, on the surface, a traditional, even uninteresting narrative of wartime masculinist culture, in which a young man comes of age thanks to violence and death. This Federico's story is markedly different from that of Federico García Lorca, who never saw frontline combat. However, the story's significance to a Canadian audience's understanding of the Spanish Civil War and queerness extends beyond a shared – and certainly common – Spanish first name. "Federico: A True Story" was written by British author Valentine Ackland, recently returned from Spain with her partner, fellow British author Sylvia Townsend Warner. Warner published an article in the same edition of *New Frontier*, in which she discussed the International Association of Writers in Defence of Culture Congress held in Madrid in July 1937 and detailed the Spanish Republic's ongoing efforts to end illiteracy in Spain ("What the Soldier Said" 12–13).[14] The journal's editorial mentions that Ackland and Warner had recently travelled to Spain together (Warner references being part of a British delegation), although the nature of their relationship is unacknowledged – they had been a couple for seven years (and would remain together for nearly four decades). The two women's presence in the pages of *New Frontier*, and the Ackland story's homonymic suggestion of another queer, foreign writer, alludes to the Spanish struggle's inextricable cosmopolitan queerness. Even if the story is not actually about Lorca, its titular character ensures the continued remembrance of the poet. The implicit queerness of the story, its context, and its authorship reflect a similar strategy of allusion, omission, and subtext examined in other chapters with regard to other racialized, gendered, and politicized situations. When understood in relation to Lorca's place in the emerging canon of global and Canadian cosmopolitan literature, what first appears to be a simple war story in fact demonstrates a complex triangulation of gender and sexual identity, nationality, and politics.

These narratives of two different Federicos – in the *Volunteer for Liberty*, as well as in the Canadian leftist press – merge in another "true story" that appeared in the pages of another Canadian leftist periodical. In "Death of a Spanish Poet: A True Story," which ran in the *Daily Clarion*, Lloyd Mallan narrates Lorca's final moments, imagining the poet's thoughts as the Guardia Civil takes him to be shot. Mallan was the English translator of many Spanish poets, including Lorca and Rafael Alberti. Mallan's narrative bears many similarities to an unattributed 4 October 1937 article of the same name in the *Volunteer for Liberty*, but provides far more detail. Mallan's account describes how, before he was shot, Lorca turned to face his captors to make a final speech, "the last defiant gesture of a great defiant poet:"

> His voice was strong and firm as he said, "For a thousand years the Spanish people lived as slaves and now that they have their freedom you try to take it away from them ... I am a Spaniard ... and proud of Spain. We have the most beautiful women and the best wines; we have a great tradition of culture: El Greco, Goya, Cervantes. Goya was a revolutionist and hated war! ... to die, a Spaniard, by a Spaniard's hand. Ugh! ... You are not my people; you are murderers! ... Beasts! Barbarians!" (6)

Lorca's speech renders his captors motionless, unable to shoot him until this final outburst, when their lieutenant shouts "Collon" and "Hijo de puta," shooting Lorca as the poet runs, striking him in the head to kill him, and then shooting his corpse (6). Lorca is left unburied "as a warning to others" (6), including the many police bystanders. Mallan's story concludes, "Oh city of the gypsies! Who will see you and not remember?" (6).

Mallan foregrounds Lorca's own poetry, locating his oeuvre within the national canon that includes El Greco, Goya, and Cervantes. Here, Lorca remembers snippets of his poems as he nears his death: "Pass if you wish to pass," "Pasan si quieren pasar," "Green that I love green" (6). These poems are remembered primarily in English translation but are explicitly connected to the cultural production of Spain. Yet the only terms that actually appear in Spanish and Catalan are the gendered insults "collon" and "hijo de puta." Even as Mallan repudiates the fascists' claims to Spanish nationality – "You are not my people" – these "Beasts! Barbarians!" and their epithets stand in for the language of El

Greco, Goya, Cervantes, and Lorca. Mallan – a translator by profession – interprets their culture for a Canadian audience, providing a shorthand for five centuries of Spanish art and framing Lorca as its last, lost scion.

Mallan's concluding question – "Who will see you and not remember?" – not only echoes Lorca's own poetry but also raises further questions about what is being seen and remembered. In the story's Spanish setting, Lorca's unburied body becomes a warning; its eventual burial in an unmarked mass grave was intended to erase his memory. For most Canadians, Granada, "the city of the gypsies," was unimaginably far away. In Lorca's own refrain in "Romance de la Guardia Civil Española" (Ballad of the Spanish Civil Guard), the poem asks "Oh city of the gypsies! / Who could see you and not remember you?" (*Collected Poems* 562–9, ll. 21–2, 61–2, 121–2). In his translation of these lines, Mallan's alternative translation, "Who could see you and not remember?" (from "¿Quién te vio y no te recuerda?"), broadens the question's scope, asking if anyone is capable of forgetting the fact, the site, or the conditions of Lorca's death.

Queerness in Canada and Spain

While Lorca's murder may have drawn many North Americans' attention to the Spanish Civil War, those who volunteered in Spain moved from one often intolerant environment to another: neither Canada nor Spain, neither the Communist Party of Canada nor the International Brigades, were accepting of homosexuality. In Canada, as in most of the world, homosexuality and "homosexual acts" remained criminalized during the 1930s. Throughout the 1950s and 1960s, the Canadian government and the RCMP targeted queer citizens, particularly public servants, through surveillance and job dismissals based on the American McCarthyists' belief that queerness and leftism were always coexistent (Kinsman 70–1). It was not until the British Wolfenden Report in 1957, and then community reactions to the indefinite prison term given to George Everett Klippert after his 1965 arrest for "gross indecency," that Canadian criminal law started to move toward reform.[15]

Homophobia was not unique to the mainstream, or to the right. Far-left politics also reinforced a homophobic distrust of queer people. Nancy Butler's research sheds light on the heteronormative, gender-normative policies of the Communist Party of Canada (CPC). As she notes, groundbreaking journalist Jean "Jim" Watts's absence from most histories and memoirs of the CPC is likely due to the stigmatization of Watts's sexuality (along with her bourgeois roots) (384–5). Butler characterizes the CPC as "actively homophobic. It persistently portrayed itself and communism as the healthy opposite of homosexual reactionary decadence"

(439).[16] In Spain, volunteers encountered a country with uneven attitudes toward homosexuality: the Second Spanish Republic had, among other reforms, decriminalized homosexual sex in 1932. The eventual fascist triumph returned homophobic laws to Spain, yet even during the war, the International Brigades likewise enacted homophobic practices.

Discrimination and prejudice against queer people is more fully understood intersectionally, as a reciprocal component of patriarchal and capitalist exploitation of racial, ethnic, and religious minorities, women and gender-nonconforming people, those with disabilities, and other groups whose values and needs threaten the hegemonic order. As I mentioned in the introduction to this chapter, the years leading up to the Spanish Civil War were marked by a collapsing distinction between homophobia and antisemitism (and the conflation of queerness, Jewishness, effeminacy, and racial otherness).[17] This conflation serves as a reminder of the overlapping identity categories at play in the writings that Lorca's death inspired. For Canadian authors, Lorca was not simply a queer writer (and it's worth remembering that he may not necessarily have been acknowledged as a queer writer by all of them): he was also a foreign Other; a Hispanophone cosmopolite; a devout Catholic; and an advocate of *gitano*, Jewish, and Black cultures and women's rights. And given Spain's proximity to the African continent and the perception that it was a cultural backwater, he may well have been perceived as an ethnic or racial other too.

But the collapsing distinctions between homophobia and antisemitism were no recent innovation in discrimination. As Daniel Boyarin, Daniel Itzkovitz, and Ann Pellegrini contend in their introduction to *Queer Theory and the Jewish Question*, "modern Jewish and homosexual identities emerged as traces of each other" (1).[18] The authors point to the stereotype of the effeminate Jewish man – and his counterpart, the Zionist ideal of the muscular, even bellicose Jewish man – as one manifestation of the intersection of gender, sexuality, and religion.[19] Warren Hoffman similarly describes the ways that Jews in the United States had to pass along sexual lines, in addition to racial and ethnic ones (see chapter 1).

Syncretism is likewise written into queer Canadian literary studies. Janice Stewart notes in the introduction to the "Queerly Canadian" special issue of *Canadian Literature* that critics who reflect on Canadian queer writings proceed from a perspective that disrupts easy identification of what it means to be Canadian or queer. She concludes the introduction by highlighting how the special issue underscores

> an important relationship between the potential for democratization in cosmopolitanism to the extent that the very acts of national identification

> are themselves complicated by hybridity and singularity ... this project of complexification is precisely the useful work that is done at the conjunction that we have here demarcated as Queerly Canadian. ("Queerly Canadian")

The earliest treatments of Lorca's life, work, and death in Canadian reportage and fiction anticipate a decades-long fascination with the ways in which his work enables the politicized process of queering both national and religious identities. We likewise see a project of complexification in the many invocations of Lorca that raise questions not only around gender and sexuality but also around national identity, ethnicity, and race. Looking to Lorca – and to a queer reading of responses to his murder – complicates the connections between Jewish Canadians and their diasporic histories. Jewish writers invested in the Spanish cause may claim a connection to Canada *and* to the Europe that they (or their ancestors) fled. These connections are also differently valenced in different regions, as sexuality and gender interact with Québécois and Spanish Catholicism and anglophone Canadian Protestantism. In writing about and fighting for Spain – an originary location of Jewish expulsion – and about Lorca – a queer, cosmopolitan potential member of the tribe – authors likewise complicate concepts of homeland and diaspora.

"Who will see you and not remember?": Early Canadian Poems for Lorca

In the years following the Spanish Civil War, many Canadian poets elegized Lorca, taking part in an international, multilingual tradition. Writing of American Lorca elegies, Cary Nelson highlights certain "continuities" within this poetic chorus, including that "poets address him [Lorca] directly by his first name and [make] affectionate, plaintive, and often rather childlike calls to him" (*Revolutionary Memory* 229). Nelson sees in their continuing attention to Lorca's death a need to elegize the man or to remember Lorca as "a touchstone for everything poetry aimed to achieve, a touchstone as well for all the forces poetry sought to resist" (*Revolutionary Memory* 233). When describing Canadian elegies to Lorca, Nicola Vulpe considers them alongside those to the blood transfusion doctor Norman Bethune. For Vulpe, these groups of poems forge ongoing connections between Canada and the Spanish cause ("This Issue" 56). Together, Vulpe's and Nelson's nationally driven perspectives on elegies to Lorca suggest a helpful framework for thinking about Lorca's aesthetic and ideological significance for North American poets. In elegizing an innovative poet and participating in a transnational literary community of remembrance, many writers were also queering this transnational literary community – through poetic and fictional engagement alike.[20]

Vulpe and Maha Albari's poetry anthology *Sealed in Struggle* groups six early Canadian Lorca elegies by Dorothy Livesay, Louis Dudek, Eldon Grier, George Woodcock, and Patrick Anderson, as well as the contemporary writer Mark Frutkin.[21] These 1940s poems fulfil and expand the tropes of American elegies that Nelson identifies, while gesturing in a variety of ways to Lorca's uniqueness – a uniqueness that, as the poems all emphasize, made him simultaneously an icon and a target. What's more, these poems emphasize a cosmopolitan, often queer vision of the world. While none of these early poets, to my knowledge, identified as Jewish, their poems underscore the experiences of marginalized minorities amid the post–Spanish Civil War, mid–Second World War moment.

The British Canadian anarchist writer and editor George Woodcock, in his "Poem for García Lorca" (in *The Centre Cannot Hold,* 1943), provides a series of directives, commanding that the reader remember Lorca "as Spain's noblest bull," "as the earth of Spain," and "as the poor of Spain" (14). In associating Lorca with a powerful, masculine symbol of Spain, with its land, and with its impoverished, oppressed citizens, Woodcock emphasizes the poet's deep and diverse connections to the country – its iconography, land, and folk inheritance. And so, in the poem's final line, when the speaker commands, "Remember Lorca, who died only for being Lorca," Woodcock asserts the poet's embodiment of Spanish traditions and culture, of Spain's geography, and of the populations the Spanish Republic sought to protect (14). The fascists' murder of Lorca represents the murder of Spain's culture, its land, and its people. Woodcock's use of the term "only" has an ironic double edge: on the one hand, it signifies the poet's singularity and originality; on the other, it gestures toward the diverse and inclusive Whitmanian self that the poem constructs: Lorca contains multitudes. That the writer was killed "only for being Lorca" might suggest any of the individual motivations to which historians have attributed his death – his politics, his cultural clout, his queerness – or all of these motivations collectively. The poem simultaneously claims Spain's national iconography and critiques Spanish nationalism by yoking Lorca to Spain as loyalists and fascists imagine it (and as both Canadian and British people might too – for Woodcock was living in England when he wrote this).

British Canadian writer and editor Patrick Anderson uses the symbol of the bull in order to place Lorca within a contested national tradition. In "For a Spanish Comrade," he depicts the last moments of an unnamed torero as he fights a bull, observed by Franco and his archbishops. The torero participates in a double fight – against the bull, but also against the gaze of the fascist leader and Catholic clergy. He is at once hunted and mourned by them, his death a foregone conclusion:

He was already dying
of the occupational disease
of his courage.

He was already racked
with the red sickness
of his pride. (10)

In the matador's performance of masculinity – the very act of bravery and resistance depicted in the poem – courage and fate join together. His "red sickness" is both communism and ritual bloodlust. Anderson's implicit comparison of the poet to a bullfighter recalls the queer Jewish American poet Edouard Roditi's "Lament," in which Lorca "nightly teased / The bulls of death" (138).

Anderson's poem is also unique for its emphasis on this bullfighter's physicality: his "athlete's body," "his thigh and his armpits," "the blood in his mouth," "his flesh," "his neck" (10–11). Yet this "athlete's body" is also softened by its juxtaposition with the "petals" of his bullfighter's cape and by his proximity to the "tomb / like a pale flower / of Andalusia" (10) – the embattled torero is no less masculine for his closeness to these typically feminine images, yet this juxtaposition seems subversive. The image of the "pale flower" resonates in Eldon Grier's later poem "In Memory of García Lorca," which refers to the poet and his words as "a flower in the lapel / of perpetual mourning" (11) – but here the flower is an image of aestheticism, decadence, and cosmopolitanism, all anathema to fascism, all inextricable from Lorca's artistry. Yet Grier's speaker's tone departs from more sympathetic addresses to the poet, asking, instead, why Lorca didn't anticipate his own murder. In contrast, Anderson's poem adopts Lorca's own language and imagery, an implicitly sympathetic gesture: the poem reflects its epigraph from Lorca's "The Goring and the Death" (La cogida y la muerte) with its explicit, visceral depiction of a bullfighter's final match. It also includes many untranslated Spanish words, mostly in reference to the bullfight – *veronica, torero, estocade,* and *pic.* However, his inclusion of the term "mariposa" (butterfly) references not only a symbol of freedom, beauty, and transformation, but also a Spanish homophobic slur.[22] At the conclusion of Anderson's multilingual depiction is a final imperative: to share this narrative of Lorca's assassination "in Glasgow / in the mountains of Shensi" (180). These concluding lines are an explicit statement of Lorca's global relevance, and they also imagine a world – from Canada to Scotland to China – in which Lorca's native tongue and culture will resonate, a cosmopolitan vision of polyglot poetry and politics.

As with Valentine Ackland's earlier "True Story" of Federico, Anderson's background and history in publishing lend a deeper significance to the elegy's queer subtext. Anderson was the editor of the influential Montreal little magazine *Preview*, where the poem "For a Spanish Comrade" first appeared (Dec. 1943, 9–11). Many other poems explicitly and repeatedly invoke Lorca; by contrast, Anderson's allusive reference appears only in an epigraph, "… *a las cinque* [*sic*] *de la tarde* / Lorca" (9; italics in the original). Anderson's poem otherwise avoids explicit references to the queer poet. Such a strategy makes practical sense, given the stakes of aligning oneself with Lorca's queer cosmopolitanism. When the poem was first published, Anderson had recently been outed in the pages of rival Montreal little magazine *First Statement* by editor John Sutherland in an article criticizing Anderson's poetry as effeminate and homoerotic ("The Writing of Patrick Anderson"). Threatening to sue, Anderson elicited a front-page retraction from Sutherland in the following issue. *First Statement* and *Preview* were both foundational to the growth of Canadian modernism and were allied with American and British modernism, respectively. As a part of these national divisions, *First Statement* writers often cast their rival publication as colonial and effeminate, aligning their own little magazine with masculine Americanness. At the time of the accusation, Anderson was married to a woman, although he would later come out as gay.[23] In this context, we might see Anderson representing himself alongside his "comrade" Lorca under the sign of the Spanish matador, engaged in a dangerous and ironic double performance of masculinity, fighting the bull under the watchful gaze of patriarchal and homophobic hegemony.[24]

Like Anderson, Dorothy Livesay in "Lorca" emphasizes the physicality, eroticism, and transnationalism of Lorca's poetry. And, like Anderson, Livesay was not openly queer until later in life.[25] While I discussed her depictions of the Spanish Civil War more broadly in the previous chapter, here I focus on the poem "Lorca," which first appeared in her poetry collection *Day and Night* (1944). This poem, like so many poems elegizing Lorca, speaks directly to the poet, with italicized, rhyming interjections throughout the stanzas that specifically describe Lorca's singular gifts. Together, these interjections read:

While you –
You hold the light
Unbroken
…
You make the flight

Unbroken
...
You hold the word
Unspoken
...
Light flight and word
The unassailed, the token! (*Day and Night* 22–4; italics in the original)

These interjections are woven into the longer poem, which meditates first on the impact of Lorca's murder as the speaker describes their bed "shrink[ing] / To single size" (22) as "we descend now down from heaven / Into earth's mold, down" (22). This gloomy night contrasts with Lorca's capacity to "*hold the light,*" a light that emanates in the poem from his very body: "When you lived / Day shone from your face," she writes (22). The speaker then describes a series of images of what could be, if Lorca were alive: the trees, the waves, and the birds would communicate with the speaker of the poem. In a moment of reverie, the poem uses couplets to imagine Lorca's resurrection and the renewal of romantic love: "In secret thicket mold / Lovers defend their hold, / Old couples hearing whisperings / Touch in a handclasp, quivering" (23). Simply by living, Lorca invigorates love and attraction among the young and the old – beds unshrunk from single size. In the poem's reversal – moving from the conditions after Lorca's death to an imagining (or a remembrance) of his life, Livesay concludes on an especially poignant note, as Lorca sings, dances, breathes, and enlivens the world.

Even in his death, Lorca would continue to animate Canadian cultural production. In her essay "Canadian Poetry and the Spanish Civil War" (1976), Livesay delineates the conflict's foundational impact on Canadian culture and letters. She highlights Lorca's influence, noting that "young activists today are putting on his plays and singing his songs" (255). In the "Spain 1936–1939" section of her memoir *Right Hand Left Hand* (1977) she includes the essay alongside her Spain poems. Reframed in this way, her poem "Lorca" is recontextualized as one of many elegies to Spain – the poet's death becomes an emblem of his country's descent into fascism.

The version of "Lorca" included in this memoir has some minor changes: notably, the epigraph changes from "For Federico Garcia Lorca, Spanish poet, shot by Franco's men" (22) in *Day and Night* to the less certain "for Federico Garcia Lorca, Spanish poet, shot, it was said, by Franco's men" (259) in *Right Hand Left Hand.* The motivation for this historical hedging is unclear, but its effect is to emphasize the ongoing mystery surrounding Lorca's murder. This mystery is compounded by the inclusion, in the midst of the poem, of the *New Frontier* image of a crucified soldier. Livesay suggests in "Canadian Poetry and the Spanish

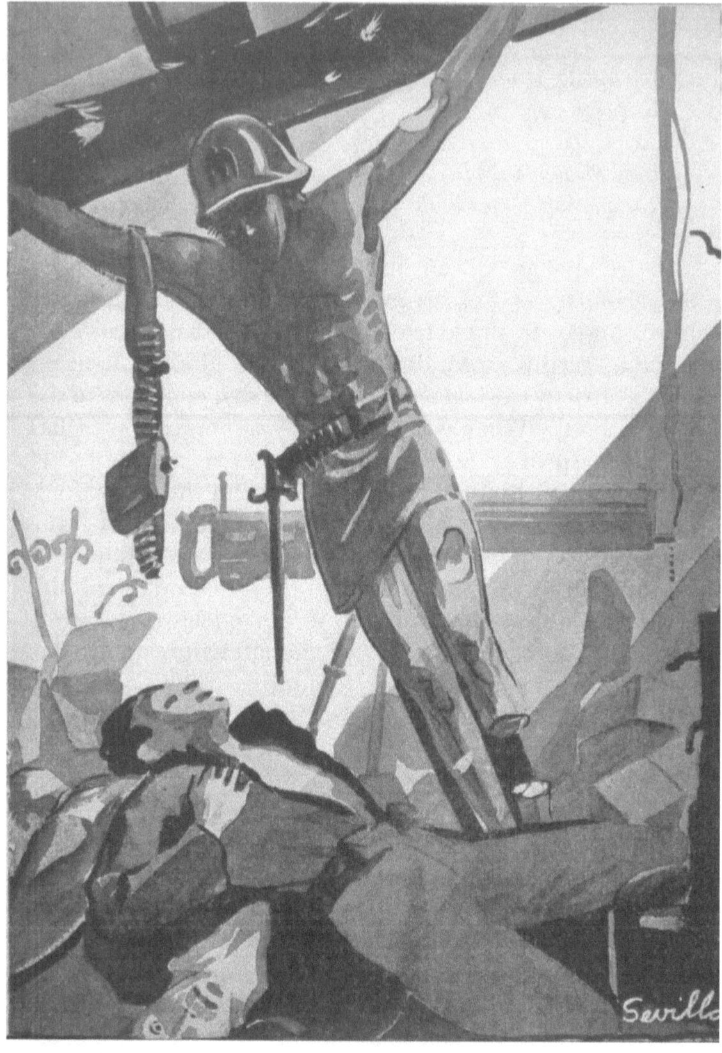

Untitled drawing of a crucified soldier by Henri Sevilla, *New Frontier*, vol. 1, no. 8 (Dec. 1936), p. 17.

Civil War" that one dominant theme of the Canadian responses is what she terms the insurgents' "betrayal of Christianity" (252). Given this religious preoccupation in the poetry, the accompanying image suggests Spain's sacrifice of Lorca. The image is clearly not intended to depict Lorca, who never fought, yet it underscores the martyrdom of an innocent poet.

Moreover, Livesay identifies two additional themes running through the Canadian poetic responses to the Spanish Civil War: the unequivocal critique of non-intervention, and the alignment of the conflict with the destruction of human progress ("Canadian Poetry" 254). These themes are evident in Canadian responses to Lorca's murder, especially, as depictions of his aesthetic promise coincide with harsh words to the world's bystanders. Eldon Grier laments Lorca's unnoticed death: "Granada let you die / like any freak" (11); while Montreal writer Louis Dudek's "García Lorca" speaks not to Lorca but to bystanders around the world. Dudek's poem first appeared in *First Statement* in 1944. It begins with this uncited historical note: "In 1936, in the outskirts of his own beloved Granada at dawn, a fascist firing squad composed of Civil Guardsmen took the young poet out and shot him" (10) (this historical note was excised when the poem was reprinted in Dudek's collection *East of the City*). Dudek's poem imagines Lorca as a flower, a child, and his work as "a friendly comedy / of loving creatures, all of flowers and happy people" (11). Amid this simplistic characterization of Lorca's plays, the speaker's accusations of the world's inaction are harsh. Lorca's murderers were "an ignorant audience" but not so different from the individualistic members of the left and the right (11). In reflecting on Lorca's murder, the poem concludes by accusing the world of collusion by inaction: "The news is a prophecy / no one heard: / a child has been taken from bed / and broken in our hands" (12). This concluding line attaches the reader to a broader, global guilt, not only for non-intervention but also for the tragedies the Spanish Civil War portended – the Second World War and the Holocaust.

Beyond the War Years: Lorca in Canadian Fiction

Lorca and his works continue to hold an important place in the Canadian cultural imaginary, whether fictionalized, elegized, sung, or performed.[26] In texts spanning the mid-century to the present, authors utilize many earlier approaches and innovate new ones. Lorca's poems continue to be translated and rewritten, his life and death narrated and reimagined; he becomes a character and an interlocutor. Fiction by Mordecai Richler and Elizabeth Ruth and poetry by Joshua Auerbach,

George Elliott Clarke, Leonard Cohen, Brian Dedora, Mark Frutkin, Susan Holbrook, Maureen Hynes, John MacKenzie, Jim Nason, Jim Smith, Steven Ross Smith, Nicola Vulpe, and J.A. Wainwright foreground Lorca's literary innovation, as earlier texts do, while emphasizing both his queerness and his ongoing global impact. In these poems and novels, many written by LGBTQ authors, I trace a continued investment in writing outsiderness into Spain and the world; as Patrick Anderson suggested earlier, Lorca remains relevant around the world, "in Glasgow / in the mountains of Shensi" (180).

Lorca's poetry plays a subtle yet important role in Jewish Montreal author Mordecai Richler's mid-century novel *The Acrobats* (1954) by signalling the queer subaltern genealogy that Lorca has come to symbolize. The novel is set in a barren, fascist mid-century Valencia, where American tourists take advantage of the weakened peseta. I discussed the novel's main plot in chapter 1; here, I want to focus on the subplot of an American International Brigades veteran's experience returning to Spain. Derek is haunted by memories of the homophobia he experienced while fighting to protect the country he volunteered to serve. He subsequently gained some fame for pseudonymously publishing a book about the Spanish Civil War, but physically returning to the country proves traumatic. In Spain, Derek is one of many characters pretending to be someone he is not. Derek's brother-in-law is a Jew trying to pass as a gentile; Kraus is a German Nazi hiding in Spain. Through Kraus, Richler connects Jewishness and queerness via the conjoined antisemitism and homophobia of Kraus's reflections on Spanish men: "He disliked Spain. The men were effeminate, Semitic, and they made poor soldiers. Even when they killed it was always from a passion, never with a sense of order" (56).

Derek's flashbacks to the war are overwritten with Lorquian imagery. He imagines a Spanish soldier – not a poet – killed by "three quick shots in the buttocks": Lorca's reported cause of death (4). Derek may have achieved professional success through his writings about Spain, but his physical labour on the battlefield was always overshadowed by fear. Richler further emphasizes Lorca's ghostly presence by presenting this excerpt from Lorca's poem "Balada de la placeta" (Ballad of the Little Square, 1919) as the epigraph to the novel's third book:

> What is it you feel
> In your red, thirsty mouth?
> The taste of the bones
> Of my big skull. (107)[27]

The threat of homophobic violence – an erotic moment leading to the taste of a skull – and the shadow of Lorca's homophobic murder both loom. In the following pages Richler depicts the particular dangers of Derek's stint in the International Brigades:

> [T]he gorgeous boy from Memphis languishing on the army cot next to him, himself gone weeks without sleep and bursting from denial, leaning over, tenderly, gently, kissing those young lips. Then the betrayal, the beating rendered by the boy that was the very stuff of their love, the shame and humiliation. (129)

Even the memory of a pleasant evening clandestinely holding hands with another soldier in the Puerta del Sol movie theatre concludes with the other soldier's leg shot off (130). In Richler's depiction, queer love is always punished, whether by homophobic violence or by the vicissitudes of warfare.

Furthermore, Derek's political beliefs must always remain separate from his personal life: he finally realizes that "those days at the front constituted the only moment of truth he had known (not the ideas or the lies or the speeches or the poems or the machines, but the men all together and angry and beautiful)" (133). Yet this realization of ideological clarity remains tempered by the secrecy and potential violence around the disclosure of his own identity. In other words, Derek comes to see his time fighting fascism as the most authentic time in his life, yet he was simultaneously living in the closet. His fellow soldiers may have been "all together," but he was still isolated amid their unity. The Spanish closet haunts Derek right up to the novel's conclusion, when the narrator reveals that Derek's Spanish boyfriend is not gay, but is using Derek to immigrate to the United States. While Derek is a sympathetic character, Richler indicts his romanticization of Spain – its cause, and then one of its people – in an ongoing unrequited love affair.

Writing sixty years later, lesbian Toronto author Elizabeth Ruth's novel *Matadora* (2013) is also haunted by Lorca as it returns repeatedly to connections between individual rights and aesthetic creativity. Ruth's immediate focus is not on the war itself: *Matadora* is set in the years leading up to the war, years of growing unrest over class and gender divisions. While I will be discussing the novel more extensively in the conclusion, it's worth noting here how often characters' discussions of artistic freedom invoke Federico García Lorca. Just as Richler's character Derek thinks about his own experiences in Spain in terms of Lorca's murder, so too do Ruth's characters understand their personal freedoms in tandem with Lorca's lived experience of difference and outsiderness. In one early scene, at an artists' salon, characters reminisce about Lorca's past performances, hoping he will join their group once he returns from Cuba. One character – later revealed to be gay – uses homophobic language to refer sarcastically to the "most famous faggot in all of Spain" (17). Later, when the main character loses her father to fascist violence, the family learns – nearly simultaneously – of Lorca's death. Her brother experiences the loss of the poet as an even harsher blow than the loss of his father: "All at once, the melancholy that had lived in Lorca's poems fell like tears upon him. He began to sob. With each Fascist victory from then on, he would struggle to hold onto poetry as if it was a fickle lover who couldn't commit" (221). For this character, an aspiring poet, the war chips away at his family and at his identity – Lorca's death, much more than his father's, politicizes him. Yet their other brother, now more firmly ensconced in his fascism, uses Lorca's death as a threat and a warning: "remember what happened to that big mouth, faggot, Lorca. They shot him twice up the ass" (247). For both Ruth and Richler, Lorca's words and life are inextricable – he is a figure both aspirational and cautionary.

Lorca in Canadian Poetry

Lorca's importance to Canadian literature is apparent primarily in verse. Jewish Montreal writer Leonard Cohen is perhaps the best-known Canadian to pay tribute to Lorca. Cohen widely acknowledged his creative debt to Lorca's poetry, even, famously, naming his daughter after the poet.[28] As recently as 2006, Cohen's collection of poems, *Book of Longing*, clearly draws inspiration from Lorca's life and art. Cohen's poem "Lorca Lives" imagines an elderly Lorca eschewing music and Andalusian culture to grudgingly live out his days in New York City: "He heard that he was shot and killed / He never was, you know / He lives in New York City / He doesn't like it though" (90). This imagined Lorca is a curmudgeon, his disappointment with the United States and queer culture (expressed in *Poeta en Nueva York*) coalesced and amplified in his old age. *Book of Longing* also includes Cohen's translation of Lorca's poem "La casada infiel" ("The Faithless Wife," in Cohen's translation, but also translated as "The Unfaithful Housewife").[29] "La casada infiel," originally published in Lorca's *Gypsy Ballads*, details the willing seduction of a married mother by a "Gypsy." Cohen's translation was set to music by Philip Glass and titled "The Night of Santiago" in the *Book of Longing* cycle (2007).

Cohen's "The Faithless Wife" retains the eroticism of the original poem, although it changes the poem's form from free verse into quatrains and simplifies the imagery and language. This translation contrasts with Cohen's earlier, better-known adaptation of another of Lorca's erotic poems. It is Cohen's song "Take This Waltz" (1986), in which the musician-poet translates "Pequeño vals vienés" (Little Viennese Waltz), transforming a Spanish poem about a Viennese romance into a Canadian waltz.[30] Cohen first recorded the song in Paris for a compilation album in tribute to Lorca's *Poeta en Nueva York* – Lorca's poetry collection composed while visiting the city in 1929–30, published posthumously in 1940.[31] Cohen's song appeared on the album *Poets in New York* (1986) alongside tributes by Spanish, Italian, Brazilian, Israeli, French, Greek, Scottish, and German musicians. He joined in a celebration of the poet's work in Granada that same year, and filmed a music video for the song in the house where Lorca was born. This multilingual, transnational record was released in memory of the fiftieth anniversary of Lorca's murder.[32] Cohen also included "Take This Waltz" (with additional female vocals) on his subsequent album *I'm Your Man* (1988).

Before he made "Take This Waltz," Cohen's music was known across Spain: during the last days of Franco's rule, in 1974, Cohen performed in Madrid and Barcelona (Alberto Manzano notes that at the end of the performance, Cohen dedicated it to Lorca, *Leonard Cohen* 202). Lorca and Cohen's words were subsequently taken up by Spanish flamenco musician Enrique Morente in his innovative flamenco fusion album *Omega* (1996).[33] Most recently, in 2011, when Cohen was awarded Spain's Prince of Asturias Award for Literature he credited Lorca's writings with helping him "to find a voice, to locate a voice; that is, to locate a self, a self that is not fixed, a self that struggles for its own existence" ("Acceptance Address" 267). Cohen's acknowledgment of Lorca's influence here alludes to a much more extensive engagement: at fifteen, Cohen first encountered Lorca through his *Selected Poems*, and began learning guitar from a Spanish immigrant to Montreal. A year later, in 1950, Cohen would first hear the Spanish Civil War protest song "Vive la Quince Brigada" alongside the other transnational protest songs included in *The People's Songbook*. According to Cohen's biographer Ira B. Nadel, "all demonstrated to Cohen that songs could be about protest, freedom, and resistance. Cohen's 'The Old Revolution,' 'The Partisan,' and 'The Traitor' all reflect what he learned from *The People's Songbook*. From that songbook, he said, he 'developed a curious notion that the Nazis were overthrown by music'" (26). Cohen's later trip to Cuba, too, was motivated by Lorca's time there as well as by a related, short-lived hope: "I thought maybe this was my Spanish civil war" (qtd in Nadel 91).

Cohen's loose translation of "Pequeño vals vienés" riffs on Lorca's imagery, and particularly the sexual language of the poem.[34] Of the original, Christopher Maurer observes that Lorca uses "the lightest, most playful cadences imaginable" to express his "darkest, most secret yearning," calling it "the most explicitly homoerotic [poem] Lorca had yet written" (Introduction xxvii). Cohen's translation maintains the explicit sexuality yet shifts the gendered language of the poem so that it is about heterosexual romance; at the same time, he utilizes the male and female singing voices to dramatize the tension.[35] Where Lorca's poem begins, "In Vienna there are ten little girls" ("muchachas"; "Little Viennese Waltz" 164–5), Cohen sings, "Now in Vienna there's ten pretty women." In a parallel move, Lorca's description, "There is a death for piano / that paints the little boys blue" ("Little Viennese Waltz" 165) becomes Cohen's "bar where the boys have stopped talking / They've been sentenced to death by the blues." The "boys" of Cohen's lyrics are boys in the colloquial sense – young men – rather than the children of Lorca's verse. In Cohen's lyrics, these "boys" become possible suitors for the "ten pretty women."

Besides aging the characters in the poem, Cohen further translates Lorca's ambiguous use of the Spanish verb *querer* to mean "to want," rather than the equally plausible translation "to love." In this way, Cohen's song becomes about sexual desire, as he sings "I want you, I want you, I want you, / On a chair with a dead magazine ... In some hallway where love's never been / On our bed ..." In contrast, Lorca's lines might read either "I love you" or "I want you" (often translated as the former), "with the armchair and the book of death, / down the melancholy hallway, / in the iris's darkened garret" ("Little Viennese Waltz" 165). Lorca places this love and desire "in the attic where the children play" ("Little Viennese Waltz" 167). Cohen's version is again more explicit, revealing "an attic where children are playing / Where I've got to lie down with you soon" – an ambiguous use of the verb "to lie down" that suggests a corruption of youth already written into his revision of girls and boys into adults. Both poem and song conclude with physical intimacy – Lorca's "I will leave my mouth between your legs" ("Little Viennese Waltz" 167) and Cohen's "my mouth on the dew of your thighs."

Cohen's song is significant not only for its success in bringing Lorca's words to a wider audience through a musical interpretation, but also for its implicit commentary on the significance of translation. Cohen's translation work does not attempt fealty to the original; rather, it uses the Spanish poem as inspiration. Cohen's images allude to Lorca's words, but the singer recomposes them into a different kind of love story. In its sound, Cohen's song remains true to the conceit of a waltz, bringing a heterosexualizing anglophone lens to Lorca's own translation of a Viennese pairs dance. Yet this translation – even in its looseness and liberties – represents a moment of cultural exchange rather than appropriation.[36]

Richler's and Ruth's fictional tributes and Cohen's remediation of Lorca's work demonstrate how Canadian authors draw on Spanish art, culture, and history to find modes of representation that can account for their own postcolonial, multiethnic, polyglot, and queer ideas of individual expression and national belonging. Lorca symbolizes an aspirational possibility and a cautionary tale. However, Cohen's contribution to the transnational compilation album *Poets in New York* also suggests that this process works in both directions – that is, Canadian writers caught in a cycle of romance and disappointment with the failed Spanish Republic mirror the way in which Spanish artists and audiences use the distancing of transnational adaptations of Lorca's work to understand their own national culture and history. For instance, the album *Poets in New York* includes zero poets from New York; in fact, the only performance recorded *in* New York is sung in Hebrew by the Israeli folk musician David Broza. Moreover, the album was never even released in North America, even though it was given wide distribution across Europe (including at least three vinyl pressings as well as release on cassette and compact disc in Spain), in addition to releases in Brazil, Argentina, and Israel. The only anglophone contributor besides Leonard Cohen is the Scottish folk-pop artist Donovan. Last, the album's title refers to Lorca's international sojourn, and both the book of poems and the album use New York as synecdoche for North America, cosmopolitanism, and multiethnic, multilingual community.

Even as Cohen de-emphasizes the queerness of Lorca's original poem, he does more than simply allude to Lorca. He also uses his anglophone Montreal Jewish persona to stand in for a version of North American heterosexual masculinity, a subtle contextual negotiation between the possibilities and the dangers Lorca represents. Cohen's manipulation of masculine identity (always complicated by his Canadianness, Montrealness, and Jewishness) is a thread that runs throughout his work, and the reappearance of "Take This Waltz" on his 1988 album *I'm Your Man*, with Jennifer Warnes's vocals added, seems a kind of resurrection after his earlier *Death of a Ladies' Man* (1977). Even so, his work, which so carefully treads the fault lines of nationality, religion, and sexuality, has been the key point of connection between Canadian audiences and Lorca as a queer emblem of the Spanish Civil War.

Recent Canadian poetry for Lorca demonstrates a broader conception of the poet's embodiment of the intersection of politics and personal identities with aesthetics. Even generations after Lorca's murder and the Spanish Civil War, poets continue to draw numerous connections between his writings and their contemporary moment. George Elliott Clarke's poetry collection *Lush Dreams, Blue Exile: Fugitive Poems: 1978–1993* locates Lorca's murder within a history of assassinations of artists, activists, and political leaders. Clarke, who is of African American, Indigenous, Nova Scotian Africadian, and Afro-Métis descent, depicts the violence done to Lorca as violence against the poet's writings. In "The Death and Life of Garcia Lorca," Clarke describes how the Guardia Civil "bust open his lines ... spill black ink over his words ... inhume his *corpus*" (19; italics in the original). Clarke uses homonyms to describe the Guardia's actions: they "riddle" the poet, bullets "scor[ing]" his blood" (19). These homonyms are ironic, in that the Guardia's violence effects the opposite of Lorca's artistic creation. Simultaneously, Lorca becomes his words, in this way attaining a kind of artistic immortality through the voices of his audience. The titular reference to Lorca's afterlife is evident in the poem's conclusion: "Seven Civil Guards now rot, unsung. / But his flesh is song in lovers' rouged mouths" (19). Lorca's murderers may be "rot[ting]," but the impact of their actions remains, even in a poem composed decades after Franco's death and Spain's democratization. In this way, "The Death and Life" both aestheticizes Lorca's murder and critiques that same aestheticization, an effect compounded by the inclusion, directly after, of the poem "Guernica," an ekphrasis of Picasso's painting depicting the aftermath of the fascist bombing of the town.

"The Death and Life of Garcia Lorca" is part of a section titled "Gehenna," a biblical reference to a site near Jerusalem where children were sacrificed, thereafter associated with destruction and sin, and even used as a synonym for Hell. Within the collection of poems in this section, Lorca joins John F. Kennedy, Robert F. Kennedy, Martin Luther King, Jr., Malcolm X, Indira Gandhi, Pierre Laporte, and Judas, alongside poems that reference Guernica, the Second World War, the Holocaust, and the Nigerian–Biafran War. Together, the poems read as a dechronologized history of personal, political, and artistic betrayal over the course of which individuals, communities, and even countries are sacrificed. The section "Gehenna" thus enacts the same dechronologized ordering that the title of the Lorca poem also suggests: death followed by life. Clarke's poems begin, rather than conclude, with death and destruction, tracing violence's widespread and ongoing reverberations.

In Clarke's Lorca poem, Lorca's writings continue to stand for love – romantic and sexual love between ungendered lovers. Yet Lorca himself is also a scapegoat for love, and – through the poem's placement alongside elegies to King and the Kennedys, X and Laporte, Gandhi and Guernica, the Biafran nation and European Jewry – a martyr for a kind of decolonial, anti-oppressive beloved community not yet attained.

More recently, in a 2015 poem, Clarke returns to Lorca, but to an earlier phase of his life. In "Garcia Lorca, Harlemite," Clarke imagines Lorca touring Harlem with Langston Hughes. Here, Clarke writes in the first person from Lorca's perspective, foregrounding both Harlem's sensorially overwhelming spaces (speakeasies, pubs, and brothels) and the

Spanish poet's own similarities to his African American host. In Lorca's formula, "Mr. Langston Hughes is the Negro poet, / and a Commie faggot, / as I am the Gypsy poet / and an anti-Fascist faggot ... / Our pens are best bayonets, not scalpels" (357–8; ellipsis in the original). Clarke's Lorca reclaims the homophobic epithet while simultaneously appropriating the title "Gypsy," thus aligning politics, race, and sexuality as equally important identity vectors. The strength of the two poets' words lies in their capacity to violently foment change (bayonets), not to dissect society (scalpels). Clarke's association of Hughes's and Lorca's poetry with tools of war (bayonets) alludes to the war to come and to both poets' roles in it. This allusion to the Spanish Civil War further echoes in the poem's subsequent mentions of censors, both Roosevelts' insincerity, and police officers' violence. The forces that ended Lorca's life – Francoist homophobia and hatred of his writing, the aggressive and emboldened Guardia Civil, and international political inaction – are here translated into an American context to demonstrate the US's dangers for Hughes and for other African Americans.

The poem concludes with Harlem's deterioration as it becomes a sepulchre, "the hustler's Athens" (359). This dispiriting conclusion is at odds with the excitement of Lorca's own poetry about New York – or, at least, the excitement those poems generate for Canadian poets, as I will discuss. I see the poem's concluding gesture as itself foreshadowing Lorca's own end back in his home country, while also resembling the suggestion, in Clarke's previous Lorca poem, of a social change not yet completely realized. Furthermore, "Garcia Lorca, Harlemite" is one part of *Canticles I (MMXVII)*, a multilingual poetry collection incorporating a wide range of historical perspectives – Lorca joins Frederick Douglass and Mao Zedong, among many others. This collection of variously voiced poems, roughly chronologically presented, underscores the multiple perspectives that are vital to understanding a particular historical moment: the need for poets' pens to serve as both bayonets and scalpels. Lorca's ongoing literary influence likewise serves to inspire both: poetry as social commentary and poetry as revolutionary instigation.

As is evident in Clarke's poems, Lorca's life, writing, and symbolism continue to resonate in contemporary texts (my conclusion additionally focuses on post-2000 fictional invocations of the Spanish Civil War). Many poets cite experiences travelling in Spain, particularly to places where Lorca lived and worked, or their own knowledge of Spanish and encounters with different forms of translation, or their own experiences of marginalization, as key influences on their writings about the poet.[37] The intersecting roles of geography, translation, and queerness are foundational to poet Brian Dedora's *Lorcation* (2015). Dedora, who is gay, grew up in the Okanagan, lives in Toronto, and has lived in Granada too, locations invoked and compared in *Lorcation* in an experimental structure of personal narrative and poetry, most of it translated into Spanish by Martín Rodríguez-Gaona.[38] Rodríguez-Gaona's translations hew closely to Dedora's words, even swapping English for Spanish when Dedora includes Spanish phrases in his poems. Included on facing pages to Dedora's poetry, these translations suggest an expansive concept of audience, as Dedora's unique perspective on Lorca's life becomes available to anglophone and Hispanophone readers alike – an echo of the Lorca/location wordplay of Dedora's title (Preface 9).

Location is also key to Dedora's approach to translation – he also translates "Pequeño vals vienés," but unlike in Cohen's revision, Dedora's approach to Lorca's oeuvre and life explicitly locates both author (Dedora) and poet-playwright (Lorca) in the spaces in which they write, read, and are read. Dedora writes in the preface about his travels through Spain as well as his growing understanding of Lorca's personal history and Spain's war, flashing back, too, to his first encounters with Lorca's words. *Lorcation* begins in Madrid, then continues through Granada, returns to Canada, and concludes with an indictment of America's squandered potential as "the place where Lorca put his hope" ("Uno soy yo = I Am One" 95). Throughout, Dedora reiterates Trescastro's boast that Lorca suffered "*two bullets in his ass for being a queer*" ("The Potboiled Simmer" 23; italics in the original), using the refrain "*Give him coffee, / lots of coffee*" ("The Potboiled Simmer" 23, "La Plaza de la Trinidad, Granada" 41; italics in the original) – the code used to authorize Lorca's death – to remind the reader of the homophobic motivations for the torture that concluded Lorca's life. In other words, Dedora prevents the reader from focusing merely on Lorca's art without also appreciating the dangerous, nationally and historically specific conditions in which he created it. Where Cohen's translation envisions an erotic if heteronormative world, Dedora's juxtaposes queer sex and queer death.

Dedora's densely allusive writings include lines from Lorca's poems and plays both in Spanish and in English translation, focusing on "Pequeño vals vienés," among others, to underscore Lorca's literary queerness. Dedora argues that the poem expresses its queerness in a time when secrecy was the norm. Highlighting this, he twice includes Lorca's line "*Dejaré mi boca entre tus piernas*" (I will leave my mouth between your legs; "The First Part of the Journey, Madrid" 15; "Uno soy yo = I Am One" 73; italics in the original), as well as a translation of the poem's conclusion:

> I will leave my mouth between your legs
> my soul in the photograph's museum of memory

> in the gilded fragrance of the lily's growth
> and in the necessary hidden footsteps of your going
> my love, my love, I want to leave
> the soaring joys of violins and the grave of the little death
> the ribbons of semen upon your body from the waltz that is our sex.
> ("The First Part of the Journey, Madrid" 15,
> "Uno soy yo = I Am One" 75)

Dedora acknowledges that his translation is a more explicit translation of Lorca's own words, which read

> I will leave my mouth between your legs,
> my soul in photographs and lilies,
> and in the dark wake of your footsteps,
> my love, my love, I want to leave
> violin and grave, the ribbons of the waltz.
> ("Uno soy yo = I Am One" 75)[39]

While Cohen's revision of Lorca's poem highlights the waltz through its music, Dedora's revision reveals the waltz as a metaphor. Instead of a heteronormative dance, waltzing, for Dedora, is a way of understanding both a sexual affair and the careful social choreography necessary to sustaining it. The clandestine romance of what he calls "the secret love that bears no name" generates an intense desire to leave tangible records – a mouth, a soul, violins, a grave, ribbons of semen ("Uno soy yo = I Am One" 73). These physical reminders – fleeting though they may be – create an implicit contrast to the lack of physical markers for Lorca's own life: buried anonymously, in an unmarked mass grave that no one can look upon and remember, but that no one can look upon and *not* remember either, as Lloyd Mallan suggested in the immediate aftermath of Lorca's assassination (Mallan 6).

Dedora's discussion of "Pequeño vals vienés" is part of the section titled "Uno soy yo = I Am One" (an allusion to Lorca's 1933 play *El público*), in which he reflects on his different experiences of reading Lorca's *Poet in New York*. In discussing *Poet in New York* as well as Lorca's other writings, Dedora highlights the importance of Lorca's refusal to apologize for his homosexuality: "Lorca gifts us, warp and woof, weaving with morality, honour and loyalty the most important homosexual testament of the early twentieth century by the mere fact that he doesn't theorize, or justify this preference; it just is, a fact of nature, a leaf on a tree, the course of a river" ("Uno soy yo = I Am One" 67). In his reflections on Lorca's queer identity, Dedora connects Lorca to nature – the foliage and rivers that are common to Spain and Canada. By emphasizing Lorca's refusal to apologize, Dedora underscores

Lorca's right not to justify his life, not to try to pass – the impossibility, even, of passing. Furthermore, in highlighting Lorca's line "Uno soy yo," Dedora's book also highlights Lorca's singularity – his exceptionality, and the unique threat he posed to fascism so that he was murdered, as George Woodcock suggested in the early 1940s, "only for being Lorca" (Woodcock 14).

Many poets, before and since, in writing about Lorca, address the poet directly or imagine his final hours. While their tone is sympathetic, their choral questioning of the dead poet makes his murder seem inevitable: describing Lorca's rejection of heteronormative codes of dress and behaviour can read as victim-blaming – for instance, Eldon Grier asks, "García Lorca, / did you think they'd let it go / Did you guess the brilliant words / had made you alien / and (strangely) / evil?" (11). Representations of Lorca's final hours from the 1930s and '40s often imagine his bravery in the face of his impending, seemingly inescapable murder, and his ability to quote his own poetry while facing down a firing squad. *Lorcation* is critical of the common literary trope of imagining – and venerating – Lorca's final hours. In the poem "Granada," Dedora condemns the bystanders in a version of Lorca's final hours that gives priority not to the poet's bravery but rather to the intense violence visited upon him:

And I think of him

you don't think
punched, kicked, slapped around
and the fag taunts
in that stonewalled room
that one light bulb room
tied to a chair

and I think of him

you don't think
of the funnel jammed into his mouth
for the jugs of castor oil
to humiliate himself
tied to a chair (35)

In this horrifying litany of the torture Lorca may have endured, Dedora refuses to overlook the pain suffered by Lorca in favour of a more soothing focus on the poet's heroic death as a martyr. Instead, Dedora's description connects Lorca's suffering to subsequent homophobia ("that stonewalled room" recalling New York's Stonewall Inn riots) and to a widespread artistic refusal to think about the visceral sufferings of a larger-than-life figure. In this gesture – and in *Lorcation*, more broadly – I see Dedora's crucial attempt to translate Lorca's words and experiences and to transform the words of previous poets' elegies into a message more human and less symbolic.

In his attempt to focus on violence, and not just on bravery, Dedora joins queer Toronto writer Jim Nason, whose poem "Apparition on the Beach: Ode to Federico García Lorca" (2013) likewise describes how "They kicked and dragged you along the street, / a bag tied over your head. / Your terror is with me, the bruises and the tears" (29). Nason further includes Spanish and English homophobic slurs, repeated throughout the poem amid more honorific language. In so doing, Nason, like Dedora, underscores Lorca's refusal to apologize – in Nason's words, addressed to Lorca, "you never caved in" (29). Nason's poem, like Dedora's *Lorcation*, is an important critique of those transnational poetic constructions of Lorca as a hero that so often ignore the realities of his life and murder, sanitizing the violence he suffered and occluding the broader struggle against homophobia.

Nason's poem first appeared in *Literary Review of Canada*, as "Ode to Federico Garcia Lorca," before its inclusion in his collection *Music Garden* (2013) with a slightly altered title. In its second publication, the poem further signals Lorca's transnational relevance. The addition to the title of "Apparition on the Beach" suggests the speaker's own located experience of encountering Lorca. As well, Nason's collection includes a series of ekphrastic poems, many of them inspired by the works of Salvador Dalí, who, Nason points out, had a sexual relationship with Lorca. Nason follows what he characterizes as Lorca's "dream of Salvador Dali" (28) with a series of poetic responses to Dalí's art, set in Madrid, and then more poems inspired by works by Manasie Akpaliapik, Henry Moore, L. Torrance Newton, Susan Low-Beer, Jean Simeon Chardin, Viktor Mitic, and Rowan Gillespie. In so doing, Nason connects Lorca's poetry to Dalí's art, and the two Spanish artists to Indigenous and settler Canadian, British, Irish, and French artists, whose works span centuries. Again, the memory of Lorca resonates around the world and across time.

Nason's international, diachronic representation of Lorca's significance anticipates lesbian Toronto writer and activist Maureen Hynes's "On Reading Lorca's *Poet in New York*," which returns to the Spanish and New York contexts of Lorca's collection. Hynes alludes to Lorca throughout her poetry collection *The Poison Colour* (2015): in "Andalusian Pianos" she describes the "Lorca houses" (52), while "Holy Week" recalls Lorca's criticism of Semana Santa: "*commercialism* … / that buries the Muslim and Jewish and Gitano / roots of life and profanes the Alhambra" (53; italics in the original). Hynes highlights a hidden history of Spain's multifaith past – and especially the oppressive treatment of these marginalized groups – and links it to Canada's own heterogeneous society and historic treatment of those outside the mainstream. *The Poison Colour* includes poems set around Toronto and across Canada, in Chile, Spain, and Ireland, in spaces as diverse as synagogues, hospitals, art galleries, and yarn shops. The collection's heterogeneous geography frames the deeply intimate "On Reading Lorca's *Poet in New York*" by connecting Lorca's life experiences to the poetic speaker's own. First published in *The Antigonish Review*, the poem addresses a younger Lorca who shares the excitement of international travel and encounters with new cultures, languages, art, and geographies. In much the same way that Lorca brought Andalusia to New York, Hynes's memory of travelling "to another teeming and seemingly ordered continent" evokes remembrances of that time overlaid with knowledge of what she would come to know (76). This reminiscence is exhilarating, as Hynes's speaker asks, "Lorca, / remember how astonishment tasted?" (76). In this direct address to Lorca, Hynes suggests how the poet might live on in his poems.

Many Canadian poets besides Hynes, Dedora, and Cohen engage with *Poet in New York*, looking to Lorca's remaining words. Halifax writer J.A. Wainwright rewrites Lorca's "Lament for Ignacio Sánchez Mejías" as a lament for Lorca himself (2012). Addressing Lorca, Wainwright elegizes the poet killed "Because you wore a bow tie ... Because you were queer ... Because your poems were louder / Than the click of rifles." In a different approach to elegy, included in *Happy Birthday, Nicanor Parra* (2012), Toronto poet Jim Smith reimagines Lorca's death in "Do and Die" as a cartoonish anvil drop in which the poem's speaker is also Lorca's murderer (54). And in "Federico García Lorca," he revises Lorca's own poem, "La cogida y la muerte" (80). Queer Windsor-based writer Susan Holbrook's poetry collection *Joy Is So Exhausting* (2009) contains a series of poems "To Federico García Lorca's *Poema del cante jondo*," each responding to one of Lorca's flamenco-inspired poems through translation and often humorous wordplay, in what poet Fred Wah calls transcreation. Elsewhere in the collection, Holbrook invokes texts as diverse as Walt Whitman's *Leaves of Grass*, the PetSmart website, and the insert from a Tampax box. Holbrook herself speaks both English and Spanish, and her playful, polyglot interpretations of Lorca – including "*Yabadabadoo*," "!¡¡!!¡¡", and a poem titled "My Drug Ada" (for Lorca's "Madrugada," or "Before Dawn," 45, 46, 47) – innovate new ways of seeing Lorca's ongoing influence. In his collection *Emanations: fluttertongue 6*, Toronto poet Steven Ross Smith includes a transcreation of Lorca's "Pequeño poema infinito" as "Peck" amid a collection of poems that "leap off an edge" of source poems ranging from Di Brandt's "Nine River Ghazals #2" to John Clare's "Sonnet: I Am" (99). Prince Edward Island poet John MacKenzie's *Letters I Didn't Write* (2008) also contains a series of Lorca poems. In "Lorca Again," MacKenzie considers Lorca's inextricability from the landscape and culture of Spain (72–3), and in "Lorca's Lament," he uses Lorca's own voice as the poem's speaker (66–7). MacKenzie provides his own translations of "Murio al amanecer" in "You Died At Dawn" (71), and of "Poema de la satea" in "Poem of the Arrow" (86–92). Montreal poet Joshua Auerbach likewise translates a Lorca poem, "Casida del llanto," as "Song of the Lament," and includes it alongside his own translations of Paul Éluard and poems that reference Rilke, Robert Frost, Shakespeare, and Theodore Roethke.

Lorca's words, if not his voice, endure in Canadian poetry. As I have discussed, George Elliott Clarke's "The Death and Life of Garcia Lorca" emphasizes Lorca's afterlife through his writings. In "Death of a Poet," American-born Ottawa writer Mark Frutkin wonders, "His grave is lost but the words remain. / What if it had been the other way round?" (176). In the following chapter I will discuss a Spanish Civil War novel by Frutkin (whose memoir identifies him with tongue in cheek as "Catholic-Jewish soon to be Buddhist-German-Russian-Irish-English-French" [*Erratic North* 17]). Here, I want to suggest that Frutkin's question articulates a sentiment that guides many other contemporary poems as they imagine Lorca alive, celebrate his words, and mourn his tragic murder and its inconclusive aftermath. In another way, Ottawa writer Nicola Vulpe laments Lorca's lost grave through a dramatic monologue that denies Lorca's very existence. In "De Falla at the Police Station," an intimidating officer states: "No one's been arrested / No one's been shot, / certainly not your friend – / Federico you said his name was?" (18).[40] Vulpe's depiction of Granadans' willful blindness recalls Eldon Grier's description of all those who "pass blandly / overhead" of Lorca's unmarked grave (11). Contemporary Canadian Lorca poems form a literary renunciation of this social denial, ensuring the poet's continued acknowledgment as a voice for Granada, for social justice, for cosmopolitanism, and for queerness.[41]

Queering Spanish Civil War Literature

Taken together, these eighty years' worth of Canadian responses to Lorca's murder showcase a collective horror at the conditions of his last hours – the homophobia, xenophobia, and jingoism that motivated it. They also reveal a growing sense of Lorca's resonant influences in Canada – the significance of studying a cosmopolitan figure in an increasingly cosmopolitan country. Despite the lack of a local memorial to Lorca, or even a definitive account of his final hours, Canadian writers – like writers from around the world – remember him. By translating his words into English (and their own words into Spanish), imagining him as an interlocutor or a spokesperson, and describing his valour in the face of fascism, authors explain Lorca's multiple significances to Canadian letters.

Elegies for Lorca form a significant canon of responses that at one time motivated transnational support for the Spanish cause, that continue to mourn the death of a great writer, and that resist or queer the tropes of war literature. Lorca was a non-combatant, uninvolved in traditional masculine aspects of war; in elegizing him, then, transnational writers write war literature about a man remembered not for his battlefield bravery but for his writerly engagement on the home front. Lorca becomes a martyr for his life and his work, "only for being Lorca" (Woodcock 14).

What I see as a literary resistance to exclusively commemorating bravery on the battlefield amplifies Lorca's own cosmopolitan projects. He famously stated, "I believe that being from Granada inclines me to a sympathetic understanding of the persecuted, gypsies, Jews, blacks, ... the Moorishness that all of us hold within" (qtd in Rogers 185). While Lorca's conflation of various experiences of persecution is undoubtedly problematic, it also suggests a cosmopolitan attempt at sympathy beyond borders, beyond race, ethnicity, religion, and nationality – an endeavour that rang true for many of the Canadians directly and indirectly involved in fighting Spanish fascism. Looking to writings about Lorca provides an expanded perspective on the war's stakes for marginalized people, as focusing on Jewish Canadian literatures of the Spanish Civil War can reveal the stakes of national inclusion within Canadian society that form the subtext of fictional works ostensibly focused on Spain's war. Tributes to Lorca simultaneously remember Lorca and underscore the threat that fascism continues to pose to individuals and cultures outside the mainstream – how fascism defines the mainstream in relation to its own pursuit of authority and control. Rejecting simply tolerance, or queer assimilation, these elegies argue that Lorca must be allowed to be Lorca.

Conclusion
Remembrance: Envisioning Spain and Canada Now

"I wonder if, in time of war, anything can be as vivid as the imagination."
Dennis Bock, *The Communist's Daughter*

The war may be over, but the struggle remains with us. In Spain, an amnesty law continues to protect those who committed crimes while serving Franco's regime, even though the UN High Commissioner for Human Rights has demanded its repeal. Another law, the 2007 Law of Historical Memory, recognizes the victims on both sides of the conflict, gives their descendants rights, and denounces Franco's regime. Since the dictator's death in 1975, families, communities, and artists have reckoned with their country's divisive history. The slow thawing of the social *pacto del olvido* (pact of forgetting) that prevented political and social discussion of the war has unleashed a deluge of novels, testimony collections, films, and documentaries about the war and postwar repression, in what has been called a memory boom.[1] New unmarked mass graves continue to be discovered and excavated, while individuals and organizations commemorating the eightieth anniversary of the war's outbreak seek to establish a museum of the war.

The struggles remain with us, too, in North America. Contemporary events are not repetitions or parallels of what happened in the 1930s, yet surely we can hear some echoes. Franco's statement eighty years ago that Spain could be made "great" again through the military support of Morocco in a war against a democratically elected government cannot help but seem the forerunner to the current US president's white supremacist heteropatriarchal election slogan "Make America Great Again." Likewise, footage of the ongoing civil war in Syria is broadcast globally while the world watches, seemingly impotent to stop the mounting bloodshed and destruction. The war in Syria is no more a civil war than Spain's was: Assad's government is supported by Russia, as Franco was once supported by Hitler and Mussolini. Meanwhile, notwithstanding the inclusion of National Aboriginal Day, Saint-Jean-Baptiste Day, and Canadian Multiculturalism Day in the festivities, 2017's "Canada 150" sesquicentennial celebrations commemorated the union of three colonies along with the genocide and oppression on which the Dominion was built. These contemporary resonances may seem tenuous and polemical, yet I would argue that ongoing global conflicts, as well as continuing debates over identity and reconciliation, may go some way toward explaining North Americans' enduring fascination with the Spanish Civil War.

The Spanish Civil War remains with us in Canadian literature, too. While throughout this book I have discussed fiction, reportage, memoir, and poetry that date from that same eighty-year span, there is simply no precedent since the time of the war itself for the growth of interest in the Spanish Civil War in post-2000 Canadian fiction. What's more, the novels and short stories published since the start of the new millennium foreground many of the concerns over identity and inclusion that, I have argued, underpin earlier Spanish Civil War literature. In so doing, many of these fictional works coincide with contemporary Holocaust and Second World War fiction, which likewise engages with histories so often subsumed within the dominant battlefront narrative. What's more, Spanish Civil War fiction often plays a pedagogical role as well, educating readers who, while familiar with Holocaust and Second World War history, may know little or nothing about Spain. Taken together, these Spanish Civil War novels and short stories demonstrate the war's ongoing power within the Canadian and transnational cultural mythology, in which brave, selfless volunteers from around the world came together to fight fascism. That narrative may be grounded in truth, but as I have suggested, it tells only one part of the story. This is to say, I do not seek to challenge the heroism of the international volunteers, or the terrifying threat that Franco and his fascist and Nazi supporters posed. Rather, I want to complicate and nuance this understanding of the Spanish Civil War's importance to and influence on North America. Looking to these contemporary works of fiction underscores what has been missing or sidelined from that mythology: the important roles played by participants who were also Jewish, female, queer, immigrants, and people of colour; and the violent legacy of Spain's and Canada's ongoing colonial entanglements, especially this legacy's impact on Indigenous populations. These contemporary texts offer us a more nuanced mosaic: they complicate and challenge how we understand the populations and generations involved in Spain's conflict.[2]

One of the Spanish Civil War's originary fictions was that it was a domestic conflict. Thousands from around the world saw through that deceit and supported the Spanish Republic against the fascist insurgency. North American Spanish Civil War literature represents transnational solidarity among the supporters of the Spanish Republic, and Nazi collusion on the opposing side. These texts are united in their appeal to the ethical imperative of participation in war. As previous chapters have argued, looking to authors and characters who have been marginalized shows how the Spanish Civil War was a more intricate conflict than the battle between democracy and fascism it is so often portrayed as having been. My approach showcases the war's stakes for oppressed populations by highlighting Francoism's relationship to an intersecting web of racism, antisemitism, Islamophobia, sexism, homophobia, and xenophobia that stretched across the Atlantic from North America to Europe and North Africa. North American authors responded to these repressive beliefs by espousing a different vision of nationalism than fascism could envision. Writers rewrote the literary genre of the war romance novel to include Jewish soldiers and foreign love interests – and to make it less romantic. They depicted the participation of colonized and diasporized African troops on both sides of the conflict, revealing the lie at the root of Spain's supposedly localized conflict. They showed how the denial of citizenship rights to women could be at least partly surmounted in transnational community groupings. And they memorialized a gay Spanish writer, whose murder generated so much global attention to what Franco and his supporters had planned for others whose identities also challenged the fascist mainstream.

Yet, these texts also unavoidably contain fictions of their own, whether due to incomplete information, political biases, or storytelling flourishes (Hemingway's controversial representation of lone wolf Robert Jordan in *For Whom the Bell Tolls* is just one example). And despite their ethical appeals, the cosmopolitan patriotism that writers espoused was often aspirational. My chapters are also guided, however, by how writers respond to a more nefarious set of fictions – the antisemitic stereotypes that stigmatized Jews as gender nonconforming and otherwise queer, that marginalized them by racializing their difference, and that deemed them unworthy of acceptance for all these failures to be part of the mainstream. There are some fictions that writings from the margins can dispel, others that are too culturally dominant to overthrow. (In eschewing literature supportive of the insurgents in this book, I have engaged in some fictionalizing of my own.)

Post-2000 works of fiction make central what had been peripheral to earlier Canadian Spanish Civil War literature. If participating in – or writing about – the Spanish Civil War gave Canadians the opportunity to critique their own young country from a geographical distance, then writing about the same war decades later – in some cases, upwards of seventy-five years on – again offers a temporal, cosmopolitan distance from the agitation of the war years. Contemporary literature about the Spanish Civil War expands and extends the ethical imperatives so many earlier texts imply. These later writings are the beneficiaries of the opening of Franco-era archives and government files and Canadians' increasing recognition of the volunteers who fought in Spain. In these works of fiction, the shared aspiration toward transnational, transcultural sympathy that all Spanish Civil War literature commemorates becomes an aspiration toward uncovering the fictions and oversights that much of the preceding literature disseminated, particularly in its obfuscation of colonialism, homophobia, antisemitism, and sexism.

The literary reclamation and expansion of Canada's Spanish Civil War history coincides with a broader Canadian interest in historical fiction – in particular, historical war fiction.[3] This renewed interest in Canadian participation in the Spanish Civil War additionally suggests nostalgia for a time of clear-cut conflicts between good and evil, democracy and fascism and, paralleling what Lisa Renée DiGiovanni sees in contemporaneous Spanish cultural production, for a time of Canadian bravery. I perceive this nostalgia in the evolving recuperation work that has been done around the Canadian communist doctor Norman Bethune, fictionalized, as I mentioned, in Hugh MacLennan's novel *The Watch That Ends the Night* (1958). Since then, Bethune has been memorialized in, among other projects, the National Film Board documentary *Bethune* (1964), Rod Langley's play *Bethune* (1975), and Philip Borsos's film *Bethune: The Making of a Hero* (1990; written by Ted Allan and starring Donald Sutherland). Most recently, Bethune's experiences in Spain and China have been fictionalized in Toronto-based author Dennis Bock's novel *The Communist's Daughter* (2007), in which Bock imagines a series of letters from Bethune to a daughter he will never meet, his daughter with Kajsa von Rothman.[4]

These representations of the heroic, maverick Dr Bethune coincide with a larger literary reconsideration of Canadian participation in the Spanish Civil War beginning in the 1980s. This reconsideration was at first fraught with nostalgia for the last great cause, in what I see as not only a parallel reaction to Franco's death and the dissolution of the *pacto del olvido*, but also a reaction to local developments such as the Quiet Revolution, the Canadian government's changing policies toward multiculturalism and Indigenous rights in the form of the Charter of Rights and Freedoms, the Canadian Multiculturalism Act, and Bill C-31's amendment to the Indian Act.[5] During the 1980s and '90s, along with George Luscombe, Mac Reynolds, and Larry Cox's play *The Mac Paps* (1980) – a choral voicing of the Canadian volunteers' experiences – fiction by Mordecai Richler, Neil Bissoondath, and Matt Cohen focused on the experiences of male characters too young to have participated directly in the Spanish Civil War, yet whose lives bear its indelible imprint. This shared narrative of a second generation looking back on the war reflects much Spanish fiction, in which Jo Labanyi notes the prevalent plot of a young protagonist piecing together his or her family history. In the Spanish context, the protagonist almost always has something to discover about a family's affiliations, be they Francoist or Republican. These fictional representations of inherited family histories also recall Marianne Hirsch's extensive work on what she terms "postmemory" in her study of the art of Holocaust survivors' children.[6] Relatedly, these Canadian works of fiction depict the discovery of a buried transnational family history – that is, a newfound international identity, one that implicitly compels the protagonist to reflect on his own relationship to Canada's changing policies around the diverse members of its own populace.

I discussed Richler's *Joshua Then and Now* (1980) in chapters 1 and 2. Short stories by Neil Bissoondath and Matt Cohen likewise weave the Spanish conflict into Canadian life through complex, emotionally fraught stories of postwar family fissures. Trinidadian-born Quebec author Bissoondath's short story "Things Best Forgotten" (1990) depicts the protagonist's discovery of how his grandfather died – not as a coward or a Franco supporter, but as a union member imprisoned by a neighbour and then put to death as a "Red."[7] This belated discovery of family activism is enlarged in Jewish Canadian author Cohen's short stories (1983). In "The Sins of Thomas Benares," an immigrant doctor in Toronto – Spanish by birth, Jewish Ukrainian by ancestry – experiences his son's death overlaid with memories of the family life in Spain that he fled before it was destroyed by Franco. In "Sentimental Meetings," published in the same volume, Cohen returns to the Benares family, this time depicting Thomas Benares's grandson's travels to France and Spain as he attempts to reconnect with family dispersed by the Spanish Civil War and the Holocaust.[8] In uncovering their families' wartime histories, these protagonists are compelled to rewrite their own stories of who they are. These late-twentieth-century writings about male characters' nostalgia connect the Spanish Civil War to broader issues – of Jewish decimation and immigration, of gender roles and family expectations, and of Canadian identity.

Since 2000, nearly a dozen Canadian works of fiction about the Spanish Civil War have followed Bissoondath, Cohen, and Richler in critiquing nostalgia for the war by depicting the ongoing effects of the conflict in tandem with ongoing issues within Canadian society, including the erasure of women, queer people, leftists – and the Spanish Civil War itself – from Canadian historical memory, developing governmental policy on multiculturalism and Indigenous rights, and an evolving historical perspective on Canada's inadequate response to the Holocaust.[9] Canadian writers depict Canadian participation and the next generations' inheritances while explicitly connecting the war to the tensions of national, racial, religious, ethnic, sexual, and gender identity I have highlighted throughout this book. For contemporary writers, the war endures as a touchstone of global engagement and social revolution. Depicting the war becomes a method of undoing some of the country's own pacts of silence around its history.[10]

To render visible the concealed labour of women and working-class people in maintaining middle-class Canadian society, Margaret Atwood's novel *The Blind Assassin* (2000) self-consciously silences the Spanish Civil War. While the war – and one character's participation in it – is far from Atwood's main plot, the conflict appears repeatedly in her novel's intersecting storylines, of a Great Depression memoir, a romance novel, and leftist science fiction stories. And interspersed throughout are news clippings reporting on, among other things, the "Reds in Spain" and the "Red Vendetta in Barcelona" (357, 410). The war's presence in Atwood's different narratives is always effected through other characters' references to a minor character, Alex Thomas, who volunteers in Spain and then dies in the Second World War. Despite Alex's own secrecy about his volunteering, the war echoes through the novel's other narratives because of him: he is the author of the didactic science fiction stories and the lover of both the protagonist and her sister. In drawing these many connections between narratives, characters, and a war taking place an ocean away, *The Blind Assassin* enacts a parallel silencing to so much of the fiction published in the immediate aftermath of the Spanish Civil War, implicitly critiquing this literary absence while providing an intertextual vision of potential ways to see Spain through the novel's overlapping narratives.

The self-conscious silences of *The Blind Assassin* around Spanish Civil War participation are not reflected in subsequent Canadian fiction, which instead spotlights the volunteers and the issues so often represented as secondary in earlier texts. And what's more, many contemporary Canadian novels allow participants to tell their own stories – breaking with the nostalgia of subsequent generations' imaginings of earlier battlefield bravery and allowing these fictionalized volunteers to speak (unlike the character Alex, as well as countless minority characters in earlier Spanish Civil War fiction). These later works create the intimacy of first-hand stories of Spanish Civil War participation. Their narratives are strikingly similar to the many 1930s novels of wartime exploits, but bring contemporary ethical and affiliative considerations to bear on volunteers' experiences.[11]

Contemporary Canadian authors reimagine the wartime novel, frequently doing so by incorporating many of the issues around colonialism, immigration, gender and racial equality, and identity that earlier fictions might only gesture toward through the tokenist deployment of minoritized characters or related subplots. In so doing, authors move beyond what scholar Leah Garrett has identified as the "cloaking" gesture of universalism that so many Jewish authors employed in their own representations of Jewish characters (221). Jewish characters – and other marginalized characters too – in contemporary Spanish Civil War fiction are not invoked as symbols or tokens, but as complex, developed characters.

The centring of working-class and Jewish experience is nowhere more apparent than in Ottawa writer Terrence Rundle West's *Not in My Father's Footsteps* (2011). The protagonist, Marty Kellenberger, is the tough Jewish hero that so many earlier Spanish Civil War novels anticipate. Instead of a flat minor character in the story of a young white anglophone man's maturation, West's Jewish hero is instead a multifaceted, sympathetic Montreal medical student and Mackenzie-Papineau soldier initially politicized by his experiences of antisemitism. These range from physical violence, to the educational fallout of the "Days of Shame" – the 1934 medical strike to protest Dr Sam Rabinovitch's appointment as chief intern at Notre-Dame Hospital – to his struggles to secure employment.[12]

In West's depiction, Marty's struggles against antisemitism are not secondary to the Spanish cause – they are the reason Marty fights. In particular, West relentlessly depicts both the fears that temporarily drive Marty to pass as a gentile, and the psychological harm that passing causes. Multiple times, Marty and his comrades are warned that if they are not naturalized citizens, the Canadian government may not allow them back into the country after their International Brigades stint. Marty, passing as an Irish Canadian, is isolated in his fears of permanent exile and deeply afraid that he will be exposed. While crossing the Atlantic with a group of Yiddish-speaking Jewish volunteers, Marty is especially ambivalent: "He was as proud of them as he was ashamed for hiding his own background. To make matters worse, they often conversed in Yiddish. It was a struggle not to laugh at their jokes, or get angry when they made fun of the others, including the bespectacled Montrealer with the Irish name" (209). Meeting a Spanish Jew, the descendant of *marranos*, finally convinces Marty to admit, in the Spaniard's words, his "true heritage" (226). Marty confesses, "I'm one of your *cobardes* [cowards] ... I'm a Jew, just like you" (227; italics in the original).

Marty's courage comes from his contact with a transnational cast of other Jewish characters. They give him the confidence to become outspoken about the oppression he has suffered: upon first encountering his former tormenter in Spain, he screams, "*J'ai passé trois ans à l'université de Montréal avant de me faire foutre dehors. KICKED OUT parce que je suis Juif. J'aurai dû être docteur si ce n'était pour le racisme et le Jeune-Canada*" (*I spent three years at the University of Montreal before I was kicked out to go fuck myself. KICKED OUT because I'm Jewish. I should have been a doctor if it weren't for the racism and Jeune-Canada*; my trans.; 275; italics in the original). It is important, too, that Marty is *not* inspired to participate in Spain because of his Judaism, but rather because of the antisemitism he experiences: as I discussed in the introduction, many Jewish volunteers identified with their political affiliations above their religion. In other words, West's narrative does not moralize about Jewish religious teachings and universalism; rather, it harshly critiques structures of discrimination.

Marty's explicit evaluation of the systemic antisemitism he has experienced is directed at another round character based in earlier tokenist representations. Dollard Desjardins is a deeply religious Québécois Catholic who eventually abandons his far-right *pure laine* politics to support the Spanish Republic. West foregrounds already marginalized Canadian characters' dawning recognition of their own myopic attitudes toward difference – a recognition catalysed by their Spanish Civil War participation, one that suggests the possibility of future reconciliation. The novel concludes where so many other Spanish Civil War novels do, before the horrors of the next global conflict – one that Marty fought so valiantly to prevent. In concluding the novel in 1939, West leaves the importance of Marty and Dollard's prescient antifascism unspoken. These male war heroes remain heroes – one murdered in war, the other left to defend Canada from fascism.

Not in My Father's Footsteps acknowledges the importance of home-front activism through the character of Marty's Jewish girlfriend. Other Canadian novels of Spain foreground female characters' heroism on the battlefields, too. Where West's novel represents an integral – and sadly unique – depiction of Jewish volunteerism, novels by Mark Frutkin, June Hutton, Elizabeth Ruth, and Gayla Reid represent women's heroism. If, as M. Cinta Ramblado-Minero has argued, Spanish women's memory texts are "acts of resistance against a collective memory" (30), then these Canadian authors' fictional accounts of Canadian and Spanish women's bravery challenge Canadian collective memory. Mark Frutkin's novel

Slow Lightning (2001) updates many of the war romance tropes I discussed in chapter 1, incorporating Spanish characters' perspectives, and particularly emphasizing the female volunteer's own subjectivity. Frutkin foregrounds Teresa's wartime experiences, including the particular dangers facing women, as in a scene when a Falangist officer offers to protect her in exchange for sex.[13] Teresa is not a plot device, in other words, but an integral – and uniquely vulnerable – player in the narrative.

Frutkin's narrative sympathy toward women's distinct struggles in war is expanded in Vancouver novelist June Hutton's *Underground* (2009). *Underground* is, in many ways, a narrative of a young man's dawning appreciation of women's rights struggles, within the frame of a traditional war novel. Furthermore, the protagonist's support of women's rights stems from his emerging recognition of his own white privilege. Early on, upon meeting women visiting their husbands at the Spanish front, one of them proudly nursing her baby, the narrator describes how the "very presence of women in the war both pleases and alarms [Albert]" (168). Albert seems to decide that he prefers being "please[d]" to being "alarm[ed]" by the women's presence: while his comrade criticizes women's participation as a "fucking mess" (169), Albert remains silent. Later interactions with women – and with his pregnant (not by him) girlfriend in particular – also challenge his sexism: his future wife is more concerned with refugees and shellings than romance, and she does not apologize for having had multiple sexual partners. She immigrates to Canada with him, and Al raises her child as his own. Her bravery in the war and her profound yet unachievable desire to return to a democratic Spain make her a constant reminder of war's ingloriousness. The transnational sympathy that Al learns is inextricable from the feminism he absorbs in Spain and imports back to Canada.

Hutton, West, and Frutkin all revise typical wartime narratives by expanding the concept of heroism. In so doing, their novels incorporate more characters (and, by extension, more individuals) into the national identity that Canadian Spanish Civil War literature constructs. But national identity remains especially tenuous for individuals from marginalized groups, as the Australian-born British Columbia writer Gayla Reid reminds us in her novel *Come from Afar* (2011). Reid represents the transnational, postcolonial connections forged and reforged by the war, as well as the perilously fragile hold that women had on their own citizenship rights. The protagonist, an Australian nurse named Clancy, volunteers in Spain after the public revelation of her English husband's homosexuality drives him to suicide. She falls in love with an injured Mackenzie-Papineau soldier, yet after he returns to the front, she marries a German International Brigades soldier so that he can immigrate to safety – an act that saves him even as it renders her stateless. Of this second marriage, she reflects: "I'd had one bizarre marriage, I decided. Why not another? At least this one might be of some use" (224). She now sees marriage's legal and social utility – not its romance – and, by extension, her own power within that framework. Their marriage gives her the surname "Thaelmann" – her new husband's name, adopted from the German battalion. Reid's novel emphasizes that national affiliation is not stable – not for women, nor for political dissidents – and that social acceptance is based in heteronormativity, so patriotism does not provide safety.

Clancy's constant struggle in Spain is against her relentlessly feminized body – and the threats posed to it. A fellow volunteer attempts to sexually assault her, and while she fends him off, she feels the movement that alerts her to her pregnancy. Dispassionately, she plans to travel to England for an abortion, but, ultimately unable to leave Spain, she reluctantly acquiesces to motherhood. Dolores is born as the war concludes, her name – Spanish for "pain" or "grief" – recalling both the war's tragedy and "La Pasionaria," Dolores Ibárruri. In contrast to the many hopeful pregnancies and births depicted in early Spanish Civil War novels – Muriel Rukeyser's *Savage Coast* and Upton Sinclair's *No Pasaran!* among them – Dolores's birth brings frustration and sadness despite Clancy's love for her. Clancy's inability to secure an abortion is a critique of historical and contemporary restrictions on women's bodily autonomy, in Canada *and* Spain.

Reid's novel, like Frutkin's novel and Gellhorn's short stories (see chapter 3), is an insistent reminder of the singularities of women's wartime experiences: concerns over reproductive choice and sexual violence overshadow any fears Clancy has about working on the battlefront. Likewise, Clancy's early relationship with her first husband expands this perspective even further through its depiction of the sometimes fatal effects of compulsory heterosexuality. *Come from Afar* brings women's wartime experiences out from the margins and asks us to consider how women and queer people regularly face threats to their physical safety, whether on or off the battlefield.

This novel has its corollary in Regina author Byrna Barclay's short story "Girl at the Window" (2004), which depicts the postwar life of a traumatized former nurse, who has been stigmatized and institutionalized by her family. "Mad Joan," as she is called, continues to live inside the Spanish Civil War, singing the Mujeres Libres anthem and bragging of her sexual exploits with Dalí, Hemingway, and the famous bullfighter Manolete (273). But Joan also lives in terror of wartime violence, warning:

"Better watch out, better get ready, the Moors are coming with Franco! ... Jarama, Brunet [*sic*], Quinto, Belchite, Fuentes de Ebro, Teruel, the Retreats and the Ebro!" (73). The war paradoxically provided both Joan and Clancy with personal freedoms unavailable to them in their home countries – the ability to travel, work, and have affairs. Yet as both stories remind us, these choices also had repercussions within their societies – not just the judgment of others, but the physical and psychological repercussions of being female in a war zone.

Both "Girl at the Window" and *Come from Afar* reclaim female wartime participation as its own narrative rather than as ancillary to masculine battlefield bravery. In so doing, they remind us of the massive stakes of the war for Spanish as well as foreign women. Elizabeth Ruth's novel *Matadora* (2013), which I briefly discussed in the previous chapter, also focuses on women's struggles against classism, sexism, and homophobia, depicting a working-class Spanish woman's glass-ceiling-shattering career alongside a queer Jewish Canadian woman's integral wartime work. *Matadora* is a bildungsroman set against the Second Spanish Republic's destruction. Like Reid's character Clancy, Ruth's Spanish protagonist Luna is singularly focused on her vocation as a bullfighter. Even when friends and family members are killed in the mounting political unrest, Luna herself does not pay attention to the impending war until it affects her work: supporters of the Spanish Republic criticize the tradition of the bullfight – its cruelty to animals and misuse of land that could otherwise be farmed for life-sustaining crops. Luna is ultimately unconvinced by these environmentalist arguments, but she later falls in love with one of these activists, a Canadian medical volunteer.

Luna remains the novel's central character, yet her love interest, Grace, is far from the sidelined girlfriend so common to heteronormative Spanish Civil War romances (recall how even the brave, professionally distinguished Lisa in *This Time a Better Earth* was criticized for daring to discuss marriage and children). Grace is Jewish, the daughter of Russian immigrants who came to Canada to escape pogroms, who wears a *mono* (coveralls) emblazoned with the Yiddish saying "*If all men pulled in one direction, the world would topple over*" (231; italics in the original). Her work in Spain – driving an ambulance – recalls Jean "Jim" Watts's own role. And her fierce beliefs – in the Spanish cause, in environmentalism – compel Luna to reconsider her own supposedly apolitical stance. Through Luna and Grace, *Matadora* represents multiple ways of being a woman within a sexist society.

Luna and Grace also vocalize debates around Canada's perceived liberalism and Spain's flailing democracy, thus summoning many current debates over dominant Canadian narratives of peaceful postcolonial social equality. During one argument, for instance, Luna blames their differing views on Grace's nationality, speculating that "[p]erhaps other Canadians were the same, innocent in the way the young are innocent, not having been corrupted by too much history" (260). Canada is, for Luna, "too young to be civilized yet" (260). Yet in the following scene, Canadian civilization is championed as Grace introduces Luna to Norman Bethune and convinces her to donate blood. There are no victor nations in *Matadora,* nor is patriotic vanity allowed for a Canadian audience.

Even as Ruth avoids aggrandizing Canada, the novel connects Spanish fascism to Spanish sexism as Grace challenges Luna to think about her own resistance to fascist gender roles. Grace explains, "according to some people, a woman fighting bulls is wrong but that hasn't stopped you" (293). Luna's long-standing obsession with becoming a bullfighter – a traditionally male career – generates much speculation, in the novel, about her gender identity: early on, she refers to herself as the masculine "torero" (40), and her professional name is "El Corazón" – "not La Corazoncito, but the masculine form, undeniable" (82). A victory over a bull generates further self-examination: "Was she still a girl? Had a taste for power and blood made her less of one?" (83). While Luna is aware of other women who have fought bulls, the narrow strictures of Spanish society – around gender as well as class – compel her to question what it means to be female in a male-dominated field. After the war begins, the sexism she experiences mounts – she is heckled as "grotesque" and "butch" by spectators who "ridicule what maleness in another torero, or in another place, would've received praise" (240). More intimately, her brother's homophobic reaction to the revelation of her relationship with Grace threatens one of her only remaining family connections.

In its characters and narrative, *Matadora* marks a significant revision of many Spanish Civil War literary tropes: it subverts gendered stereotypes; incorporates Spanish, Jewish, queer, and female characters; complicates the battlefield romance; and refuses to cast Canada as the nation that Spain should strive to emulate. All these textual moves together make Ruth's concluding gesture intriguing: like many of the novels I have discussed, *Matadora* concludes before the war's end. Yet instead of alluding to a future, peaceful Spain, Ruth emphasizes Francoist sexism, homophobia, and antisemitism so as to render the fate of Grace and Luna an unspoken, unspeakable certainty. Even as *Matadora* is written from an arguably more tolerant time (at least relative to Franco's Spain), Ruth avoids a happy ending. In so doing, she offers a trenchant critique of our own readerly expectations of historical fiction, for nostalgia for a good cause and confirmation of our own society's superiority.

Fictional texts by Barclay, Frutkin, Hutton, Reid, Ruth, and West not only undo the silences around Spanish Civil War participation that Atwood identifies, but also foreground the brave volunteerism of marginalized individuals – marginalized because they are Jewish, Québécois, immigrant, female, and queer. In remembering Spain from today's vantage point, these authors may allude to contemporary connections, but their narratives' chronologies remain bound by the previous century. Fiction that depicts the next generations' inheritances – as Barclay, Bissoondath, Cohen, and Richler's stories do – are able to more explicitly yoke the Spanish Civil War to ongoing warfare as well as to additional experiences of oppression among colonized and immigrant populations. In addition to centring the narratives of individuals marginalized in earlier Spanish Civil War literature, Barclay, Hutton, and Stephen Collis further expand the stories and characters that Spanish Civil War literature considers, writing characters and narratives previously untold.

Virginia Woolf contends in *Three Guineas*, her pacifist tract composed in the midst of the Spanish Civil War, that warmaking always leads to more war – there can be no fighting for peace, even in the most seemingly noble or justified of conflicts. This perspective is writ large in Barclay's "Girl at the Window." The character Joan takes a celebratory perspective on her own wartime experiences as a nurse, yet the story also considers the horrors of wartime conditions for other women, both in Spain and in Iraq. Barclay suggests that if "Mad Joan" is doomed to live the war on an endlessly repeating loop, there are other women who are still unable to avoid being drawn into new wars. The protagonist encounters a former Spanish refugee, who expresses her frustration with the men who make war: "I wish I could talk to Mr. [Colin] Powell up there on the TV. I'd tell him all about WAR" (296; capitalization in the original). Barclay also thwarts easy nostalgia for the "last great cause," as this same Spanish refugee details the horrors she survived in Spain. However, implicit in the story's chronology is a commentary on the increasingly complex nature of global warfare: while "Mad Joan" believed she was living in a state of war until she died, that war was the Spanish Civil War – a conflict that ended definitively before the Second World War broke out. Her granddaughter, the protagonist, also exists in a world at war, and here, the ambiguous motivations and massive bloodshed of the Iraq War serve both as a reminder of Spain's earlier supposedly civil conflict and the perils of non-intervention, and as a foil to the distinctions between the two sides. Barclay's "Girl at the Window" constructs a single narrative out of ongoing conflicts that are regionally limited in name only – first Spain, then Iraq – and from the perspective of Canada's own tenuous non-participation in the Iraq War.

Where Barclay connects Canadian participation in the Spanish Civil War to another global conflict, British Columbia author and activist Stephen Collis in his novel *The Red Album* (2013) demonstrates how the causes and repercussions of the war in Spain radiated outwards through the country's colonies. *The Red Album* is framed as a mysterious, incomplete novel by Gloria Personne (Glorious No One) emailed to Collis, and including an extensive paratextual apparatus of "documentos" – editorial commentary through essays and footnotes, poetry, a short play, and essays ostensibly written by characters – after its "narración," the novel itself. This apparatus, along with the novel's inclusion of the actual current work of the Association for the Recovery of Historical Memory (ARMH), and Collis's use of a complex group of real, pseudonymous, and heteronymous character names – Lorca, Alfred Noyes, Ramon Fernandez (Wallace Stevens's character and real-life critic), Dioscuro Galindo (a teacher murdered alongside Lorca), and Gloria Personne among them – blur the lines between fiction and non-fiction, the history we learn and the history we uncover. As Collis puts it in an essay on the 1936 revolution in Catalonia, history comes to us "second or third hand, highly mediated and saturated with the textures added by its various storytellers, its interested parties and government recollectors" (180).[14]

The Red Album's main narrative recounts the journey of a South American man, Dioscuro Galindo, to Barcelona to attend a ceremony to honour his great-uncle's memory and rebury his remains. Dio's great-uncle was murdered by Spanish fascists, and now the ARMH seeks to appropriately commemorate him. Yet Dio has never heard of this great-uncle – in his story, too, the line between fiction and non-fiction seems blurred as Dio grapples with his family's hidden history. It is not just the familiarity of Dio's family history that is challenged by his trip to what he calls "the old world" (13); his very identity feels under attack as the Barcelonans struggle to understand his Spanish, his jetlagged dreams blend into his waking experiences, and, in the narrative's climax, he discovers that a revolution has begun in his home country, trapping his family and preventing his homecoming. Dio's bewilderment over his changing sense of himself and his family history parallels his perplexed reaction to the Spanish and Catalan history that surrounds him, the feeling that "[s]omething ... had been dug up, and now needed proper burial – if only to keep it buried once and for all" (33). At the ceremony to honour his great-uncle – another proper burial – an ARMH official comments on Spain's need to reckon with its civil war past in order to attain "liberation" (69). Despite these formal efforts toward reconciliation, Dio is angered by what he sees as "ceremony bullshit" when "real justice" is called for (100). Collis's novel suggests that ceremonies are not enough to lay the past to rest: proper burials still conceal the country's previous wrongdoings – the religious oppression, the colonial expansion, and the violence that even a post-Franco Spain remains built upon. The minimal concern with Spain's colonies evident in earlier fictional representations of Spain (other than the predominantly racist representations of Franco's "Moors"; see chapter 2) is here expanded so that it is from the perspective of the colonies that this newly democratic Spain is judged.

Collis's rewriting of Spain's history is also a rewriting of family history, as the character Dio's frustration with the ARMH's work reveals the ways in which historical retellings – even those sensitive to the plight of the underdog – can still gloss over systemic oppression. Dio soon learns that the mysterious great-uncle he is in Spain to honour was rejected by his own family because of their suspicion that he was gay. While the ceremony recounts his murdered family member's integral work as a journalist, poet, and activist – including his close friendship and collaboration with Federico García Lorca – his queerness remains unspoken. Both Dio's family and Dio's ancestral country sustain a homophobic revision of history.

Throughout the novel, Dio's country of origin remains mysterious, his home city's name, La Ciudad (the City), offering no clue. But Dio does allude to a postcolonial identity that feels more important than any connection to Spain. He has difficulty communicating in the shared language of colonizer and colonized (recalling, of course, that Catalan is the other official language of Barcelona – Catalonia has its own fraught history within Spain, including the stigmatization of the Catalan language under Franco's rule). As well, his home country's government bears the imprint of postcolonial instability and foreign intervention: with both "right-wing and left-wing governments ... the difference is not always discernable at the local level. Usually, what changes is how the government talks to other countries, to the United States, and the oil and mining interests" (28). This home – along with his family – is ripped from him with the revolution that breaks out at the novel's end: "He should be home but he wasn't, he couldn't be, he suddenly thought he might never be" (148). *The Red Album* connects Dio's family history of migration to Spain's civil war, and more broadly to Spain's history of colonialism. Furthermore, the legacy of this colonialism – the social instability of Dio's home country – again enforces his family's fissuring, just as the revolution in Barcelona once drove his family to South America.

The revolutionary moment in Spain is woven through many of Collis's works. In an earlier book of poetry about the Spanish anarchists, *Anarchive* (2005), Collis describes "the Empires committing suicide / carrying within themselves / the seeds of their own dissolution" ("Dear Reclus"

17). The poem's colonial imagery of suicide by dissolution refracts through *The Red Album* as Spain's colonial implosion engulfs its former colonies. Spain's long-standing colonial projects allowed for the country's rise and, eventually, precipitated its fall. In addition to acknowledging its own civil war history and honouring its dead, Spain must also recognize its far longer history of colonial violence and oppression, both before and since the late-1930s conflict. Collis's representations demand a centuries-long view of the Spanish conflict. Acknowledging, even centring, peripheral participants is not enough, nor is the "ceremony bullshit" of monuments and honorary Spanish citizenship for former international volunteers: *The Red Album* calls for a larger-scale reckoning with the unquantifiable, perpetual wounds that colonialism originated.

Nor is it enough to critique Spanish colonialism from a North American distance. As *Matadora* reminds us, there is no room for Canadian smugness when analysing the originary fictions of the Spanish Civil War. Collis's emphasis on Spain's colonial history parallels Hutton's emphasis on the colonial heritage of both Spain and Canada. As I discussed earlier, the protagonist of *Underground*, Al, develops his understanding of feminism from an emerging recognition of his white privilege – a privilege explicitly yoked to the oppression of both Indigenous and immigrant populations. Throughout the novel, Hutton depicts Al's complicity in the ambient racism of his predominantly white community in both Canada and Spain. In addition to his early silence when hearing anti-Chinese jokes and attitudes – a prejudice that dissipates when a Chinese Canadian man saves his life during a strike – Al is challenged in his assumption of normative whiteness. To hide from the police after the strike, he travels to Whitehorse, where a friend of a friend has offered to house him. Albert is surprised to realize that this man, Johnny, is Indigenous, and then quickly recognizes the racism underscoring his surprise. When Albert decides to volunteer in Spain, Johnny and his wife again protect him, offering Albert the identification papers of their own deceased son. By adopting their son's identity Al avoids incarceration and travels to Spain. His very name becomes a constant reminder of his and his country's massive, unrepayable debt to Indigenous peoples.

Al's new awareness extends to Spain, where he perceives the racist biases of the Spanish Republicans against their colonial subjects: upon encountering a Moroccan POW, for instance, he reflects that the man "bears no resemblance to the murderous Moors who creep out at night to slit the throats of babies and rape their mothers" (214). Al rejects the negative stereotypes around Moroccan participants in favour of calm observation – a tacit acknowledgment of the Moroccan soldier's historic connection to Spain. Furthermore, he implores himself to "Be like the Moor ... Don't show emotion. Don't give anything away" (216) – a lesson that saves his life when he is able to escape imprisonment. While these characters might recall the tokenized minoritized figures I have highlighted in earlier Spanish Civil War novels, Hutton's representation of one man's coming of age emphasizes that his personal growth comes not from the supposed glories of the battlefield but from intimate contact with others. Hutton foregrounds marginalized characters who are completely absent from earlier literary depictions. What's more, these characters are represented as developed, complex individuals. In this way, Collis and Hutton enact analogous historical projects, tracing Spain and Canada's colonial histories and legacies. Within what could have been a triumphal narrative of Canadian transnational participation, Hutton underscores Canadian systemic racism toward Indigenous peoples and Chinese immigrants, connecting the Spanish Civil War to Canada's head tax and subsequent punitive immigration policies, indeed, to Canada's very basis in settler colonialism.

The Spanish Civil War remains with us – its international warfare as well as its intrinsic conflicts over colonialism, gender equality, racial integration, immigration, and sexual freedom. As I have argued throughout this book, looking to literary representations of marginalized characters compels another powerful rethinking of how we understand the Spanish Civil War: its stakes in Spain and in North America for overlapping populations of Jews, African Americans, people of colour, women, queer people, and immigrants as they struggled for social and legal recognition. Post-2000 Canadian fiction demands that we remember the war not simply as a foundational moment in the construction of a transnationally sympathetic Canadian nationalism – although it certainly was that – but as a means to continue to expand our own local and transnational sympathies, even our own notion of national identity.

These contemporary works of fiction present new narratives, of the war's relationship to more and more global conflicts in which the chemical warfare Franco practised in Morocco continues to have devastating effects, of Spain's continual struggle to understand its history, and of our own ongoing failures in Canada and the United States to recognize and counteract the systemic discrimination faced by marginalized populations. Jewish Canadian characters are far more prominent in this contemporary literature than in previous writings, and these characters are joined by others who are new to Canadian depictions of the Spanish Civil War – members of colonized populations from Canada and former Spanish colonies, other immigrant populations, and female and queer characters.

At the conclusion of British Canadian author Hugh Garner's mid-century novel *Cabbagetown* (1968), his protagonist, newly arrived in Spain, reflects of the breaking day: "The dawn is a widened earth – a populated earth" (415). Garner's protagonist could not have known in that moment how the war would conclude or what would await him if he returned to Canada – what that widened, populated earth would look like. Our national inheritances from the Spanish Civil War continue to inspire Canadian writers to bring more marginalized and hidden narratives to the fore, and to examine ever more candidly and assertively what the conflict means, here in Canada, for a widened, populated mosaic. We can only imagine what fictions they may uncover and what new truths they may show us.

Notes

Introduction

1 Franco's coalition referred to themselves as "Nationalists," a term that some historians argue legitimizes the invasion. Following María Rosa de Madariaga, I prefer the term "Insurgents" (*Los moros* 17).

2 For the sake of clarity, I use the terms "Canadians" and "Canadian citizens," even when referring to pre-1947 designations.

3 For more on Canadian antisemitism during this time, see Robinson 59–101; Klein, *Nazi Germany*. For analyses of Canada's regional antisemitisms, see Davies.

4 There was little support for the Spanish Republic in French Canada or among francophone artists, although Vulpe highlights the contributions of the Montreal communist newspaper *Clarté* ("This Issue" 32).

5 Eventually, nearly all Canadian volunteers were allowed to return, although they were not given veterans' benefits. Momryk cites at least three examples of Jewish Canadians who were prevented from re-entering Canada because of their "alien" status, who went on to settle in Mexico, Palestine, and Great Britain (17). Canada was the last of all the countries involved in the war to welcome its citizens home. Acknowledgment of their sacrifice is still controversial: Levangie notes, "all monuments erected to the Canadian volunteers were conceived of and funded by grassroots efforts, or were gifts from the government of the People's Republic of China" ("From Union Station").

6 For a detailed analysis of Allan and Watts's differing paths to Spain, see Murphy.

7 Momryk cites thirty-eight (5), Petrou fifty-two (22–3). While the number of Jewish-identified Canadian volunteers may seem small, Penslar suggests that "the low numbers might be explained by Canada's Foreign Enlistment Act, which prohibited its citizens' enlistment in the armed forces 'of any

foreign state at war with any friendly state,' and which technically applied to Canadians fighting on either side in Spain" (201). Zaagsma estimates that between 3,500 and 4,000 of all the foreign volunteers were Jewish (2).

8 Most were affiliated with the Communist Party but often split along ethno-national lines. According to Momryk's research, at least twenty-four of the Jewish-identified volunteers were members of a communist group – the Young Communist League, or the Communist Parties of Canada, the United States, or Spain (7). See also McKay, *Rebels* 145–217. Of the Jewish Canadian volunteers whose ancestry could be traced, half identified themselves as Canadian, while the rest came from the United States, Ukraine, Hungary, Finland, Poland, Denmark, Lithuania, Belarus, and Russia (Petrou 10–25).

Looking internationally, Zaagsma cautions against ascribing volunteers' decisions to travel to Spain to their Jewish identity, seeing this as an after-the-fact categorization of Jewish participation in Spain as resistance to Hitler (28–9). Furthermore, such categorization overlooks their individual motivations: "This is especially problematic because important questions need to be asked about nationality politics within the brigades, competition among national and/or ethnic groups and … the existence of anti-Semitism and/or anti-Semitic stereotypes" (Zaagsma 19).

9 The Canada and the Spanish Civil War Project, of which I am co-director with Bart Vautour and Kaarina Mikalson, has assembled a bibliography of Canadian cultural production around the Spanish Civil War currently totalling 390 pages. See also Carlsen, Peck, and Vulpe and Albari. Wald's overview of American writings on the Spanish Civil War – in and out of print – is an additional useful resource (*Trinity* 266–7n40).

There has also been minimal historical research into Canada's role in the conflict. Petrou's *Renegades: Canadians in the Spanish Civil War* (2008) provides a much-needed overview. See also earlier research by Hoar, Beeching, and Zuehlke. Gerassi's *The Premature Antifascists* (1986) includes some Canadian volunteers' first-person accounts but emphasizes Americans.

10 See Moss, as also Sugars, for discussions of the nuances of nationalism and colonialism's joint legacy in Canada.

11 See also Miller, "Documentary/Modernism"; Rabinowitz, *They Must*; and, in the Spanish context, Mendelson. I have argued elsewhere for the integral role of feminist ekphrasis in Spanish Civil War reportage: see "Mary Low's" and "Pacifying Bloomsbury."

The 1930s saw the creation of Canadian documentary institutions: in 1936, the Canadian Broadcasting Corporation was established, and in 1939, the National Film Board. Documentary forms and norms also made their way into modernist Canadian literature, as Livesay's essay "The Documentary Poem: A Canadian Genre" (1969) and her poetry collection *The Documentaries: Selected Longer Poems* (1968) suggest.

12 Gibbon's book was also part of a broader middle-class North American interest in the photographed lives of others – immigrants and the working classes, especially, in texts such as Agee and Evans's *Let Us Now Praise Famous Men* (1939) and Riis's *How the Other Half Lives* (1890).

13 As Hart describes in his history of Jewish Canadian literature,

> While functioning as a trope of inclusive plurality, a mosaic simultaneously depicts through each of its constituent fragments an exclusive singularity. The overall pattern of perceived wholeness proves illusory, cleaved by the mosaic's individual, bordered segments. Although the mosaic may invite readings and interpretations which suggest uniformity, consensus, and stasis, its tessellated nature produces an ongoing kinesis of recontextualization, re-reading, and reinterpretation. (363)

14 For more on Gibbon's exclusion of Indigenous and non-white populations, see Smith, "Cement" 55–6.

15 While Jewish immigrants were, during Gibbon's time, viewed as non-white, subsequent waves of immigration have contributed to the whitening of many Canadian Jews. Singer explains, "Jews can drop their 'colour' and become white, but only because there are new minority groups who are compelled to take up the lower social positions" (20). In the American context, Freedman notes, "Jewish middle-class assimilation frequently involved not only the acceptance of whiteness but also the active rejection of blackness – and often, of African Americans themselves" (29). For more on the growth of the category of "white ethnic," see Roediger, Brodkin.

16 Coleman analyses the trope of the infantile immigrant encountering Canadian civility, arguing, "the allegory of national maturation therefore articulates the hierarchies of race and gender in such a way that categories of privilege such as whiteness, Britishness, heterosexuality, and masculinity are naturalized as leading the vanguard of modernity, and people are placed at higher or lower stages of civil advancement on the basis of how many of these categories they can claim" (172). For Antonia Smith, Gibbon's emphasis on female immigrants enforces how intermarriage might render "the negative elements of their 'race' easily bred out" (54).

17 Gilman argues that American and European discourses of multiculturalism similarly evolve in tandem with – and possibly out of – Jewish experience, arguing that the "Jew" becomes "the litmus test for the possibility, necessity, and danger of the multicultural" (*Multiculturalism* 45).

18 The Botwin Company has received little critical attention. Zaagsma's new book *Jewish Volunteers, the International Brigades, and the Spanish Civil War* is a long overdue exploration; see especially 37–57. For more on international Jewish participation, see Penslar 201–7, Brossat and Klingberg 95–129.

Often, volunteers were able to switch battalions: for instance, Hugh Garner left the American volunteers to serve with the British, while George Orwell selected his enlistment based on where he hoped to be posted.

19 For a wide-ranging analysis of Spain's historical and contemporary treatment of its Jewish heritage, see Linhard's *Jewish Spain.* Greckol's poetry collection *No Line in Time* (2018) examines this Spanish connection to contemporary Jewish Canadian experience.

20 In a different way, the title of Robbins's *Perpetual War: Cosmopolitanism from the Viewpoint of Violence* ironically invokes Kant's "perpetual peace."

21 For more on the Orientalist aspects of Hispanist discourse, see Faber, *Anglo-American Hispanists*; and DeGuzmán.

22 For discussion of an earlier version of Canadian cosmopolitan nationalism, see Bentley.

23 "The cosmopolitan patriot can entertain the possibility of a world in which *everyone* is a rooted cosmopolitan, attached to a home of his or her own, with its own cultural particularities, but taking pleasure from the presence of other, different, places that are home to other, different, people. The cosmopolitan also imagines that in such a world not everyone will find it best to stay in a natal patria, so that the circulation of people among different localities will involve not only cultural tourism ... but migration, nomadism, diaspora" (Appiah 91–2; italics in the original).

24 The titles of two of Tulchinsky's books, *Taking Root: The Origins of the Canadian Jewish Community* (1993) and *Branching Out: The Transformation of the Canadian Jewish Community* (1998), emphasize this desire for rooted growth. The title of Allan's novel *This Time a Better Earth* and Duddy Kravitz's fixation on landownership in Richler's *The Apprenticeship of Duddy Kravitz* are fictional examples.

25 Amanda Anderson argues for detachment as a characteristic cosmopolitan aspiration, one that can never be actualized, but that rather becomes a position from which to consider the "cultural origins that one can no longer inhabit in any unthinking manner" (121). Favret further considers how cosmopolitan detachment functions in watching or reading about war from a distance, characterizing it as a "two-step between identification and separation" (227).

26 For more on Canadian modernism's preoccupation with cosmopolitanism, see Gerson, and also Trehearne 3–40.

27 For more on this propaganda, see Preston, *Spanish Holocaust* 34–51; Zaagsma 4.

28 For more on editorial practice and occasional literature, see Vautour, "Politics."

29 Garrett identifies a similar phenomenon among Jewish American authors depicting the Second World War (220).

30 There are, of course, many other relevant identity categories, both chosen and non-, including class, age, ability, and education.

31 In this approach I also do not intend to allegorize the figure of the Jew; as Boyarin and Boyarin rightly point out in "Diaspora," allegorizing is a problematic theoretical tendency that obliterates difference as it reaches for universality.

32 Edwards explains that the archive of Black transnational literature is "not so much ... a site or mode of preservation of a national, institutional, or individual past, but instead ... a 'generative system': in other words, a discursive system that governs the possibilities, forms, appearance, and regularity of particular statements, objects, and practices – or, on the simplest level, that determines 'what can and cannot be said'" (*Practice* 7). Irvine, in discussing Canadian leftist literary history, notes that "by calling attention to which kinds of textual materials are cast aside at a given historical moment, we may begin to reassess the processes of cultural selection that shape the canons, histories, and critical traditions that we have for the most part passively accepted without ever knowing what was left out in the first place and what interests and values motivated these originary acts of omission" (24).

33 Doyle emphasizes aesthetic forms and party affiliations, thereby providing an alternative genealogy to the more broadly leftist one I construct here.

34 Jewish Canadian poet Irving Layton would mock this title and Franco's egotistical power in "El Caudillo" (1964).

35 Preston explicitly connects the Spanish Civil War to the Holocaust in the title of his book *The Spanish Holocaust.* For more on Jewish experiences after the Spanish Civil War, see Zaagsma 109–13.

1 Love

1 In a departure, the Jewish American writer Michael Blankfort's novel *The Brave and the Blind* (1940) focuses on Spanish participation on both sides of the conflict, with a romantic subplot between a French male combatant and a Spanish woman. Except for allusions to Franco's Army of Africa, the novel emphasizes Spanish instead of transnational experiences.

2 Silber explains that after the American Civil War, the imagery of the powerful, logical, masculine man of the North marrying and taming the "tempestuous and romantic belle" of the South became, in the North, both a symbol of and a justification for reunification (7). In the postcolonial context, Levine describes how "white men sleeping with women of colour was seen merely as a natural extension of their residence in the colonies" (135). Sheffer's study of minority women authors argues for the multiple purposes of interracial romance plots in envisioning the nation as a family: "(1) they reveal a history of exploitation of racialized women by white men; and (2) they offer a multiracial model of national identity that promises a

more egalitarian future for minorities in the United States or those affected by its imperial reach" (2–3).

3 Herrick, in particular, counteracts the stereotype of passive Jewish men by presenting diverse Jewish characters in *Hermanos!* (1969), from Jake, a hard-line activist called "the voice and the hand" of the party in Spain, to the cruel higher-up Vlanoc, to Mack Berg, a Harvard graduate, to Eaman O'Hara Levy, "who spoke Yiddish with a brogue, having been born and bred in Dublin" (70). Elsewhere, the novel refers to Yiddish as "the esperanto [*sic*] of the International Brigades" (186). For more on Jewish masculinities, see Rosenberg, Breines.

4 See also Sol. For an early Canadian example of the interfaith romance novel, see Gwethalyn Graham's *Earth and High Heaven* (1944).

5 Taro's death was widely publicized internationally, and her funeral, organized by the French Communist Party, was attended by hundreds: "Taro's death propelled her into a type of martyrdom" (Vautour, Introduction xxi). For readers of Allan's novel in the 1930s and 1940s, the parallels between Taro and the character Lisa would therefore have been clear. For an extensive account of the relationship between Allan and Taro, see Norman Bethune Allan, "Gerda."

6 The heteronormative dimension of passing as gentile is a counterpoint to the antisemitic feminization of Jewish men – which, building on Sander Gilman's research, Hoffman explains affected every body part "from his tongue (speech) to his foot (making him unfit to serve in the military) to the circumcised (often read as castrated) penis" (9).

7 This final scene recalls the conclusion of Sinclair's Spanish Civil War novel *No Pasaran!*, in which the main character returns to the battlefield in what Sinclair describes as a "state of exaltation" (94), undistracted by thoughts of his girlfriend or home. Dickinson points out the relentless triangulation of male homosocial relationships in Canadian nationalist fiction; see 11–38.

8 Rottenberg argues against reading Jewish American novels such as *The Rise of David Levinsky* as assimilation narratives, emphasizing the complexities of passing and assimilating: "the subject's desire to live up to the norms associated with a particular category ... is always multifaceted and riddled with ambivalence" (11).

9 The extent to which Harrison identified – or was identified – as Jewish is unclear. His scrapbooks of press clippings demonstrate that the Yiddish press's reviews of *Meet Me on the Barricades* identify him as a Jewish author, while English-language publications do not mention his religion (Harrison, "Scrapbook 1").

10 For discussion of the novel's reception, see Sharpe and Vautour xxi–xxvi.

11 For more on the politics of Harrison's modernist aesthetics, see Sharpe and Vautour xv–xx.

12 See Coleman 168–210; Smith, "Cement" 37–60; Garrett 4.

13 As Garrett argues of post–Second World War fiction, "Intentionally or not, the Jewish American soldier stood in stark contrast to the negative stereotype of the passive Holocaust victim: America had transformed the Jew from a weak sufferer into a proactive warrior who fights and slays the enemy" (4).

14 For more on Richler's interest in the war, see Kramer, *Mordecai Richler* 74–6.

15 For more on Richler's critique of Québécois nationalism, see Ravvin, "The War and Before" 205–7.

16 Singer explains how being perceived as white is tantamount to being accepted as a Canadian: in *The Apprenticeship of Duddy Kravitz*, "Duddy's desire for land is an aspirational desire, a desire to become a part of the upwardly mobile middle class – the class that, perhaps best, embodies the invader-settler belief that the highest achievement is owning land: a belief that the rewards of citizenship stem from becoming a shareholder in 'Canada'" (18). Such fixation on land and Canadianness is evident across Richler's fiction.

17 As Jewish American former volunteer Alvah Bessie critiques the novel in *The Un-Americans* (1957), "the shattering struggle of twenty-eight million people for survival and decency was subordinated to an endless episode in a sleeping bag, and the phrase 'the earth moved' was quoted by bohemians and bourgeois with a leer on their faces" (211–12). See Wald, *Trinity* 16–45.

18 Bessie's *The Un-Americans* explicitly contrasts the experiences of two Spanish Civil War veterans, one Jewish, one gentile, compelled to testify before the House Un-American Activities Committee – as Bessie himself was. Both characters ruin their romantic relationships, in part through sublimating sexual desire into volunteerism. See also Bessie's *Men in Battle* (1939), *The Heart of Spain* (1952), and *Spain Again* (1975). Bessie's earlier works – especially the memoir *Men in Battle* – explicitly connect Spanish Civil War participation with the need to prove masculinity. For a discussion of his activism and poetry, see Nelson, "International Context" 1–7.

Jewish American former volunteer Milton Wolff published the novel *Another Hill* (1994), in which he sympathetically portrays American and Spanish women who are romantically involved with North American volunteers.

19 In this way, Richler joins a broader category of Jewish North American novelists of the time who foreground women's roles in both leftism and the Spanish Civil War – for example, William Herrick with *Kill Memory* (1983) and Chaim Potok with *Davita's Harp* (1985). These two American novels present the war from female characters' perspectives – Potok, through the eyes of a young American girl, and Herrick, in his final fictional representation of the war, through a former nurse's reminiscences. In *Hermanos!*, Herrick inverts the typical romance narrative: the protagonist

pursues a relationship with a fellow volunteer against the Communist Party's wishes.

20 In Richler's non-fiction *This Year in Jerusalem* (1994), a study of Israel and Palestine, he reflects on his own sense of belonging in Canada and criticizes a form of Jewish identity defined against adversaries:

> But many of us, unapologetically Jewish, do feel at home in North America, the most open of societies, and even harbor a sneaking, subversive sympathy for gentiles, who must find a number of our apparatchiks exasperating and endlessly kvetchy. For if we once rebuked the *goyim* for supporting quotas on Jewish students at universities, as well as maintaining country clubs, hotels, and neighborhoods that were *judenrein*, there are those Jews who now mourn the passing of most of these restrictions, and complain that it is by dint of having become so acceptable that we are menaced today. (259; italics in the original)

2 Sympathy

1 Petrou's study of Canadian volunteers tracks ethnicity but not race and does not record any Canadian volunteers of African descent (22–3). Many of the Italian soldiers who fought with Franco had first served in Ethiopia; see Keene 1–17. For more on African American responses to the invasion of Ethiopia, see Hochschild 25.

2 Naison points out that Popular Front politics in Harlem extended beyond the Spain–Ethiopia intersection to connect "the cause of Ethiopia with that of China and Loyalist Spain … the persecution of Jews in Germany with that of blacks in the United States" (194). See also Dolinar's discussion of Langston Hughes's writings as a prescient articulation of the Double-V campaign (72). More recently, Potok's novel *Davita's Harp* (1985) also connects the stakes of the Ethiopian and Spanish causes.

3 Kea's name is frequently spelled "Kee" – in fact, she herself spelled it both ways.

4 See Donlon, "Thyra Edwards" 114–15.

5 For more on Morocco's colonial history, see Balfour, Sueiro Seoane, and Alás-Brun. Franco's forces were also aided by international volunteers. For a discussion of literary depictions of Morocco by anglophone fascist supporters, see Keene 254–5.

6 Thomas notes that a delegation from a "committee of Moroccan nationalist action" applied to the Republican government, but the government was unresponsive until 1937, when it "did take steps to try and stir up Morocco against Franco. For example, on 19 February 1937, they proposed to Britain and France concessions in Morocco favourable to both countries (perhaps an assignment of all Spanish Morocco to France) if they would change their minds over non-intervention" (561). See also Kelley 33.

7 For more on this propaganda, see Preston, *Spanish Holocaust* 34–51. Rein suggests that Francoist Spain "tried to appropriate the achievements of the Jewish and Muslim cultures that had flourished in Spain during the Middle Ages until Isabella and Ferdinand took steps to extirpate them from Spanish soil ... Franco portrayed himself as a defender of Islam and an enemy of colonialism and European imperialism" (196).

8 According to Thomas, among Franco's supporters, German soldiers in Spain numbered at most 10,000, and Italian soldiers as many as 75,000; there were also several thousand Portuguese soldiers. Moroccan soldiers numbered at least 75,000 (940). Jensen points out that there were also North Africans among the International Brigades, numbering 700 (514). Some Moroccans supported Republican Spain's continued presence in the colony, fearing that without Spain's protection, France would colonize the entire region. For insight into the conditions under which the Moroccan troops enlisted and fought, see de Madariaga, *Los moros* and "The Intervention." After the war, Franco's government scapegoated the Moroccan soldiers as the perpetrators of the most violent war atrocities.

9 For more on divergent attitudes toward the Moroccan soldiers, see Høgsbjerg 168–76. Many soldiers on the Republican side attempted to entice Moroccan soldiers to switch sides, mostly to no avail; see Seidman 103–4.

10 For more on Edwards's writing on the treatment of Moroccan soldiers, see Andrews 104–5. Donlon contends that such journalistic reports were often in contrast to the dominant Republican message: "Republican propaganda often portrayed the 'Moors' as barbarian, savage invaders, but Hughes, Cunard, and others viewed them as victims of colonialism exploited by Franco" (*Poetry* 33n55). In Canada, coverage in the *Daily Clarion* and in *New Frontier* included anonymously authored articles as well as one by Cunard, reprinted in the *Clarion*: see "Moors."

11 Edwards notes that McKay also discusses Spanish colonialism more explicitly in an obscure essay titled "A Little Lamb to Lead Them: A True Narrative." See "Taste" 967–9. For more on Wright's depictions of Spain and Morocco, see Kennedy 107–10; Reid-Pharr 180–213.

12 Alás-Brun explains that Republican propaganda "portrayed the much-feared Moroccan troops that fought with Franco as black, or at least with rather dark skin and some exaggerated features usually associated with caricatures of black Africans ... By contrast, the image of the heroic Moroccan soldier was systematically whitened in propaganda drawings and paintings created by Franco's supporters" (167).

13 I have been unable to find any documentation explaining the decision to excise this section. For other examples of literary revisions to remove references to Morocco, see Lindberg's consideration of W.E.B. Du Bois, Berry's examination of Richard Wright's excisions from *Pagan Spain* (xiii),

and Høgsbjerg's analysis of the different editions of C.L.R. James's *The Black Jacobins: Toussaint L'Ouverture and the San Domingo Revolution.*

14 See Jensen 510–14 for answers to some of these questions.

15 See too Hughes's "Negroes in Spain" and "'Organ Grinder's Swing' Heard above Gunfire in Spain – Hughes." Wright makes a similar observation in *Pagan Spain,* although he also comments that he was frequently stared at, wondering of one woman whether he "remind[ed] her of Moors" (9) and recounting how his appearance even prompted a postal worker to cross herself (29).

16 Thurston connects Hughes's representation of the Moroccan soldiers' historic claim to Spain – as former colonizers and rulers – to the more recent invasion of Ethiopia, suggesting that in Hughes's journalism "the 'Moors' are avatars, then, for Haile Selassie's kingdom" ("Bombed" 122).

17 Thurston notes that Hughes's poetry and his essay "Negroes in Spain" were the only texts to analyse race in the conflict in the *Volunteer for Liberty* (*Making* 130). "Negroes in Spain" raises important questions around gender, too, in describing how Franco's troops relied on Moroccan women to do their washing and cooking.

18 Edwards contends that the encounter implies "that a diaspora is necessarily translated and mediated" ("Langston Hughes" 694). For more on the translation of Hughes's poetry into Spanish, and his collaborative translations of Lorca from Spanish into English, see Scaramella.

19 In his memoir, Hughes describes how the Popular Front attempted to foster class-based connections (*I Wonder* 353).

20 Yates, another African American volunteer, relates Cobb's story in his memoir (127–8).

21 Calihman notes Williams's writerly debt to his time in Spain (158n5).

22 See Dobson 73; Walcott 87–8.

23 As Crunden points out, "since the Spanish Civil War gave Joshua and his friends a meaningful cause, the loss of it is a threat to their present identity" (248).

24 Richler's earlier representation of an antisemitic Jewish woman performing in blackface in *The Acrobats* similarly pushes the boundaries of religious and racial affiliations.

25 In discussing Richler's attitude toward race during the Civil Rights era, Kramer contends that "Richler simply didn't know what he was talking about" when the author claimed an absence of Canadian racism (*Mordecai Richler* 207). Kramer explains that Richler and his writings could be racially demeaning and insensitive: he satirized Black people in the same way that he satirized Jews, without considering the differing social dynamics of their lived experiences.

26 This scene also recalls one I discuss in chapter 3, from Richler's novel *The Acrobats,* in which a Jewish American tourist meets a Jewish immigrant to Spain (114–15).

27 Writing in 2011, Rinaldo Walcott describes a multiplicity of perspectives on Canadian multiculturalism: "Thus, it might be argued that the only consensus on Canadian multiculturalism in the last thirty-plus years is that it has become a fundamental Canadian entity, but a consensus on what it means and how it should work continues to elude us. Ideas and practices of multiculturalism remain contested sites and so they should be" (94).

28 For more on literary representations of Black–Jewish relationships, see for instance Budick, Newton, Sundquist. Key to understanding the intersecting representations of Black and Jewish diasporas is Gilroy's *The Black Atlantic*: "Acknowledging the intercultural history of the diaspora concept and its transcoding by historians of the black dispersal into the western hemisphere remains politically important not just in North America, where the story of its borrowing could be used to open up the long and complicated relationship between blacks and Jews in radical politics, but in Europe too, where Ethiopianism and Africentricity have exhibited both Zionism and anti-Semitic features" (211).

29 Calihman details Williams's use of Spanish Civil War nostalgia throughout his oeuvre; see 141–2.

30 Reilly notes: "Blackman is a figure particularized by William's provision of a biography for him that includes the personal feelings of love, frustration, and ambition, but, as his name insists, he is equally a figure typifying the collective enterprise of Blacks seeking participation in history as conscious actors" (5).

31 Kelley poses related questions about African American participation:

> How did African Americans feel among their white fellow Americans, particularly in a social setting? For that matter, how comfortable were they with white European International brigadists for whom language served as a major barrier? To what extent were they treated as objects (i.e., representatives of a race and examples of an ideal) as opposed to thinking, feeling subjects? (35).

3 Community

1 For more on Livesay's frequent comparison of the natural and social worlds in her Spanish Civil War poetry, see Vautour, "From Transnational Politics."

2 Gellhorn, Parker, and Hellman have been represented as war tourists rather than the journalists they were, an issue compounded, in Gellhorn's case, by literary critics' frequent conflation of Hemingway's fictional character Dorothy Bridges with Gellhorn in his play *The Fifth Column*. Hemingway even, apparently, infuriated Gellhorn by trying to take credit for her press credentials and voyage to Spain – a voyage she paid for with earnings from her own writing.

3 In discussing women's writings about the First World War, Debra Rae Cohen notes a similar intersecting of the private and public spheres, in which women sought to create alternative spaces in their fiction: "enclosures – whether fantasy structures, architectural motifs, or narrative frames – become privileged temporary spaces for the interrogation of wartime rhetorics" (8).

4 Linhard contends that "it is necessary to challenge such binaries as combat experience and civilian experience in order to reveal the radical heterogeneity of women's participation, and to show that the aforementioned 'legitimate' experience of war, as it appears in hegemonic narratives, represents only an extremely limited and usually patriarchal perspective" (*Fearless Women* 4).

5 I focus here on texts in which the Spanish Civil War is the animating issue. Works like Herbst's novel *Rope of Gold* (1939) incorporate allusions to the Spanish Civil War into a broader discussion of American labour struggles and family life. On this, see Rabinowitz, *Labor* 157–72; Shulman 131–2.

6 See Byron on Ibárruri's own memoirs and their representation of women's collective activism – an important contextualization of Ibárruri's own, at times tokenized, role.

7 Preston writes that in much of Spain, "the woman rash enough to put her head over the parapet and intrude upon the patriarchal territory of politics faced accusations of being brazen and ... from there it was but a short step to being seen as a whore" (*Doves* 411).

8 See also Ellis.

9 For instance, North American women's contributions are evident in the pamphlet *Writers Take Sides: Letters about the War in Spain from 418 American Authors* (1938), published by the League of American Writers. At least forty-nine of the respondents among the loyalists' supporters are women, with many more women signatories to that side. An earlier, similar questionnaire of English Canadians published by *New Frontier*, "Where I Stand On Spain," includes only two women (1.8 Dec. 1936, 13–16). *Writers Take Sides* was the American counterpart to the publication *Authors Take Sides on the Spanish War* (1937), created by the British activist and writer Nancy Cunard.

10 McDonald notes that women were a mere 10 per cent of the CPUSA membership in the 1930s, but constituted half its membership by 1943 – including an increasing membership of Black women (4–5).

11 White Canadian women gained the right to vote in federal elections beginning in 1917, but provincial voting rights varied: women in Quebec – which had a large Jewish population – could not vote until 1940. Asian men and women did not gain voting rights until 1948. Indigenous people did not gain the federal vote until 1960.

12 As Herrmann describes, "women from left-of-center political and syndicalist organizations received rudimentary military instruction, were encouraged to expand their physical sphere of existence by changes as prosaic as wearing pants, to take active posts in their unions, to seek out vocational training, to initiate armed reappropriations of farmlands, and generally to participate in the making of revolution" ("Voices" 12). See Nash 50–1, 110.

13 In a similar appeal to their audience's sensibilities, reportage by the British Cuban writer Mary Low and the American journalist Josephine Herbst likewise considers women's self-presentation. See Low and Breá's *Red Spanish Notebook* and Herbst's "The Starched Blue Sky of Spain." North American women's representations of Spanish women are at odds with the Spanish media's ambivalent representation of militant women; see Linhard, *Fearless Women* 39–41.

14 Ackerman points out inconsistencies in Hellman's account of her involvement in the Spanish cause in *An Unfinished Woman* (218–21). Buller undertakes an extensive comparison of Hellman's memoirs and personal papers; see especially 118, 120–1, and 123–4 for an examination of Hellman's process in rewriting her Spanish Civil War journalism into *An Unfinished Woman.*

15 For memoirs by American women embedded with the insurgents, see Davis, *My Shadow in the Sun* (1940) and *A Fearful Innocence* (1981), and Cowles, *Looking for Trouble* (1941). Keene further examines pro-Franco American women's memoirs and journalism (249–52, 260–4).

16 Most of Kea's archival documents are undated, but the four memoirs and many drafts housed at the Tamiment Library and Robert F. Wagner Labor Archives and at the Marx Memorial Library span approximately forty years. In addition to "A Negro Nurse," Kea wrote a much longer and more detailed account of the same time period, titled "While Passing Through." Dating this memoir is more complicated: one historian speculates that it was also written in 1938 (Patai, "Salaria Kea O'Reilly" 1), while the typed copy of "While Passing Through" (the only complete draft of which I am aware) housed in the Tamiment has "1973" written on the front, along with other minor edits also in Kea's hand. One page of that copy is typed on the back of a 1960 article about Kea.

The Tamiment also contains two narratives from after 1966, the year of Kea's retirement: "May Every Knock Be a Boost" is a much-shortened version of Kea's life, and the handwritten "Hope: To Serve God and my country. Reflection of my Life" was composed for Kea's Bible study class. These two memoirs follow the same timeline and omit Kea's volunteering in Spain, but the latter emphasizes Catholicism's centrality to her daily life. Excerpts from "While Passing Through" have appeared in *The Beacon, Magazine of the Beacon Journal,* and *Health and Medicine: Journal of the Health and Medicine Policy Research Group*, and in Patai's article in *Nursing History Review*. The excerpt from *Health and Medicine* was also excerpted in Fyrth and Alexander's *Women's Voices from the Spanish Civil War*.

17 For instance, Donlon cites an article by Nancy Cunard about Kea that also appears in Kea's later memoir "While Passing Through"; see "Thyra Edwards" 115.

18 For further discussion of Kea's involvement, see Brandt; Carroll and Fernández; Graham, *Spanish Civil War*; Hine; Katz; Kelley; Plummer; and Sharpe, "Salaria Kea." Collum's book includes a short biography of Kea and reprints her pamphlet, "A Negro Nurse in Republican Spain."

19 Thompson's memoir outlines her different activities while in Spain, including her brief meeting with Kea (10–11). For more on Edwards, see Andrews; and Donlon, "Thyra Edwards." For more on Robeson, see her own account, Ransby 125–31.

20 For instance, in *Into the Fire*, Kea states:

> See I didn't know much about fascism. Here's the thing that brought everything to me: it was the way that Germany was treating Jews. I never really thought that white people do against white people because we don't look at you as French or Italian – you're white. I had met a lot of Jewish people who had left Germany and they told us about what Hitler was doing to them. It was like the Ku Klux Klan. So now we're matching what is happening in Germany to the Jews to us here in the United States. So I went downtown to this meeting, and the meeting was all these people from foreign countries. And they said to me that they hoped to go to Spain to work with the Republican side. So they said, "would you like to go with us?" I said, "Yes!" The next thing I knew, I was accepted to go to Spain. (5:00–5:44)

In both this documentary and *The Good Fight*, Kea describes her singular role in Spain, but she does not mention any negative experiences. More recently, the documentary *Invisible Heroes* describes Kea's work but omits any direct quotations from her writings (43:15–43:43, 44:45–45:50).

21 For extensive analysis of these efforts to keep Kea's writings unpublished, see Reid-Pharr 64–71. In a letter to former International Brigades soldier Martin Balter, Patai defends her decision:

> It's all a figment of her imagination ... It's totally absurd that [Dr Donald] Pitts (who may have been a not-good person and a sexist) would make such an outlandish racist insult. Had he done so the AMB [American Medical Bureau] personnel and the Lincoln volunteers on the boat would have been up in arms ... none of us wants such an untrue lie to dim the glory of the history of the US volunteers ... However, the fact that Salaria may have confused fact with fiction does not in any way diminish her bravery, courage, nobility in volunteering. (27 Dec. 1990)

Patai's determination not to "dim the glory" presupposes a shared politics among all Americans volunteering in Spain. As Reid-Pharr notes of Patai's rationalization, "a single incident from one (obviously sexist but surprisingly nonracist) aboard the S.S. *Paris* would throw the entire logic underwriting the heroism of the Lincoln brigadiers into disarray" (67). In her writings, Patai at times excerpts parts of Kea's memoirs, but never those sections that discuss the racist incident or the fascist capture. See her "Heroines of the Good Fight: Testimonies," "Heroines of the Good Fight: U.S. Women Volunteers," and "Salaria Kea O'Reilly."

22 In an interview with Gerassi, Hutchins further describes how, once they arrived in Spain, Pitts insisted that Kea and all the other female volunteers be tested for syphilis. See Gerassi 113. I have not yet found any mention of this incident by Kea. Patai cites Gerassi's book in some of her drafts, and the majority of the letters dismissing Kea's claims were written after its publication; however, none of these writers ever mentions Hutchins's support for Kea's claims.

Most often, volunteers and historians cite mistakes or inconsistencies in Kea's narratives as evidence that she fabricated them. For instance, she claims to have travelled to Europe on a British ship, when she was in fact on a French one. In an early account, she credits two soldiers with British accents with rescuing her from the fascists, but in later accounts she stipulates that one rescuer was either Canadian or French. She describes her prison cell as five floors underground in some accounts, but not in others.

23 Kea's decision to omit her time in Spain from later memoirs may have been politically motivated, for many former volunteers, including Kea, had a difficult time finding employment because of their supposed ties to the Communist Party. They were hounded by, among others, the House Un-American Activities Committee. In a letter to Fredericka Martin, Kea worries, "Do you think I might be on Nixon's Enemies list" (9 Jan. 1974).

24 For more on Claudia Jones's use of the term, see McDonald 26.

25 The longer manuscript gives an extensive description of each African American soldier with whom Kea came in contact, as well as the story of how she met and married her husband, an Irish soldier named John O'Reilly. Donlon further analyses the omission of Kea's romantic relationships in Spain, including the possibility that she was first married to the African American soldier Oliver Law ("Thyra Edwards," 116). See Gates for a discussion of the framing of slave texts. Donlon sees Kea's reliance on press coverage as another technique to stake her authority while writing about her oppression: see "Thyra Edwards" 115.

26 For more on Gellhorn's Second World War fiction, see Lassner. Gellhorn herself disparaged her own role in Spain in *The Face of War* (16).

27 Much has been written about these poems. See, for instance, Shulman 231; Mariani; Kennedy-Epstein, "Whose fires."

28 Dorothy B. Hughes published *The Fallen Sparrow* (1942), a murder mystery about Spanish Civil War veterans.

29 In studying Rukeyser's other Spanish Civil War texts, many critics point to Rukeyser's relationship with the German Olympian Otto Boch. See, for instance, Mariani.

30 Irvine notes her nearly mythic position as "the one individual who persistently traverses modernist and leftist cultural formations and reappears at key moments of crisis and transformation of magazine cultures" (27). See also Irr 215–16.

31 In *Archive for Our Times*, for instance, see "Man Asleep" (45), "Spain" (54–5), "Reply to a Time Server" (67), "The Bethune Wind" (205). In *Collected Poems* see "Catalonia" (98–101). For more analysis of Livesay's inclusion of sexuality in her representations of war, see Rifkind, *Comrades* 66; Pierce.

32 See, for instance, Reiter 208–9.

33 For more on "The Exiles: Spain" and kinship, see Tetzlaff 2–3.

34 Sánchez-Pardo González also cites the unpublished poem "We of 1937," in which Waddington "undertakes a critique of a militaristic male-dominated elite" (179). The poem is not included in Panofsky's *The Collected Poems of Miriam Waddington.*

35 See "Dog Days" (81), "Icons" (435–8), "The Nineteen Thirties Are Over" (500). There is also a photograph by Michael Semak of a museumgoer looking at Picasso's *Head of a Horse, Sketch for Guernica* in Waddington's *Call them Canadians: A Photographic Point of View.* Picasso painted *Guernica* in 1937 in response to the fascist bombing of the Basque town (187).

36 Rifkind similarly observes of Waddington's literary criticism, "For Waddington, the poet works Janus-faced, with one eye to the future and one to the past" ("Collection" 258).

37 "With the flexible and sometimes threatening power of that which crosses boundaries, Jewishness serves modernism as a sort of multipurpose tool whose components can be adapted to nearly any task. When modernists consider the possibilities for disinterested art, they think about the stereotype of the greedy Jew. When they work to create a modernism that supersedes masculine realism, they rely on the paradigm provided by the Christian supersession of Judaism. When they think about modernity, racial continuity, or timelessness, they enlist the plastic Jew to support their exploration of these temporal modes" (Linett 188–9).

38 Hochschild explains that under Franco "the position of women was far worse than in Hitler's Germany. Women were legally considered dependents of their fathers or husbands, whose permission they needed to open a bank account, own property, file a lawsuit, apply for a job, or take a trip away from home. A husband had the right to kill his wife if he caught her committing adultery" (347).

39 Kennedy-Epstein, too, notes that recovery work often repositions women's contributions; see Introduction xi.

4 Inclusion

1 In emphasizing this virtual space of war in which a queer writer was mourned and celebrated, I also want to point to the integral roles that other queer writers have played in our understanding of the conflict, including Langston Hughes, Virginia Woolf, Nicolás Guillén, Jean "Jim" Watts, William Rollins, Jr., Muriel Rukeyser, Stephen Spender, Josephine Herbst, Dorothy Livesay, and Edna St Vincent Millay. My approach is also distinct from those of scholars who examine Lorca's poetic influence on others, or queerness in his own poetry. See, for instance, Álvarez; Binding; Gibson, *"Caballo azul"*; Herrero; Kennedy 120–5; Perriam; Soto, "'To Hear'" and "Crossing Over"; Woods.

2 Nelson explains that in the United States, "the war produced a small number of highly focused topics – the defense of Madrid, the murder of the poet Federico García Lorca, the role of the Internationals who came to fight for the Republic – that were unlike anything in the poetry of the first half of the decade" (*Revolutionary Memory* 218). See also Infante 81–116, Rogers 163–98. Not only the left mourned Lorca, either: South African writer Roy Campbell, author of *Flowering Rifle: A Poem from the Battlefield of Spain* and a Franco supporter, translated Lorca's poetry into English.

3 Referring to José Esteban Muñoz's analysis of terrorist drag, Puar explains, "homosexuals have been traitors to the nation, figures of espionage and double agents, associated with communists during the McCarthy era, and, as with suicide bombers, have brought on and desired death through the AIDS pandemic (both suicide bomber and gay man always figure as already dying, a decaying or corroding masculinity). More recent exhortations place gay marriage as 'the worst form of terrorism' and gay couples as 'domestic terrorists'" (xxxi).

4 Stainton observes that the Falange squad that murdered Lorca called him "queer" during their attack, explaining: "Many Granadans assumed he was a communist. Others hated him for his homosexuality. Behind his back they called him 'the queer with the bow tie'" (449). Preston suggests that while the Falange may have claimed Lorca was murdered "because of an apolitical private feud related to his homosexuality ... Lorca was anything but apolitical ... Since he was an immensely famous and popular poet and playwright, his politics and his sexuality provoked the loathing of the Falange and the rest of the right" (*Spanish Holocaust* 173–4).

5 For an extensive discussion of how Lorca's murder was reported in Spain, see Sahuquillo 36–7. For a literature review of critical responses to Lorca's queerness, see Sahuquillo 33–65.

6 Reid-Pharr's analysis of the similar popular preoccupation with Langston Hughes and Lorca's sexual orientations is an important reminder of the easy assumptions many make about the scholar's ability (or responsibility)

to prove queer identity: "I have begun to suspect that we remain far too comforted by the assumption that no matter the complexity of the questions that we confront in our cultural studies, these might ultimately be resolved through reference to biography" (139).

7 See Boyarin, Itzkovitz, and Pellegrini. For more on the proximity of queerness to racialization during the same time period, see Pérez.

8 Mayhew notes that, in addition to the extensive poetic responses of Black and gay poets, many Jewish poets have also written Lorca poems. Mayhew contends that the lack of a discussion of Jewish "markers of identity" in these poems makes any analysis hypothetical (46); I suggest that Jewish content and Jewish authorial identity need not always coexist.

9 Lorca also referred to his poem "Thamar and Amnon" as "Gypsy-Jewish," in its genesis from an Old Testament song he had heard Andalusian Roma people singing (Stainton 127). For more on Lorca's use of Jewish figures and imagery in his poetry, see Glass, "El cementerio judío"; Nordlund.

10 Stainton suggests that these parallels were often based on simplifications and generalizations about Black and *gitano* primitivism and experiences of persecution (221).

11 I have not found any documentation of a Canadian publisher producing a volume of Lorca's works, although Vulpe does note that in the 1930s, *New Frontier* and *Canadian Forum* published translations of Spanish poetry ("This Issue" 33).

12 Mayhew offers an extensive critique of the Americanization of Lorca through "inadequate translations ([Ben] Belitt, [Robert] Bly), apocrypha ([Paul] Blackburn, [Jack] Spicer, [Robert] Creeley), and weak imitations of Lorquian surrealism ([Amiri] Baraka, [Jerome] Rothenberg, [Robert] Bly)" (179).

13 Rogers traces the different ways Lorca became a symbol, noting, too, that his death almost immediately prompted multiple translations of his works (186–7). See also Reid-Pharr's chapter on Lorca's mutual influence with African American intellectuals and artists, "Lorca's Deathly Poetics" 72–117.

14 Warner had previously published her article "Barcelona" in *New Frontier* 1.9, reprinted from the English *Left Review* (9–10).

15 Noting that Klippert worked as a mechanic's helper, Goldie additionally explores the classed dimensions of Klippert's arrest and classification as a dangerous sexual offender ("Queer Nation?" 18). For more on the impact of the Charter of Rights and Freedoms' entrenchment on queer rights in Canada, see Miriam Smith.

16 Ian McKay envisions a future "queer leftism," but notes that it is "not a historically significant counter-hegemonic formation that can be documented in Canadian left history" (*Rebels* 133). In describing the

American Communist Party, Wald notes that the "policy since the 1930s had purportedly been to prohibit gay people from joining it, associating homosexuality with social decadence" (*American Night* 118).

17 As Sherry argues, in the United States after the Second World War, antisemitic fears of Jewish control of the media soon morphed into homophobic fears of a "Homintern." See also Wald, *American Night* 117–49.

18 The authors trace this intersection to the nineteenth century, as has Gilman's work on the feminized Jewish man: see *Jew's Body* 125–6.

19 Simply analogizing queer and Jewish experiences effaces their intersections, as the title of Jakobsen's chapter, "Queers Are Like Jews, Aren't They?" demonstrates. Jakobsen also cautions against erasing the homophobic discourse that initially brought the term "queer" to what is now an area of study.

20 Through a series of anglophone anthology projects, Lorca's poetry – and poetry dedicated to Lorca – has remained central within literary remembrance projects of the 1930s and beyond. Lorca's own words were included in a series of pamphlets, *Les poétes du monde défendent le peuple espagnole* (1936–1937), published by Nancy Cunard and Pablo Neruda. M.J. Benardete and Rolfe Humphries's collection ... *and Spain Sings: Fifty Loyalist Ballads Adapted by American Poets* (1937) omits Lorca's own writings but contains poems dedicated to Lorca. Alan Calmer's *Salud! Poems, Stories and Sketches of Spain by American Writers* (1938) emphasizes Lorca through elegies written in English, by the Jewish American immigrant poet S. Funaroff and gay Canadian-born poet John Malcolm Brinnin, among others. *Poems for Spain* (1939), edited by Stephen Spender and John Lehmann, likewise includes a section of elegies to Lorca.

In the 1950s, Jewish American Spanish Civil War veteran Alvah Bessie edited *The Heart of Spain: Anthology of Fiction, Non Fiction, and Poetry* (1952), which includes Lorca's own poem "Ballad of the Spanish Civil Guard," translated by Langston Hughes (18–21), alongside elegies to him.

The 1970s and '80s saw the greatest production of anthologies paying tribute to Lorca. Murray A. Sperber's anthology *And I Remember Spain* (1974) brings together a range of international responses. Valentine Cunningham's collection *The Penguin Book of Spanish Civil War Verse* (1980) includes a section of Lorca elegies titled "The Crime Was in Granada." Carl Bauer's *Cries from a Wounded Madrid* (1984) excerpts and translates three Spanish-language anthologies originally published during the war: *Romancero de la guerra civil, Poetas en la España leal,* and *Homenaje de despedida a las Brigadas Internacionales.* Bauer also includes three translated elegies. Another anglophone anthology, *Winds of the People* (1986), edited by Michael Rossman and Richard Vernier, highlights Lorca's influence. Rossman and Vernier self-published their translations of Spanish-language Spanish Civil

War poetry, placing Lorca's own poetry alongside poems by Guillén, Prados, and Neruda and including Neruda's essay eulogizing Lorca. The same year, John Miller's *Voices Against Tyranny* memorialized Lorca through multiple artists' prose reflections on Lorca's murder alongside a single poem by Lorca himself, "Lament for Ignacio Sánchez Mejías" (54–62).

Most recently, *Sealed in Struggle: Canadian Poetry and the Spanish Civil War* (1995), edited by Nicola Vulpe and Maha Albari, includes a cluster of poems about Lorca from as early as the 1940s. Cary Nelson's *The Wound and the Dream: Sixty Years of American Poems about the Spanish Civil War* (2002) incorporates poetry from the late 1930s through 1999, with at least fifteen Lorca elegies. Jim Jump's *Poems from Spain: British and Irish International Brigaders on the Spanish Civil War* (2006) brings together poetry primarily by soldiers.

21 Another contemporary poem, "Spain, You Hurt Me," by the Jewish Ottawa author and translator Seymour Mayne, elegizes Peruvian poet César Vallejo. Its eerie opening lines, "Spain, you hurt me – / said the poet – " (145), also allude to the many poets killed in Spain. See also Mayne's *Dragon Trees.*

22 Anderson's usage also recalls Lorca's use of the term in his poem to Walt Whitman – an allusion with its own queer significance, as Sahuquillo points out (47).

23 For more on Sutherland's attack on Anderson, and the alignment of *Preview* with older, British cosmopolitanism and of *First Statement* with newer, American nativism, see Barton 14–16, Dickinson 71–3.

24 Anderson's explicitly transnational concluding gesture recalls Infante's analysis of Lorca's influence on the Berkeley Renaissance: the poets "lack[ed] local models for the generational and historical transmission for the practice of their own queerness ... [but through these poetics could] turn their local and private experience into a poetry that aimed to express a public and universal need" (87).

25 Goldie and Frew note the complications around designating Livesay the first well-known lesbian Canadian poet when she did not "actively participat[e] in and celebrat[e] lesbian relationship" until her later life (865).

26 Lorca's continuing influence on the Canadian stage merits further study. I have found little documentation of performances of Lorca's plays before his death, but performances of Lorca's plays as well as performances inspired by Lorca's work span the 1950s to the present time; they include the Radio Canada presentation of a French-language *Bodas de Sangre* (1951), CenterStage Theatre's production of *La Casa de Bernarda Alba* (1987), Daniel MacIvor and Daniel Brooks's *The Lorca Play* (1992), and Esmeralda Enrique Spanish Dance Company's *¡Lorca! In Search of Duende* (2009).

27 Richler includes the same quotation in *Images of Spain* (15). His quotation omits the fact that the poem is spoken responsively; "Children" pose the question, and "Poet" replies (Barea 79).

28 Manzano notes, "En una identificación irracional, el judío Leonard había creído reconocer en la tinta lorquiana su propia sangre gitana, y, en las cuerdas de la guitarra española, sus venas" (In an irrational identification, the Jewish Leonard believed he recognized his own *gitano* blood in Lorca's ink, and his veins in the chords of the Spanish guitar; my trans. *Leonard Cohen* 31). Boucher analyses Cohen's writings in the context of Lorca's theory of the poetries of imagination and inspiration, 158–9. See also Tordjman.
29 Manzano translates both these poems into Spanish; see *Leonard Cohen* 306–9.
30 The song also supplies the title for Sarah Polley's film about a heterosexual Torontonian couple's romantic ennui, *Take This Waltz* (2011).
31 Lorca's *Poet in New York* includes the historic and "prophetic" poem "Cementerio judío" (Jewish Cemetery), which depicts Jews boarding ships to travel to their deaths (Glass, "El cementerio judío" 34), as well as "Oda a Walt Whitman" (Ode to Walt Whitman), in which Lorca's speaker critiques the realities of gay life compared to Whitman's idealized imaginings.
32 For more on Cohen's reception in Spain, see Somacarrera 50–1.
33 See Bosque.
34 Diehl-Jones comments in her detailed analysis of the structure of "Take This Waltz" that even without the song's first line it is immediately recognizable for its connection to Vienna and "the tradition of the lover's dance" (78). Manzano includes a line-by-line comparison of Lorca's poem and Cohen's lyrics, using his own translations; see *Leonard Cohen* 259–61.
35 I base this reading on Simon and White's 1988 translation, in Maurer's critical edition of *Poet in New York*.
36 For more on Cohen's translation process, see Manzano, "I'm Your Man" 218, 222.
37 See personal communication with Clarke, Dedora, Frutkin, Holbrook, Hynes, Nason, Smith, Vulpe, Wainwright. A writers' retreat organized by writer Gerry Shikatani, "Lorca's Granada," has inspired a wealth of Canadian literary responses to Lorca, Granada, and the Spanish Civil War, including those by Dedora and Hynes.
38 The bilingual book was published in both Canada, by Book*hug, and in Spain, by Visor.
39 This translation, supplied by Dedora, is the same one included in the Maurer edition of *Poet in New York*.
40 This poem is also included in Vulpe's recent collection *Insult to the Brain*.
41 Dave McGimpsey parodies this impulse to translate Lorca into Canada in "As vast as the vastlands of this vast land, poet, are you to yonder skies, breads, and local cheeses."

Conclusion

1 The recent documentary *The Silence of Others* poignantly demonstrates these laws' long-term reverberations, as well as some hopeful signs of overdue change. Faber describes how, in the days after the passing of the Law of Historical Memory,

> Spain's public sphere witnessed a series of curious phenomena that had all the trappings of eerie returns of the repressed: exhumations of seventy-year-old mass graves followed by emotional reburial ceremonies; scores of historical novels, movies, documentaries and television programs dealing with the Republic, the Civil War, and Francoism; the frequent appearance of both Francoist and Republican flags at political rallies and other public events; an "obituary war," with newspapers on the Left and Right publishing ever-larger death notices for people killed in 1936; and the reemergence into the limelight of Spain's fascist party, Falange Española, as a plaintiff in one of the three cases brought against Judge Baltasar Garzón, the investigative magistrate who in 2008 initiated a legal investigation of crimes against humanity committed under the Franco regime. ("'¿Usted, qué sabe?'" 12)

Labanyi traces the roots of the memory boom to the decade after Franco's death, when two filmmakers, Julio Llamazares and Antonio Muñoz Molina, were "able to adopt a more detached stance toward the topic . . . driven by a genealogical imperative to transmit to future generations tragic events experienced by their elders" (95).

2 As Wyile notes of contemporary Canadian writers' engagement with received histories and historical figures, "this dialogue is particularly important in the case of those whom the historical record has tended to exclude – women, the working class, and racial(ized) minorities." (4).

3 Writing of twenty-first-century historical novels, Wyile explains:

> The phenomenon is itself arguably the product of historical circumstances, such as the overthrow of a colonial mentality in which Canadian history was dismissed as negligible, even oxymoronic; an increasing desire to interrogate and challenge a narrowly defined national past and to venture beyond its boundaries; the influence of a wider questioning of the epistemological and ideological basis of history; an anxiety about distinguishing Canadian culture and identity from that of the United States in an era of increasing economic, cultural, and political integration; and an increasingly global, postnational culture that has perhaps cultivated (as a kind of compensation) a preoccupation with the nation's past. Finally, there is no discounting the fact that writers may gravitate to historical fiction for the simple reason that it is popular with readers. (5–6)

For a helpful overview of literary criticism about Canadian historical fiction, see Cabajsky and Grubisic.

4 While the existence of a daughter is completely speculative on Bock's part, the epistolary form allows Bock to humanize Bethune by imagining his dawning recognition of his own mortality as well as his motivations for travelling to Spain and China. For Bock's own reflections on fictionalizing Bethune, see his "Searching." For more on representations of Bethune, see Levangie, "Born a Bourgeois."

5 Margolis explains: "In the 1980s, the country's new official government policies of multiculturalism created a place for Canada's Jews to promote their distinctive culture, in particular in the realm of the arts. Ethnic culture was promoted and supported by government programs that encouraged Jewish voices. Meanwhile, in the 1970s, in Quebec, separatist politics that aggressively valorized the French language excluded a majority of the province's Jewish population, which comprised immigrants from Eastern Europe who had acculturated from Yiddish into the historically dominant English-speaking minority" (433).

6 For the applications of postmemory to Spanish Civil War literature, see Faber, *Memory Battles* 174–7.

7 Bissoondath's earlier, haunting short story, "Counting the Wind," seems set in Francoist Spain. For Bissoondath's reflections on his sustained fascination with Spain, Spanish history, and Lorca, see "L'Espagne: l'inconnu qui m'est familier."

8 Greenstein connects these two stories to Cohen's novel *The Spanish Doctor* (1984) as part of the author's examination of Spain's history of antisemitism. See Greenstein 191–6. Cohen himself reflected: "The destruction of Spanish Jewry – through the Inquisition and the expulsion – was to be the most tragic event in Jewish history until the Second World War" ("Outside Spain" 185).

9 Labanyi discusses the ethical risks of looking back to the Spanish Civil War with an idealized, historically detached perspective of the conflict: "There is a danger, in the texts that are opting for documentary realism, of producing a 'feel-good factor' that makes readers or spectators feel morally improved by having momentarily 'shared' the suffering represented in the text, without going on to make any connection with the present" (112).

10 See personal communication with Barclay, Collis, West; "Elizabeth Ruth on *Matadora*."

11 While I do not discuss young adult fiction in this study, John Wilson's two novels *Lost in Spain* (2000) and *Lost Cause* (2012) are a significant contribution to the adventure genre.

12 West explains that his Jewish protagonist and Montreal setting were purposeful, "a microcosm of all the tensions tearing the country apart at the time" ("Re").

13 Frutkin highlights several characters with mental disabilities – an important topic for future study.

14 For more on the ARMH's work and its constructions of history, see Faber, *Memory Battles* 61.

References

Abella, Irving. *A Coat of Many Colours: Two Centuries of Jewish Life in Canada.* Lester & Orpen Dennys, 1990.

Ackerman, Alan. *Just Words: Lillian Hellman, Mary McCarthy, and the Failure of Public Conversation in America.* Yale UP, 2011.

Ackland, Valentine. "Federico: A True Story." *New Frontier*, vol. 2, no. 5, Oct. 1937, pp. 9–10.

Agee, James, and Walker Evans. *Let Us Now Praise Famous Men.* Houghton Mifflin, 1939.

Alás-Brun, Montserrat. "The Shattered Mirror: Colonial Discourse and Counterdiscourse about Spanish Guinea." *Arizona Journal of Hispanic Studies*, no. 8, 2004, pp. 163–76.

Allan, Norman Bethune. "Gerda." *Ted Allan: A Partial Biography*, www.normanallan.com/Misc/Ted/nT%20ch%202.htm. Accessed 30 June 2018.

Allan, Ted. *Lies My Father Told Me.* Playwrights Canada, 1983.

– "Lisa: A Story." *Harper's*, vol. 177, no. 2, July 1938, pp. 187–93.

– *This Time a Better Earth.* 1939. Edited by Bart Vautour. U of Ottawa P, 2015.

Álvarez, Enrique. "Queer Arcadia: On Cultural Landscapes, Violence, and Power and Federico García Lorca's 'Poema doble del lago Eden.'" *Revista Canadiense de Estudios Hispánicos*, vol. 34, no. 2, Winter 2010, pp. 265–83.

Anderson, Amanda. *The Powers of Distance: Cosmopolitanism and the Cultivation of Detachment.* Princeton UP, 2001.

Anderson, Patrick. "For a Spanish Comrade." *Preview*, no. 17, Dec. 1943, pp. 9–11.

Andrews, Gregg. *Thyra J. Edwards: Black Activist in the Global Freedom Struggle.* U of Missouri P, 2011.

Appiah, Kwame Anthony. "Cosmopolitan Patriots." *Cosmopolitics: Thinking and Feeling Beyond the Nation*, edited by Pheng Cheah and Bruce Robbins. U of Minnesota P, 1998, pp. 91–114.

Atwood, Margaret. *The Blind Assassin.* Doubleday, 2000.

Auerbach, Joshua. "Song of the Lament (Translation of Federico Garcia Lorca's *Casida del llanto*." *Radius of Light*. Livres DC Books, 2007, p. 5.
Balfour, Sebastian. *Deadly Embrace: Morocco and the Road to the Spanish Civil War*. Oxford UP, 2002.
Barclay, Byrna. "Girl at the Window." *Girl at the Window*, Coteau Books, 2004, pp. 269–97.
– "Questions about 'Girl at the Window.'" Received by Emily Robins Sharpe, 12 Dec. 2018.
Barea, Arturo. *Lorca: The Poet and His People*. Cooper Square, 1973.
Barton, John. Introduction. *Seminal: The Anthology of Canada's Gay Male Poets*, edited by John Barton and Billeh Nickerson. Arsenal Pulp P, 2007, pp. 7–30.
Bauer, Carl, ed. *Cries from a Wounded Madrid: Poetry of the Spanish Civil War*. Swallow P, 1984.
Beagan, Tara. *Jesus Chrysler*. 2011.
Beeching, William C. *Canadian Volunteers, Spain, 1936–1939*. Hignell Printing, 1989.
Benardete, M. J., and Rolfe Humphries, eds. *... And Spain Sings: Fifty Loyalist Ballads Adapted by American Poets*. Vanguard P, 1937.
Benjamin, Walter. "On the Concept of History." *The Walter Benjamin Archive*, translated by Dennis Redmond, 1940, www.marxists.org/reference/archive/benjamin/1940/history.htm.
Bentley, D.M.R. *The Confederation Group of Canadian Poets, 1880–1897*. U of Toronto P, 2004.
Berry, Faith. Introduction. *Pagan Spain*, by Richard Wright, 1957. Banner Books, 1995, pp. ix–xxvii.
Bessie, Alvah. *Men in Battle: A Story of Americans in Spain*. 1939. Chandler and Sharp, 1975.
– *Spain Again*. Chandler and Sharp, 1975.
– *The Un-Americans*. Cameron Associates, 1957.
Bessie, Alvah, ed. *The Heart of Spain: Anthology of Fiction, Non-Fiction, and Poetry*. Veterans of the Abraham Lincoln Brigade, 1952.
Bethune. Directed by Donald Brittain. National Film Board of Canada, 1964.
Bethune: The Making of a Hero. Directed by Philip Borsos, written by Ted Allan, performance by Donald Sutherland. Filmline International, 1990.
"Bibliographies." *Canada and the Spanish Civil War: Canadian Cultural History about the Spanish Civil War*, 2019, spanishcivilwar.ca/content/bibliographies. Accessed 30 December 2019.
Binding, Paul. *Lorca: The Gay Imagination*. GMP Publishers, 1985.
Bissoondath, Neil. "Counting the Wind." *Digging Up the Mountains*. Penguin Books, 1986, pp. 224–47.
– "L'Espagne: l'inconnu qui m'est familier." *Espagnes imaginaires du Québec*, edited by Carmen Mata Barreiro. P de l'U Laval, 2012, pp. 19–26.
– "Things Best Forgotten." *On the Eve of Uncertain Tomorrows*. Bloomsbury Publishing, 1990, pp. 255–71.

Blankfort, Michael. *The Brave and the Blind.* Bobbs-Merrill, 1940.

Bock, Dennis. *The Communist's Daughter.* Alfred A. Knopf, 2007.

– "Searching for Bethune's Beating Heart." *Rediscovering Norman Bethune,* edited by M. Darrol Bryant, Yan Li, and Margaret Loewen Reimer. Pandora P, 2017.

Bosque, Daniel. "When Cohen, Lorca, rock and flamenco came together." *The Local,* 18 Nov. 2016, www.thelocal.es/20161118/when-leonard-cohen-lorca-rock-and-flamenco-came-together.

Boucher, David. *Dylan and Cohen: Poets of Rock and Roll.* Continuum, 2005.

Boyarin, Daniel, and Jonathan Boyarin. "Diaspora: Generation and the Grounds of Jewish Identity." *Critical Inquiry,* vol. 19, no. 4, Summer 1993, pp. 693–725.

Boyarin, Daniel, Daniel Itzkovitz, and Ann Pellegrini. "Strange Bedfellows." Introduction. *Queer Theory and the Jewish Question,* edited by Daniel Boyarin, Daniel Itzkovitz, and Ann Pellegrini. Columbia UP, 2003, pp. 1–18.

Brandt, Joe, ed. *Black Americans in the Spanish People's War against Fascism, 1936–1939.* Veterans of the Abraham Lincoln Brigade, [1979].

Breines, Paul. *Tough Jews: Political Fantasies and the Moral Dilemma of American Jewry.* Basic Books, 1990.

Brodkin, Karen. *How Jews Became White Folks and What That Says about Race in America.* Rutgers UP, 1998.

Brossat, Alain, and Sylvia Klingberg. *Revolutionary Yiddishland: A History of Jewish Radicalism.* Translated by David Fernbach. Verso, 2016.

Brown, Judith. "Turning Words on a Loom: *The Last Landscape* by Miriam Waddington." Review of *The Last Landscape,* by Miriam Waddington, *Essays on Canadian Writing,* no. 55, Spring 1995, p. 269.

Budick, Emily Miller. *Blacks and Jews in Literary Conversation.* Cambridge UP, 1998.

Buller, Erin Bartels. "Vouching for Evidence: The New Life of Old Writing in Lillian Hellman's Memoirs." *Arizona Quarterly,* vol. 70, no. 1, Spring 2014, pp. 109–34.

Butler, Nancy. "Mother Russia and the Socialist Fatherhood: Women and the Communist Party of Canada, 1932–1941, with specific reference to the activism of Dorothy Livesay and Jim Watts." Dissertation, Queen's University, 2010.

Byron, Kristine. "Writing the Female Revolutionary Self: Dolores Ibárruri and the Spanish Civil War." *Journal of Modern Literature,* vol. 28, no. 1, Fall 2004, pp. 138–65.

Cabajsky, Andrea, and Brett Josef Grubisic. Introduction. *National Plots: Historical Fiction and Changing Ideas of Canada,* edited by Andrea Cabajsky and Brett Josef Grubisic. Wilfrid Laurier UP, 2010, pp. vii–xxiv.

Cahan, Abraham. *The Rise of David Levinsky.* 1917. Penguin Books, 1993.

Calihman, Matthew. "Black Power beyond Black Nationalism: John A. Williams, Cultural Pluralism, and the Popular Front." *MELUS,* vol. 34, no. 1, Spring 2009, pp. 139–62.

Calmer, Alan, ed. *Salud! Poems, Stories and Sketches of Spain by American Writers.* International Publishers, 1938.

Campbell, Roy. *Flowering Rifle: A Poem from the Battlefield of Spain.* Longmans and Co., 1939.

Los Canadienses. Directed by Albert Kish. National Film Board of Canada, 1975.

Carlsen, Jørn. "Canadian Literature and the Spanish Civil War." *The Dolphin,* no. 16, 1988, pp. 41–53.

Carroll, Peter N., and James D. Fernández, eds. *Facing Fascism: New York and the Spanish Civil War.* New York UP, 2007.

Cinta Ramblado-Minero, M. "Sites of Memory/Sites of Oblivion in Contemporary Spain." *Revista Canadiense de Estudios Hispánicos,* vol. 36, no. 1, Fall 2011, pp. 29–42.

Clarke, George Elliott. "The Death and Life of Garcia Lorca." *Lush Dreams, Blue Exile: Fugitive Poems: 1978–1993.* Pottersfield P, 1994, p. 19.

– "Garcia Lorca, Harlemite (1929)." *Canticles I (MMXVII).* Guernica Editions, 2017, pp. 357–59.

– "Re: questions about and copyright permissions for Lush Dreams, Blue Exile." Received by Emily Robins Sharpe, 27–8 Feb. 2019.

Cohen, Debra Rae. *Remapping the Home Front: Locating Citizenship in British Women's Great War Fiction.* Northeastern UP, 2002.

Cohen, Leonard. "Acceptance Address for the Prince of Asturias Award." 2011. *The Flame: Poems, Notebooks, Lyrics, Drawings.* Farrar, Straus and Giroux, 2018. 267–9.

– "The Faithless Wife." *Book of Longing.* HarperCollins, 2006, pp. 147–8.

– *I'm Your Man.* Columbia, 1988.

– "Lorca Lives." *Book of Longing.* HarperCollins, 2006, p. 90.

– "Take This Waltz." *Poets in New York,* CBS, 1986.

– "The Traitor." *Recent Songs,* CBS, 1979.

Cohen. Matt. "Outside Spain." *Canadian Literature,* Autumn–Winter 1994, pp. 142–3, 183–7.

– "Sentimental Meetings." *Café le Dog.* Penguin Books, 1985, pp. 117–35.

– "The Sins of Tomas Benares." *Café le Dog.* Penguin Books, 1985, pp. 73–101.

Coleman, Daniel. *White Civility: The Literary Project of English Canada.* U of Toronto P, 2006.

Collis, Stephen. "Dear Reclus." *Anarchive.* New Star Books, 2005, pp. 17–19.

– "Re: The Red Album." Received by Emily Robins Sharpe, 2 June 2018.

– *The Red Album.* Book*hug, 2013.

Collum, Danny Duncan, ed. *African Americans in the Spanish Civil War: "This Ain't Ethiopia, But It'll Do."* G.K. Hall, 1992.

Cowles, Virginia. *Looking for Trouble.* Harper, 1941.

Crunden, Robert M. "A Joshua for the Historians." *World Literature Written in English,* vol. 22, no. 2, 1983, pp. 235–54.

Cunard, Nancy. "Moors Promised Jobs, Inveigled into Spain." *The Daily Clarion*, 7 July 1938, p. 4.

Cunard, Nancy, ed. *Authors Take Sides on the Spanish War.* Left Review, 1937.

Cunard, Nancy, and Pablo Neruda, eds. *Les poétes du monde défendent le peuple espagnole.* Hours P, 1936–37.

Cunningham, Valentine, editor. *The Penguin Book of Spanish Civil War Verse.* 1980. Penguin, 1996.

Davies, Alan, ed. *Antisemitism in Canada: History and Interpretation.* Wilfrid Laurier UP, 2006.

Davis, Frances. *A Fearful Innocence.* Kent State UP, 1981.

– *My Shadow in the Sun.* Carrick and Evans, 1940.

Dawahare, Anthony. *Nationalism, Marxism, and African American Literature between the Wars: A New Pandora's Box.* UP of Mississippi, 2002.

"Death of a Spanish Poet." *Volunteer for Liberty*, vol. 1, no. 17, 4 Oct. 1937, pp. 3–4.

Dedora, Brian. Facebook message. Received by Emily Robins Sharpe, 3 June 2018.

– "The First Part of the Journey, Madrid." *Lorcation*, pp. 12–15.

– "Granada." *Lorcation*, pp. 26–37.

– *Lorcation*, translated by Martín Rodríguez-Gaona. Book*hug, 2015.

– "La Plaza de la Trinidad, Granada." *Lorcation*, pp. 40–43.

– "The Potboiled Simmer." *Lorcation*, pp. 18–25.

– Preface. *Lorcation*, pp. 7–10.

– "Uno soy yo = I Am One." *Lorcation*, pp. 66–95.

DeGuzmán, María. *Spain's Long Shadow: The Black Legend, Off-Whiteness, and Anglo-American Empire.* U of Minnesota P, 2005.

Dickinson, Peter. *Here Is Queer: Nationalisms, Sexualities, and the Literatures of Canada.* U of Toronto P, 1999.

Diehl-Jones, Charlene. "Re-Membering the Love Song: Ambivalence and Cohen's 'Take This Waltz.'" *Canadian Poetry*, vol. 33, no. 9, 1993: 74–87.

DiGiovanni, Lisa Renée. "Return to Galicia: Nostalgia, Nation, and Gender in Manuel Rivas's Spain." *Remembering Home in a Time of Mobility: Memory, Nostalgia, and Melancholy*, edited by Maja Mikula. Cambridge Scholars, 2017, pp. 15–34.

Dionne, Bernard. "Bibliographie en français sur le Canada, la guerre civile en Espagne et l'engagement des communistes et du bataillon Mackenzie-Papineau." *Canada and the Spanish Civil War: Canadian Cultural History about the Spanish Civil War*, spanishcivilwar.ca/content/bibliography/francophone-sources. Accessed 31 June 2018.

Dobson, Kit. *Transnational Canadas: Anglo-Canadian Literature and Globalization.* Wilfrid Laurier UP, 2009.

Dolinar, Brian. *The Black Cultural Front: Black Writers and Artists of the Depression Generation.* UP of Mississippi, 2012.

Donlon, Anne. *Poetry, Politics, and Friendship in the Spanish Civil War: Langston Hughes, Nancy Cunard, and Louise Thompson.* CUNY Poetics Document Initiative, vol. 3, no. 1, Fall 2012.

– "Thyra Edwards's Spanish Civil War Scrapbook: Black Women's Internationalist Writing." *To Turn the Whole World Over: Black Women and Internationalism,* edited by Keisha N. Blain and Tiffany M. Gill. U of Illinois P, pp. 101–22.

Dos Passos, John. *Adventures of a Young Man.* Constable, 1939.

Doyle, James. *Progressive Heritage: The Evolution of a Politically Radical Literary Tradition in Canada.* Wilfrid Laurier UP, 2002.

Dudek, Louis. "Garcia Lorca." *East of the City.* Ryerson P, 1946, pp. 37–8.

– "García Lorca." *First Statement,* vol. 2, no. 9, Oct.–Nov. 1944, pp. 10–12.

Edwards, Brent Hayes. "Langston Hughes and the Futures of Diaspora." *American Literary History,* vol. 19, no. 3, 2007, pp. 689–711.

– *The Practice of Diaspora: Literature, Translation, and the Rise of Black Internationalism.* Harvard UP, 2003.

– "The Taste of the Archive." *Callaloo,* vol. 35, no. 4, Fall 2012, pp. 944–72.

"Elizabeth Ruth on *Matadora.*" *The Next Chapter,* hosted by Shelagh Rogers. CBC Radio, 14 July 2014.

Ellis, Jonathan. "'A Curious Cat': Elizabeth Bishop and the Spanish Civil War." *Journal of Modern Literature,* vol. 27, no. 1–2, Autumn 2003, pp. 137–48.

Enjuto Rangel, Cecilia. *Cities in Ruins: The Politics of Modern Poetics.* Purdue UP, 2010.

Faber, Sebastiaan. *Anglo-American Hispanists and the Spanish Civil War: Hispanophilia, Commitment, and Discipline.* Palgrave Macmillan, 2008.

– *Memory Battles of the Spanish Civil War: History, Fiction, Photography.* Vanderbilt UP, 2018.

– "'¿Usted, qué sabe?' History, Memory, and the Voice of the Witness." *Revista Canadiense de Estudios Hispánicos,* vol. 36, no. 1, Fall 2011, pp. 9–27.

"Fascists Shoot Spanish Author." *Daily Clarion,* 15 Sept. 1936, p. 1.

Favret, Mary A. *War at a Distance: Romanticism and the Making of Modern Wartime.* Princeton UP, 2009.

Fiedler, Leslie A. "Genesis: The American-Jewish Novel through the Twenties." *Midstream,* 1958, pp. 21–33.

Freedman, Jonathan. *Klezmer America: Jewishness, Ethnicity, Modernity.* Columbia UP, 2008.

Frutkin, Mark. "Death of a Poet." Vulpe and Albari, p. 176.

– *Erratic North: A Vietnam Draft Resister's Life in the Canadian Bush.* Dundurn P, 2008.

– "Re: Slow Lightning." Received by Emily Robins Sharpe, 2 June 2018.

– *Slow Lightning.* Raincoast Books, 2001.

Fyrth, Jim. Foreword. *Women's Voices from the Spanish Civil War*, edited by Jim Fyrth and Sally Alexander. Lawrence and Wishart, 2008, pp. 23–30.

Fyrth, Jim, and Sally Alexander, eds. *Women's Voices from the Spanish Civil War*. Lawrence and Wishart, 2008.

García Lorca, Federico. *Collected Poems*, edited by Christopher Maurer. Farrar, Straus and Giroux, 1991.

– "Pequeño vals vienés" and "Little Viennese Waltz." *Poet in New York*, edited by Christopher Maurer, translated by Greg Simon and Steven F. White. Farrar, Straus and Giroux, 1988, pp. 164–7.

Garner, Hugh. *Cabbagetown*. Expanded ed., McGraw-Hill Ryerson, 1968.

– *One Damn Thing after Another! The Life Story of a Canadian Writer*. McGraw-Hill Ryerson, 1973.

– "The Stretcher Bearers." *Best Stories*. 1963. Edited by Emily Robins Sharpe. U of Ottawa P, 2015, pp. 161–7.

Garrett, Leah. *Young Lions: How Jewish Authors Reinvented the American War Novel*. Northwestern UP, 2015.

Gates, Henry Louis, Jr. "Preface to Blackness: Text and Pretext." *Afro-American Literature: The Reconstruction of Instruction*, edited by Dexter Fisher and Robert Stepto. MLA, 1978, pp. 44–69.

Gellhorn, Martha. "About Shorty." *The Honeyed Peace*, Doubleday, 1953, pp. 119–31.

– *The Face of War*. 1959. Atlantic Monthly P, 1986.

– *Good Will to Men*. *The Heart of Another*, pp. 186–267.

– *The Heart of Another*. Charles Scribner's Sons, 1941.

– "Luigi's House." *The Heart of Another*, pp. 1–33.

– "A Sense of Direction." *The Heart of Another*, pp. 138–70.

– *Till Death Do Us Part*. *The Novellas of Martha Gellhorn*. Alfred A. Knopf, 1993, pp. 271–309.

– *The View from the Ground*. Atlantic Monthly P, 1988.

– "Zoo in Madrid." *The Heart of Another*, pp. 123–8.

Gerassi, John. *The Premature Antifascists: North American Volunteers in the Spanish Civil War, 1936–1939, an Oral History*. Praeger, 1986.

Gerson, Carole. "'The Most Canadian of all Canadian Poets': Pauline Johnson and the Construction of a National Literature." *Canadian Literature*, no. 158, Autumn 1998, pp. 90–107.

Gibbon, John Murray. *Canadian Mosaic: The Making of a Northern Nation*. McClelland and Stewart, 1938.

Gibson, Ian. *"Caballo azul de mi locura": Lorca y el mundo gay*. Planeta, 2009.

– *Federico García Lorca: A Life*. Pantheon Books, 1989.

Gilman, Sander L. *The Jew's Body*. Routledge, 1991.

– *Multiculturalism and the Jews*. Routledge, 2006.

Gilroy, Paul. *The Black Atlantic: Modernity and Double Consciousness*. Harvard UP, 1993.

Girón Echevarría, Luis Gustavo. "Langston Hughes's Spanish Civil War Verse." *Anuario de Estudios Filológicos*, no. 28, 2005, pp. 91–101.

Glaser, Amelia, and David Weintraub, eds. *Proletpen: America's Rebel Yiddish Poets*, translated by Amelia Glaser. U of Wisconsin P, 2005.

Glass, Elliot S. "'El cementerio judío': García Lorca's Historical Vision of the Jews." *Hispanófila* vol. 75, no. 5, 1982, pp. 33–49.

Glass, Philip. *Book of Longing*. Orange Mountain Music, 2007.

Gold, Michael. *Jews Without Money*. 1930. Carroll and Graf, 2004.

Goldie, Terry. "Queer Nation?" *In a Queer Country: Gay and Lesbian Studies in the Canadian Context*. Edited by Terry Goldie. Arsenal Pulp P, 2002. pp. 7–26.

Goldie, Terry, and Lee Frew. "Gay and Lesbian Literature in Canada." *The Oxford Handbook of Canadian Literature*, edited by Cynthia Sugars. Oxford UP, 2016. pp. 863–76.

Goldstein, Eric L. *The Price of Whiteness: Jews, Race, and American Identity*. Princeton UP, 2006.

The Good Fight: The Abraham Lincoln Brigades in the Spanish Civil War. Directed by Noel Buckner. First Run Features, 1984.

Gordon, Sybil M. "Three Spanish Women." *New Frontier*, vol. 1, no. 8. Dec. 1936, pp. 9–10.

Graham, Gwethalyn. *Earth and High Heaven*. New Canadian Library, 1944.

Graham, Helen. *The Spanish Civil War: A Very Short Introduction*. Oxford UP, 2005.

Greckol, Sonja Ruth. *No Line in Time*. Tightrope Books, 2018.

Greenstein, Michael. *Third Solitudes: Tradition and Discontinuity in Jewish-Canadian Literature*. McGill–Queen's UP, 1989.

Grier, Eldon. "In Memory of García Lorca." *Selected Poems 1955–1970*. Delta Canada, 1971, p. 11.

Griffin, Harold. *Hostage*. 1937. Simon Fraser University Special Collections and Rare Books, Burnaby, Harold Griffin Fonds, MsC 44.

– *Underground*. 1936. Simon Fraser University Special Collections and Rare Books, Burnaby, Harold Griffin Fonds, MsC 44.

Hannant, Larry. "'My God, are they sending women?': Three Canadian Women in the Spanish Civil War, 1936–1939." *Journal of the Canadian History Association / Revue de la Société historique du Canada*, vol. 15, no. 1, 2004, pp. 153–76.

Harrison, Charles Yale. *Meet Me on the Barricades*. 1938. Edited by Bart Vautour and Emily Robins Sharpe. U of Ottawa P, 2016.

– "Scrapbook 1." Charles Yale Harrison Papers, MS 0560, Box 12; Rare Book and Manuscript Library, Columbia University.

Hart, Alexander. "Scrolls, Scrapbooks, and Solitudes: An Overview of Jewish Canadian Literature." *Canada's Jews: In Time, Space and Spirit*, edited by Ira Robinson. Academic Studies P, 2013, pp. 361–411.

Hellman, Lillian. "A Bleached Lady: A Short Story." *New Masses*, 11 Oct. 1938, pp. 20–1.
– "The Little War." *This Is My Best*, edited by Whit Burnett. Dial P, 1942, pp. 989–96.
– *An Unfinished Woman: A Memoir.* Little, Brown and Co., 1969.
Hemingway, Ernest. *The Fifth Column and Four Unpublished Stories of the Spanish Civil War.* Scribner, 1970.
– *For Whom the Bell Tolls.* 1940. Scribner, 2003.
Herbst, Josephine. *Rope of Gold.* Harcourt, Brace and Co., 1939.
– "The Starched Blue Sky of Spain." *The Starched Blue Sky of Spain and Other Memoirs.* HarperPerennial, 1992, pp. 129–78.
Herrero, Javier. *Lorca, Young and Gay: The Making of an Artist.* Juan de la Cuesta Hispanic Monographs, 2014.
Herrick, William. *Hermanos!* Penguin, 1969.
– *Kill Memory.* New Directions, 1983.
Herrmann, Gina. "Voices of the Vanquished: Leftist Women and the Spanish Civil War." *Journal of Spanish Cultural Studies*, vol. 4, no. 1, 2003, pp. 11–29.
– *Written in Red: The Communist Memoir in Spain.* U of Illinois P, 2010.
Hine, Darlene Clark. *Black Women in White: Racial Conflict and Cooperation in the Nursing Profession, 1890–1950.* Indiana UP, 1989.
Hirsch, Marianne. *The Generation of Postmemory: Writing and Visual Culture after the Holocaust.* Columbia UP, 2012.
Hoar, Victor. *The Mackenzie-Papineau Battalion: Canadian Participation in the Spanish Civil War.* Copp Clark, 1969.
Hochschild, Adam. *Spain in Our Hearts: Americans in the Spanish Civil War, 1936–1939.* Mariner Books, 2016.
Hoffman, Warren. *The Passing Game: Queering Jewish American Culture.* Syracuse UP, 2009.
Høgsbjerg, Christian. "'The Fever and the Fret': C.L.R. James, the Spanish Civil War, and the Writing of *The Black Jacobins.*" *Critique*, vol. 44, nos. 1–2, 2016, pp. 161–77.
Holbrook, Susan. "To Federico García Lorca's *Poema del cante jondo.*" *Joy Is So Exhausting.* Coach House Books, 2009, pp. 40–9.
– "Re: Joy Is So Exhausting." Received by Emily Robins Sharpe, 5 June 2018.
Hollinger, David A. *Cosmopolitanism and Solidarity: Studies in Ethnoracial, Religious, and Professional Affiliation in the United States.* U of Wisconsin P, 2006.
Hughes, Dorothy B. *The Fallen Sparrow.* Duell, Sloan and Pearce, 1942.
Hughes, Langston. "Hughes Finds Moors Being Used as Pawns by Fascists in Spain." 30 Oct. 1937. Mullen, pp. 106–10.
– *I Wonder as I Wander: An Autobiographical Journey.* Hill and Wang, 1956.
– "Letter from Spain." *The Collected Poems of Langston Hughes*, edited by Arnold Rampersad and David Roessel. Vintage, 1995, pp. 201–2.

– "Negroes in Spain." 13 Sept. 1937. Mullen, pp. 96–8.

– "'Organ Grinder's Swing' Heard above Gunfire in Spain – Hughes." 6 Nov. 1937. Mullen, pp. 111–14.

– "Postcard from Spain." *The Collected Poems of Langston Hughes*, edited by Arnold Rampersad and David Roessel. New York: Vintage, 1995, pp. 202–3.

– "Song of Spain." *The Collected Poems of Langston Hughes*, edited by Arnold Rampersad and David Roessel. Vintage, 1995, pp. 195–7.

– "Walter Cobb, Driving Captured Fascist Truck, Mistaken by Own Men for Moor, but Language Saves Him." 22 Jan. 1938. Mullen, pp. 139–40.

Hunter, O.H. "700 Calendar Days." Bessie, *The Heart of Spain*, pp. 286–304.

Hutton, June. *Underground*. Cormorant Books, 2009.

Hynes, Maureen. "Andalusian Pianos." *The Poison Colour*, p. 52.

– "Holy Week." *The Poison Colour*, p. 53.

– "On Reading Lorca's *Poet in New York*." *The Poison Colour*, p. 76.

– *The Poison Colour*. Pedlar P, 2015.

– "Re: The Poison Colour." Received by Emily Robins Sharpe, 22 June 2018.

Infante, Ignacio. *After Translation: The Transfer and Circulation of Modern Poetics across the Atlantic*. Fordham UP, 2013.

Into the Fire: American Women in the Spanish Civil War. Directed by Julia Newman. First Run Features, 2002.

Invisible Heroes: African Americans in the Spanish Civil War. Directed by Alfonso Domingo and Jordí Torrent. Argonauta Producciones and Duende Pictures, 2015.

Irr, Caren. *The Suburb of Dissent: Cultural Politics in the United States and Canada during the 1930s*. Duke UP, 1998.

Irvine, Dean. *Editing Modernity: Women and Little-Magazine Cultures in Canada, 1916–1956*. U of Toronto P, 2008.

Jaher, Frederic Cople. "The Quest for the Ultimate *Shiksa*." *American Quarterly*, vol. 35, no. 5, 1983, pp. 518–42.

Jakobsen, Janet R. "Queers Are Like Jews, Aren't They? Analogy and Alliance Politics." *Queer Theory and the Jewish Question*, edited by Daniel Boyarin, Daniel Itzkovitz, and Ann Pellegrini. Columbia UP, 2003, pp. 64–89.

James, C.L.R. *The Black Jacobins: Toussaint L'Ouverture and the San Domingo Revolution*. 1938. Revised, Vintage Books, 1989.

Jensen, Geoffrey. "Military Memories, History, and the Myth of Hispano-Arabic Identity in the Spanish Civil War." *Memory and Cultural History of the Spanish Civil War*, edited by Aurora G. Morcillo, Brill, 2014, pp. 495–532.

Jump, Jim. *Poems from Spain: British and Irish International Brigaders on the Spanish Civil War*. Lawrence and Wishart, 2006.

Katz, William Loren. "Salaria Kea: From Harlem Hospital to Madrid." *The Black World Today*, 10 Apr. 2001.

Kea, Salaria. "Hope: To Serve God and my country. Reflection of my Life." Frances Patai Papers; ALBA 131, series 1, box 2, folder 12. Tamiment Library/Robert F. Wagner Labor Archives, New York University.

– Letter to Fredericka Martin, 9 Jan. 1974. Fredericka Martin Papers, ALBA 001, series 1, box 9, folder 30. Tamiment Library/Robert F. Wagner Labor Archives, New York University.

– "May Every Knock Be a Boost." Patai Papers, ALBA 131, series 1, box 2, folder 12. Tamiment Library/Robert F. Wagner Labor Archives, New York University.

– "A Negro Nurse in Republican Spain" [published anonymously.] 1938. Collum, pp. 123–34.

– [Draft of "While Passing Through"]. Fredericka Martin Papers; ALBA 001, series 1, box 9, folder 33. Tamiment Library/Robert F. Wagner Labor Archives, New York University.

– [Draft of "While Passing Through"]. Spanish Civil War Archives, box D-2:D/1. Marx Memorial Library.

– "While Passing Through." *Health and Medicine: Journal of The Health and Medicine Policy Research Group*, vol. 4, no. 1, Spring 1987, pp. 11–13.

– "While Passing Through." Frances Patai Papers, ALBA 131, series 1, box 2, folder 12. Tamiment Library/Robert F. Wagner Labor Archives, New York University.

Keene, Judith. *Fighting for Franco: International Volunteers in Nationalist Spain during the Spanish Civil War, 1936–1939.* Leicester UP, 2001.

Kelley, Robin D.G. "This Ain't Ethiopia, But It'll Do." Collum, pp. 5–57.

Kennedy, Brittany Powell. *Between Distant Modernities: Performing Exceptionality in Francoist Spain and the Jim Crow South.* UP of Mississippi, 2015.

Kennedy-Epstein, Rowena. "Introduction." *Savage Coast* by Muriel Rukeyser, edited by Rowena Kennedy-Epstein. Feminist P at the City U of New York, 2013, pp. vii–xxxvi.

– "'Whose fires would not stop': Muriel Rukeyser and the Spanish Civil War, 1936–1976." *Journal of Narrative Theory*, vol. 43, no. 3, Fall 2013, pp. 384–414.

Kessler-Harris, Alice. *A Difficult Woman: The Challenging Life and Times of Lillian Hellman.* Bloomsbury P, 2012.

Kinsman, Gary. "The Canadian Cold War on Queers: Sexual Regulation and Resistance." *Queerly Canadian: An Introductory Reader in Sexuality Studies*, edited by Maureen FitzGerald and Scott Rayter, Canadian Scholars' P, 2012, pp. 65–79.

Klein, A.M. "Of Castles in Spain." *Complete Poems*, edited by Zailig Pollock. U Toronto P, 1990, pp. 473–4.

Klein, L. Ruth, ed. *Nazi Germany, Canadian Responses: Confronting Antisemitism in the Shadow of War*, McGill–Queen's UP, 2012.

Koestler, Arthur. *L'Espagne ensanglantée: Un livre noir sur l'Espagne.* Editions du Carrefour, 1937.

Kramer, Michael P. "Race, Literary History, and the 'Jewish' Question." *Prooftexts,* vol. 21, no. 3, Fall 2001, pp. 287–349.

Kramer, Reinhold. *Mordecai Richler: Leaving St Urbain.* McGill–Queen's UP, 2008.

Kymlicka, Will, and Kathryn Walker. "Rooted Cosmopolitanism: Canada and the World." *Rooted Cosmopolitanism: Canada and the World,* edited by Will Kymlicka and Kathryn Walker. UBC P, 2013, pp. 1–27.

Labanyi, Jo. "Memory and Modernity in Democratic Spain: The Difficulty of Coming to Terms with the Spanish Civil War." *Poetics Today,* vol. 28, no. 1, Spring 2007, pp. 89–116.

Langley, Rod. *Bethune: A Play.* Talon Books, 1975.

Lassner, Phyllis. "'Camp Follower of Catastrophe': Martha Gellhorn's World War II Challenge to the Modernist War." *Modern Fiction Studies,* vol. 44, no. 3, Fall 1998, pp. 792–812.

Layton, Irving. "El Caudillo." *The Tamarack Review* 30, Winter 1964, p. 45.

Levangie, Kevin. "'Born a Bourgeois. Died a Communist': Cultural Portrayals of Dr Norman Bethune." *Canada and the Spanish Civil War: Canadian Cultural History about the Spanish Civil War,* 2014, spanishcivilwar.ca/born-a-bourgeois. Accessed 31 June 2018.

– "From Union Station to Rideau Hall: Public Commemoration of the Canadian Contribution to the Spanish Civil War." *Canada and the Spanish Civil War: Canadian Cultural History about the Spanish Civil War,* 2014, spanishcivilwar.ca/public-commemoration. Accessed 20 Sept. 2019.

Levine, Philippa. "Sexuality and Empire." *At Home with the Empire: Metropolitan Culture and the Imperial World,* edited by Catherine Hall and Sonya O. Rose. Cambridge UP, 2006, pp. 122–42.

Levy, Lital, and Allison Schachter. "Jewish Literature/World Literature: Between the Local and the Transnational." *PMLA,* vol. 130, no. 1, Jan. 2015, pp. 92–109.

Lindberg, Kathryne V. "W.E.B. Du Bois's *Dusk of Dawn* and James Yates's *Mississippi to Madrid.*" *Massachusetts Review,* vol. 35, no. 2, Summer 1994, pp. 283–308.

Linett, Maren Tova. *Modernism, Feminism, and Jewishness.* Cambridge UP, 2007.

Linhard, Tabea Alexa. *Fearless Women in the Mexican Revolution and the Spanish Civil War.* U of Missouri P, 2005.

– *Jewish Spain: A Mediterranean Memory.* Stanford UP, 2014.

Livesay, Dorothy. *Archive for Our Times: Previously Uncollected and Unpublished Poems of Dorothy Livesay,* edited by Dean J. Irvine. Arsenal Pulp P, 1998.

– "Canadian Poetry and the Spanish Civil War." *Right Hand Left Hand,* pp. 250–5.

– "Catalonia." *Collected Poems: The Two Seasons.* McGraw-Hill Ryerson, 1972, pp. 98–101.

– "Comrade." *Right Hand Left Hand*, p. 262.
– "Lorca." *Day and Night*. Ryerson, 1944, pp. 22–4.
– "Lorca." *Right Hand Left Hand* pp. 259, 261–2.
– *The Documentaries: Selected Longer Poems*. Ryerson, 1968.
– "The Documentary Poem: A Canadian Genre." *Contexts of Canadian Criticism*, edited by Eli Mandel, U of Chicago P, 1971, pp. 267–81.
– "The Lizard: October, 1939." *Right Hand Left Hand*, p. 268.
– *Right Hand Left Hand: A True Life of the Thirties: Paris, Toronto, Montreal, the West and Vancouver. Love, Politics, the Depression, and Feminism*. Press Porcepic, 1977.
– "V-J Day" [also published as "In Time of War"]. *Poems for People*. Ryerson, 1947, np.
Low, Mary, and Juan Breá. *Red Spanish Notebook: The First Six Months of the Revolution and the Civil War*. City Lights Books, 1979.
Luscombe, George, Mac Reynolds, and Larry Cox. *The Mac Paps*. Toronto Workshop Productions Archives, 1980.
MacKenzie, John. *Letters I Didn't Write*. Nightwood Editions, 2008.
– "Lorca Again." *Letters I Didn't Write*, pp. 72–3.
– "Lorca's Lament." *Letters I Didn't Write*, pp. 66–7.
– "Poem of the Arrow." *Letters I Didn't Write*, pp. 86–92.
– "You Died at Dawn." *Letters I Didn't Write*, p. 71.
MacLennan, Hugh. *Two Solitudes*. 1945. New Canadian Library, 2003.
– *The Watch That Ends the Night*. Charles Scribner's Sons, 1959.
Madariaga, María Rosa de. "The Intervention of Moroccan Troops in the Spanish Civil War: A Reconsideration." *European History Quarterly*, vol. 22, no. 1, Jan. 1992, pp. 67–97.
– *Los moros que trajo Franco. La intervención de tropas coloniales en la guerra civil española*. Ediciones Martínez Roca, 2002.
Mallan, Lloyd. "Death of a Spanish Poet." *Daily Clarion*, 24 Apr. 1939, p. 6.
Mangini, Shirley. *Memories of Resistance: Women's Voices from the Spanish Civil War*. Yale UP, 1995.
Manzano, Alberto. "I'm Your Man" [interview], May 1988. *Leonard Cohen on Leonard Cohen: Interviews and Encounters*, edited by Jeff Burger. Chicago Review P, 2014, pp. 214–24.
– *Leonard Cohen. Lorca, el flamenco, y el judío errante*. Ediciones Alfabia, 2012.
Margolis, Rebecca. "Across the Border: Canadian Jewish Writing." *The Cambridge History of Jewish American Literature*, edited by Hana Wirth-Nesher. Cambridge UP, 2016, pp. 432–46.
Mariani, Gigliola Sacerdoti. "'Barcelona, 1936' – A Moment of Proof for Muriel Rukeyser." *RSA: Rivista di studi anglo-americani*, vol. 6, no. 8, 1990, pp. 387–96.
Maurer, Christopher. Introduction. *Poet in New York*, by Federico García Lorca, edited by Christopher Maurer, translated by Greg Simon and Steven F. White. Farrar, Straus and Giroux, 1988, pp. ix–xxix.

– "Violet Shadow." *Sonnets of Dark Love and The Tamarit Divan,* translated and introduced by Jane Duran and Gloria García Lorca, Enitharmon P, 2017, pp. 23–33.

Maxwell, William J. *New Negro, Old Left: African-American Writing and Communism between the Wars.* Columbia UP, 1999.

May, Barbara Dale. "The Endurance of Dreams Deferred: Rafael Alberti and Langston Hughes." *Red Flags, Black Flags: Critical Essays on the Literature of the Spanish Civil War,* edited by John Beals Romeiser, Studia Humanitatis, 1982, pp. 13–54.

Mayhew, Jonathan. *Apocryphal Lorca: Translation, Parody, Kitsch.* U of Chicago P, 2009.

Mayne, Seymour. *Dragon Trees. Friday Circle Chapbooks: Series I.* U of Ottawa Creative Writing Program, 2003.

– "Spain, You Hurt Me." Vulpe and Albari, p. 145.

McDonald, Kathlene. *Feminism, the Left, and Postwar Literary Culture.* UP of Mississippi, 2012.

McDuffie, Erik S. *Sojourning for Freedom: Black Women, American Communism, and the Making of Black Left Feminism.* Duke UP, 2011.

McGimpsey, David. "As vast as the vastlands of this vast land, poet, are you to yonder skies, breads, and local cheeses." *The Walrus,* 12 July 2012, https://thewalrus.ca/as-vast-as-the-vastlands.

McKay, Claude. *A Long Way From Home.* 1937. Edited by Gene Andrew Jarrett. Rutgers UP, 2007.

McKay, Ian. *Rebels, Reds, Radicals: Rethinking Canada's Left History.* Between the Lines, 2005.

Mendelson, Jordana. *Documenting Spain: Artists, Exhibition Culture, and the Modern Nation, 1929–1939.* Pennsylvania State UP, 2005.

Millay, Edna St Vincent. "Say That We Saw Spain Die." *Huntsman, What Quarry?* Harper and Brothers, 1939, pp. 35–6.

Miller, John, ed. *Voices against Tyranny: Writing of the Spanish Civil War.* Charles Scribner's Sons, 1986.

Miller, Tyrus. "Documentary/Modernism: Convergence and Complementarity in the 1930s." *Modernism/modernity,* vol. 9, no. 2, Apr. 2002, pp. 226–41.

Momryk, Myron. "'Canadian Jewish Boys in Spain': Jewish Volunteers from Canada in the Spanish Civil War, 1936–39." 29 ts pages.

Morente, Enrique. *Omega.* El Europeo Música, 1996.

Morra, Linda M. *Unarrested Archives: Case Studies in Twentieth-Century Canadian Women's Authorship.* U of Toronto P, 2014.

Moss, Laura. "Is Canada Postcolonial? Introducing the Question." *Is Canada Postcolonial? Unsettling Canadian Literature,* edited by Laura Moss. Wilfrid Laurier UP, 2003, pp. 1–23.

Mullen, Edward J., ed. *Langston Hughes in the Hispanic World and Haiti.* Archon, 1977.

Munro, H.T. "To a Guitar." *Daily Clarion,* 16 Sept. 1936, p. 4.

Murphy, Emily Christina. "Jean Watts and the Spanish Civil War: Writing, Politics, and Contexts." *Canada and the Spanish Civil War: Canadian Cultural History about the Spanish Civil War*, 2016, spanishcivilwar.ca/case-studies/jean-watts. Accessed 31 June 2018.

Nadel, Ira B. *Various Positions: A Life of Leonard Cohen.* Random House Canada, 1996.

Naison, Mark. *Communists in Harlem during the Depression.* U of Illinois P, 2005.

Nash, Mary. *Defying Male Civilization: Women in the Spanish Civil War.* Ardeon P, 1995.

Nason, Jim. "Apparition on the Beach: Ode to Federico García Lorca." *Music Garden.* Frontenac House Poetry, 2013, pp. 28–9.

– "Ode to Federico Garcia Lorca." *Literary Review of Canada*, July–Aug. 2012, reviewcanada.ca/magazine/2012/07/ode-to-federico-garcia-lorca.

– "Re: copyright permissions for Jim Nason's Music Garden." Received by Emily Robins Sharpe, 15 Mar. 2019.

Nelson, Cary. "The International Context for American Poetry about the Spanish Civil War." Introduction. *The Wound and the Dream: Sixty Years of American Poems about the Spanish Civil War*, edited by Cary Nelson. U of Illinois P, 2002, pp. 1–61.

– *Revolutionary Memory: Recovering the Poetry of the American Left.* Routledge, 2003.

Nelson, Cary, ed. *The Wound and the Dream: Sixty Years of American Poems about the Spanish Civil War.* U of Illinois P, 2002.

Newton, Adam Zachary. *Facing Black and Jew: Literature as Public Space in Twentieth-Century America.* Cambridge UP, 1999.

Nordlund, David E.C. "'Cementerio judío': Lorca's Cryptic Dream of the Wandering Jew." *Revista Hispánica Moderna*, vol. 51, no. 1, June 1998, pp. 46–63.

North, Joseph. "Notebook From Spain." Bessie, *The Heart of Spain*, pp. 274–83.

Panofsky, Ruth. "Guest Editor's Introduction." *Studies in American Jewish Literature*, vol. 35, no. 2, 2016, pp. 137–46.

– Introduction. Miriam Waddington. *The Collected Poems of Miriam Waddington*, vol. 1, edited by Ruth Panofsky. U of Ottawa P, 2014, pp. xi–xlii.

Panofsky, Ruth, ed. *The New Spice Box: Canadian Jewish Writing.* New Jewish Press, 2017.

Patai, Frances. "Heroines of the Good Fight: Testimonies of U.S. Volunteer Nurses in the Spanish Civil War, 1936–1939." *Nursing History Review*, no. 3, 1995, pp. 79–104.

– "Heroines of the Good Fight: U.S. Women Volunteers in the Spanish Civil War." Frances Patai Papers, ALBA 131, series 2, box 5, folders 5–9. Tamiment Library/Robert F. Wagner Labor Archives, New York City.

– Letter to Martin Balter, 27 Dec. 1990. Frances Patai Papers, ALBA 131, series 1, box 2, folder 12. Tamiment Library/Robert F. Wagner Labor Archives, New York University.

– "Salaria Kea O'Reilly (1913–1990): A Heroine in Two Lands." Frances Patai Papers, ALBA 131, series 1, box 2, folder 12. Tamiment Library/Robert F. Wagner Labor Archives, New York University.

Peck, Mary. *Red Moon over Spain: Canadian Media Reaction to the Spanish Civil War, 1936–1939.* Steel Rail, 1988.

Penslar, Derek. *Jews and the Military: A History.* Princeton UP, 2013.

Pérez, Hiram. *A Taste for Brown Bodies: Gay Modernity and Cosmopolitan Desire.* NYU P, 2015.

Perriam, Chris. "Gender and Sexuality." *A Companion to Federico García Lorca,* edited by Federico Bonaddio. Tamesis, 2007, pp. 149–69.

Petrou, Michael. *Renegades: Canadians in the Spanish Civil War.* UBC P, 2008.

Pierce, Jonathan C. "A Tale of Two Generations: The Public and Private Voices of Dorothy Livesay." *A Public and Private Voice: Essays on the Life and Work of Dorothy Livesay,* edited by Lindsay Dorney, Gerald Noonan, and Paul Tiessen. U of Waterloo P, 1986, pp. 19–32.

Pierson, Ruth Roach. "Nations: Gendered, Racialized, Crossed with Empire." *Gendered Nations: Nationalisms and Gender Order in the Long Nineteenth Century,* edited by Ida Blom, Karen Hagemann, and Catherine Hall. Berg, 2000, pp. 41–61.

Plummer, Brenda Gayle. *Rising Wind: Black Americans and U.S. Foreign Affairs, 1935–1960.* U of North Carolina P, 1996.

Pollock, Griselda. *Encounters in the Virtual Feminist Museum: Time, Space, and the Archive.* Routledge, 2007.

Pollock, Zailig. "Duddy Kravitz and Betrayal." *Perspectives on Mordecai Richler,* edited by Michael Darling, ECW P, 1986, pp. 123–37.

Potok, Chaim. *Davita's Harp.* Alfred A. Knopf, 1985.

Preston, Paul. *Doves of War: Four Women of Spain.* Northeastern UP, 2002.

– *The Spanish Holocaust: Inquisition and Extermination in Twentieth-Century Spain.* W.W. Norton, 2012.

Puar, Jasbir K. *Terrorist Assemblages: Homonationalism in Queer Times,* expanded ed. Duke UP, 2017.

Rabinowitz, Paula. *Labor and Desire: Women's Revolutionary Fiction in Depression America.* U of North Carolina P, 1991.

– *They Must Be Represented: The Politics of Documentary.* Verso, 1994.

Ramazani, Jahan. "'Cosmopolitan Sympathies': Poetry of the First Global War." *Modernism/modernity,* vol. 23, no. 4, Nov. 2016, pp. 855–74.

Rampersad, Arnold. *The Life of Langston Hughes,* vol. I: *1902–1941, I, Too, Sing America.* Oxford UP, 2002.

Ransby, Barbara. *Eslanda: The Large and Unconventional Life of Mrs Paul Robeson.* Yale UP, 2013.

Ravvin, Norman. *A House of Words: Jewish Writing, Identity, and Memory.* McGill–Queen's UP, 1997.

– "The War and Before in Canadian Literary Life." *Nazi Germany, Canadian Responses: Confronting Antisemitism in the Shadow of War,* edited by L. Ruth Klein, pp. 183–217.

Reid, Gayla. *Come from Afar.* Cormorant Books, 2011.

Reid-Pharr, Robert F. *Archives of Flesh: African America, Spain, and Post-Humanist Critique.* NYU P, 2016.

Reilly, John M. "The Reconstruction of Genre as Entry into Conscious History." *Black American Literature Forum*, vol. 13, no. 1, Spring 1979, pp. 3–6.

Rein, Raanan. "In Pursuit of Votes and Economic Treaties: Francoist Spain and the Arab World, 1945–1956." *Spain and the Mediterranean since 1898*, edited by Raanan Rein. Frank Cass, 1999, pp. 195–215.

Reiter, Ester. *A Future without Hate or Need: The Promise of the Jewish Left in Canada.* Between the Lines, 2016.

Richler, Mordecai. *The Acrobats.* 1954. New Canadian Library, 2002.

– *The Apprenticeship of Duddy Kravitz.* 1959. New Canadian Library, 1989.

– *Images of Spain.* Photographs by Peter Christopher. Thames and Hudson, 1977.

– *Joshua Then and Now.* Alfred A. Knopf, 1980.

– *This Year in Jerusalem.* Alfred A. Knopf, 1994.

Rifkind, Candida. "'A Collection of Solitary Fragments': Miriam Waddington as Critic." *Wider Boundaries of Daring: The Modernist Impulse in Canadian Women's Poetry*, edited by Di Brandt and Barbara Godard. Wilfrid Laurier UP, 2009, pp. 253–74.

– *Comrades and Critics: Women, Literature, and the Left in 1930s Canada.* U of Toronto P, 2009.

Riis, Jacob A. *How the Other Half Lives.* Charles Scribner's Sons, 1890.

Robbins, Bruce. *Perpetual War: Cosmopolitanism from the Viewpoint of Violence.* Duke UP, 2012.

Robeson, Eslanda Goode. "Journey Into Spain." Bessie, *The Heart of Spain*, pp. 245–8.

Robinson, Ira. *A History of Antisemitism in Canada.* Wilfrid Laurier UP, 2015.

Roditi, Edouard. "Lament." 1939. Nelson, *The Wound and the Dream*, p. 138.

Roediger, David R. *Working toward Whiteness: How America's Immigrants Became White.* Basic Books, 2005.

Rogers, Gayle. *Modernism and the New Spain: Britain, Cosmopolitan Europe, and Literary History.* Oxford UP, 2012.

Rosenberg, Warren. *Legacy of Rage: Jewish Masculinity, Violence, and Culture.* U of Massachusetts P, 2001.

Rossman, Michael, and Richard Vernier, editors and translators. *Winds of the People: Poetry of the Spanish Civil War.* Berkeley, 1986.

Rottenberg, Catherine. *Performing Americanness: Race, Class, and Gender in Modern African-American and Jewish-American Literature.* Dartmouth CP, 2008.

Rukeyser, Muriel. *The Book of the Dead.* 1938. West Virginia UP, 2017.

– *Mediterranean.* 1937. Nelson, *The Wound and the Dream*, pp. 67–73.

– *Savage Coast.* 1936. Edited by Rowena Kennedy-Epstein. Feminist P at the City U of New York, 2013.

Ruth, Elizabeth. *Matadora.* Cormorant Books, 2013.

Sahuquillo, Ángel. *Federico García Lorca and the Culture of Male Homosexuality.* Translated by Erica Frouman-Smith. McFarland & Co., 2007.

Sánchez-Pardo González, Esther. "Transitional Spaces: Constructions of the Modernist 'I' in Miriam Waddington's Poetry." *Revista canaria de estudios ingleses,* vol. 54, no. 1, 2007, pp. 169–80.

Scaramella, Evelyn. "Translating the Spanish Civil War: Langston Hughes's Transnational Poetics." *Massachusetts Review,* vol. 55, no. 2, Summer 2014, pp. 177–8.

Schreier, Benjamin. *The Impossible Jew: Identity and the Reconstruction of Jewish American Literary History.* NYU P, 2015.

Sedgwick, Eve Kosofsky. *Between Men: English Literature and Male Homosocial Desire.* Columbia UP, 1985.

Seidman, Michael. *Republic of Egos: A Social History of the Spanish Civil War.* U of Wisconsin P, 2002.

Sharpe, Emily Robins. "Mary Low's Feminist Reportage and the Politics of Surrealism." *Journal of Surrealism and the Americas,* vol. 5, no. 1, 2011, pp. 77–97.

– "Pacifying Bloomsbury: Virginia Woolf, Julian Bell, and the Spanish Civil War." *The Theme of Peace and War in Virginia Woolf's Writings: Essays on Her Political Philosophy,* edited by Jane M. Wood. Edwin Mellen, 2010, pp. 153–70.

– "Salaria Kea's Spanish Memoirs." *The Volunteer: Founded by the Veterans of the Abraham Lincoln Brigade,* 4 Dec. 2011, pp. 17–19.

Sharpe, Emily Robins, and Bart Vautour. Introduction. *Meet Me on the Barricades* by Charles Yale Harrison, edited by Bart Vautour and Emily Robins Sharpe. U of Ottawa P, 2016, pp. xi–xxix.

Sheffer, Jolie A. *Romance of Race: Incest, Miscegenation, and Multiculturalism in the United States, 1880–1930.* Rutgers UP, 2012.

Sherry, Michael S. *Gay Artists in Modern American Culture: An Imagined Conspiracy.* U of North Carolina P, 2007.

Shulman, Robert. *The Power of Political Art: The 1930s Literary Left Reconsidered.* U of North Carolina P, 2000.

Silber, Nina. *The Romance of Reunion: Northerners and the South, 1865–1900.* U of North Carolina P, 1993.

The Silence of Others. Directed by Almudena Carracedo and Robert Bahar. Semilla Verde Productions, 2018.

Sinclair, Upton. *No Pasaran! A Story of the Battle of Madrid.* Pasadena, 1937.

Singer, Melina Baum. "'Is Richler Canadian Content?': Jewishness, Race, and Diaspora." *Canadian Literature,* vol. 207, Winter 2010, pp. 11–24.

Smethurst, James E. *New Red Negro: The Literary Left and African American Poetry, 1930–1946.* Oxford UP, 1999.

Smith, Antonia. "'Cement for the Canadian Mosaic': Performing Canadian Citizenship in the Work of John Murray Gibbon." *Race/Ethnicity: Multidisciplinary Global Contexts*, vol. 1, no. 1, 2007, pp. 37–60.

Smith, Jim. "Do and Die." *Happy Birthday, Nicanor Parra*. Mansfield P, 2012, p. 54.

– "Exit Interview: Federico García Lorca." *Happy Birthday, Nicanor Parra*. Mansfield P, 2012, p. 80.

Smith, Miriam. *Lesbian and Gay Rights in Canada: Social Movements and Equality Seeking, 1971–1995*. U of Toronto Press, 1999.

Smith, Steven Ross. "Re: Inquiry about 'Peck' from Emanations: fluttertongue 6." Received by Emily Robins Sharpe, 5 April 2019.

– "Peck." *Emanations: fluttertongue 6*. Book*hug, 2015, pp. 49–50.

Sol, Adam. "Longings and Renunciations: Attitudes Towards Intermarriage in Early Twentieth Century Jewish American Novels." *American Jewish History*, vol. 89, no. 2, 2001, pp. 215–30.

Somacarrera, Pilar. "Contextual and Institutional Coordinates of the Transference of Anglo-Canadian Literature into Spain." *Made in Canada, Read in Spain: Essays on the Translation and Circulation of English-Canadian Literature*, edited by Pilar Somacarrera. De Gruyter, 2013, pp. 21–53.

Soto, Isabel. "Crossing Over: Langston Hughes and Lorca." *Studies in Liminality and Literature 2*, edited by Isabel Soto. Gateway, 2000, pp. 115–35.

– "'To Hear Another Language': Lifting the Veil between Langston Hughes and Federico García Lorca." *Border Transits: Literature and Culture across the Line*, edited by Ana María Manzanas. Editions Rodopi, 2007, pp. 101–7.

Spender, Stephen, and John Lehmann, editors. *Poems for Spain*. Hogarth, 1939.

Sperber, Murray A., editor. *And I Remember Spain: A Spanish Civil War Anthology*. Macmillan, 1974.

Stainton, Leslie. *Lorca: A Dream of Life*. Farrar, Straus, and Giroux, 1999.

Stevens, Peter. *Miriam Waddington and Her Works*. ECW, 1984.

Stewart, Janice. "Queerly Canadian." Introduction. *Canadian Literature*, vol. 205, Summer 2010, canlit.ca/article/queerly-canadian.

Sueiro Seoane, Susana. "Spanish Colonialism during Primo de Rivera's Dictatorship," translated by Jessica Brown. *Spain and the Mediterranean since 1898*, edited by Raanan Rein. Frank Cass, 1999, pp. 48–64.

Sugars, Cynthia. "Unhomely States." Introduction. *Unhomely States: Theorizing English-Canadian Postcolonialism*, edited by Cynthia Sugars. Broadview, 2004, pp. xiii–xxv.

Sundquist, Eric J. *Strangers in the Land: Blacks, Jews, Post-Holocaust America*. Harvard UP, 2005.

Sutherland, John. "The Writing of Patrick Anderson" *First Statement*, vol. 1, no. 19, 1943, pp. 3–6.

Take This Waltz. Directed by Sarah Polley, performances by Michelle Williams and Seth Rogen. Magnolia Pictures, 2011.

Tetzlaff, Liz. "Miriam Waddington's Poetry Enters Spain Stage Left." *Canada and the Spanish Civil War: Canadian Cultural History about the Spanish Civil War,* 2016, spanishcivilwar.ca/sites/spanishcivilwar.ca/files/Tetzlaff-MiriamWaddingtonsPoetry.pdf. Accessed 31 June 2018.

Thomas, Hugh. *The Spanish Civil War,* 4th ed. Penguin Books, 2012.

Thompson [Patterson], Louise. "Chapter 7, Paris Conference and Spain" [untitled memoir]. Stuart A. Rose Manuscript, Archives and Rare Book Library, Emory University, Atlanta, collection 869, box 20, folder 6.

Thurston, Michael. "'Bombed in Spain': Langston Hughes, the Black Press, and the Spanish Civil War." *The Black Press: New Literary and Historical Essays,* edited by Todd Vogel. Rutgers UP, 2001, pp. 140–58.

– *Making Something Happen: American Political Poetry between the World Wars.* U of North Carolina P, 2001.

– "Montage of a Dream Destroyed: Langston Hughes in Spain." *Montage of a Dream: The Art and Life of Langston Hughes,* edited by John Edgar Tidwell and Cheryl R. Ragar. U of Missouri P, 2007, pp. 195–208.

Tordjman, Gilles. "Leonard Cohen, un art de la guerre." *Les revolutions de Leonard Cohen,* edited by Chantal Ringuet and Gérard Rabinovitch. P de l'U du Québec, 2016, pp. 21–35.

Trehearne, Brian. *The Montreal Forties: Modernist Poetry in Transition.* U of Toronto P, 1999.

Tulchinsky, Gerald. *Branching Out: The Transformation of the Canadian Jewish Community.* Stoddart, 1998.

– *Canada's Jews: A People's Journey.* U of Toronto P, 2008.

– *Taking Root: The Origins of the Canadian Jewish Community.* Brandeis UP, 1993.

Ugarte, Michael. "The Question of Race in the Spanish Civil War." *Teaching Representations of the Spanish Civil War,* edited by Noël Valis. MLA, 2007, pp. 108–16.

Vautier, Marie. *New World Myth: Postmodernism and Postcolonialism in Canadian Fiction.* McGill–Queen's UP, 1998.

Vautour, Bart. "From Transnational Politics to National Modernist Poetics: Spanish Civil War Poetry in *New Frontier.*" *Canadian Literature,* no. 204, Spring 2010, pp. 44–60.

– Introduction. *This Time a Better Earth* by Ted Allan, edited by Bart Vautour. U of Ottawa P, pp. xiii–xxxiii.

– "The Politics of Recovery and the Recovery of Politics: Editing Canadian Writing on the Spanish Civil War." *Editing as Cultural Practice in Canada,* edited by Dean Irvine and Smaro Kamboureli. Wilfrid Laurier UP, 2016, pp. 139–47.

Vulpe, Nicola. "De Falla at the Police Station." *Blue Tile.* BuschekBooks, 2004, p. 18.

– *Insult to the Brain.* Guernica Editions, 2019, p. 35.
– "Re: Slow Lightning." Received by Emily Robins Sharpe, 29 June 2018.
– "This Issue Is Not Ended (An Essay in Lieu of an Introduction)." Vulpe and Albari, pp. 19–65.
Vulpe, Nicola, and Maha Albari, eds. *Sealed in Struggle: Canadian Poetry and the Spanish Civil War.* Centre for Canadian Studies, 1995.
Waddington, Miriam. *Call them Canadians: A Photographic Point of View,* edited by Lorraine Monk, produced by the National Film Board of Canada, Roger Duhamel, 1968.
– *The Collected Poems of Miriam Waddington.* Edited by Ruth Panofsky. U of Ottawa P, 2014. 2 vols.
– "The Exiles: Spain." *The Collected Poems,* p. 2.
– *The Last Landscape.* Oxford UP, 1992.
– "Spanish Lovers Seek Respite." *The Collected Poems,* p. 4.
– "The Woman in the Hall." *The Collected Poems,* pp. 768–70.
Wainwright, J.A. "Lament for Federico García Lorca." *The Walrus,* 12 Sept. 2012, thewalrus.ca/lament-for-federico-garcia-lorca.
– "Re 'Lament for Federico García Lorca." Received by Emily Robins Sharpe, 5 June 2018.
Walcott, Rinaldo. "Disgraceful: Intellectual Dishonesty, White Anxieties, and Multicultural Critique Thirty Years Later." 2011. *Queer Returns: Essays on Multiculturalism, Diaspora, and Black Studies.* Insomniac, 2016, pp. 79–110.
Wald, Alan M. *American Night: The Literary Left in the Era of the Cold War.* U of North Carolina P, 2012.
– *Exiles from a Future Time: The Forging of the Mid-Twentieth-Century Literary Left.* U North Carolina P, 2012.
– *Trinity of Passion: The Literary Left and the Antifascist Crusade.* U of North Carolina P, 2007.
Walker, James. "Claiming Equality for Canadian Jewry: The Struggle for Inclusion, 1930–1945." Klein, *Nazi Germany, Canadian Responses,* pp. 218–62.
Warner, Sylvia Townsend. "Barcelona." *New Frontier,* vol. 1, no. 9, Jan. 1937, pp. 9–10.
– "What the Soldier Said." *New Frontier,* vol. 2, no. 5, Oct. 1937, pp. 12–13.
Watts, Jean. "Madrid Senoritas [*sic*] Work For Victory." *Daily Clarion,* 26 May 1937, p. 3.
– "With Dr Bethune in Spain Ministering to the Wounded." *Daily Clarion,* 26 Mar. 1937, p. 2.
– "Woman First Time Producer of Play: Work of Late García Lorca, Murdered by Fascists." *Daily Clarion,* 20 Oct. 1937, p. 4.
Weintraub, Stanley. *The Last Great Cause: The Intellectuals and the Spanish Civil War.* Weybright and Talley, 1968.

West, Terrence Rundle. *Not in My Father's Footsteps.* General Store Publishing House, 2011.

– "Re: Not In My Father's Footsteps." Received by Emily Robins Sharpe, 4 June 2018.

"Where I Stand on Spain." *New Frontier*, vol. 1, no. 8, Dec. 1936, pp. 13–16.

Williams, John A. *Captain Blackman.* 1972. Coffee House, 2000.

Willmott, Glenn. *Unreal Country: Modernity in the Canadian Novel in English.* McGill–Queen's UP, 2002.

Wilson, John. *Lost Cause.* Orca, 2012.

– *Lost in Spain.* Fitzhenry and Whiteside, 2000.

Wolff, Milton. *Another Hill.* U of Illinois P, 1994.

Woodcock, George. "Poem for García Lorca." *The Centre Cannot Hold.* Routledge, 1943, pp. 13–14.

Woods, Gregory. *Homintern: How Gay Culture Liberated the Modern World.* Yale UP, 2016.

Woolf, Virginia. *Three Guineas.* Harcourt, 1938.

Wright, Richard. "American Negroes in Key Posts of Spain's Loyalist Forces." 20 Sept. 1937. Collum, pp. 119–22.

– *Pagan Spain.* 1957. Introduction by Faith Berry. Banner Books, 1995.

Writers Take Sides: Letters about the War in Spain from 418 American Authors. League of American Writers, 1938.

Wyile, Herb. Introduction. *Speaking in the Past Tense: Canadian Novelists on Writing Historical Fiction*, edited by Herb Wyile. Wilfrid Laurier UP, 2007, pp. 1–24.

Yates, James. *Mississippi to Madrid: Memoir of a Black American in the Abraham Lincoln Brigade.* Open Hand, 1989.

Zaagsma, Gerben. *Jewish Volunteers, the International Brigades, and the Spanish Civil War.* Bloomsbury Academic, 2017.

Zangwill, Israel. *The Melting-Pot: Drama in Four Acts.* 1905. Macmillan, 1911.

Zuehlke, Mark. *The Gallant Cause: Canadians in the Spanish Civil War, 1936–1939.* Whitecap Books, 1996.

Index

Page numbers for illustrations are in **bold**.

www.ingramcontent.com/pod-product-compliance
Lightning Source LLC
LaVergne TN
LVHW040150080826
844660LV00014B/900/J

* 9 7 8 1 4 8 7 5 0 1 4 2 6 *